Praise for *Th*

"My work with Robert Goldstein truly changed my life. Learning to ask for my deepest longings transformed my family relationships and friendships. This book will show you how to overcome your fear of disapproval and reclaim your personal power. Buy it now!"

—Linda Medley, retired school principal and educator

"*The Craft of Life* enabled me to uncover hidden beliefs formed in my early childhood that had influenced my unconscious behavior throughout my life. Using the book's models and techniques, written in simple yet vivid language, I was able to identify, forgive, and reframe behaviors that had held me captive for years. It has awakened the unconscious realm of my being, making my days more fulfilling, joyous, and complete."

—Michael Jakes, business executive

"Robert Goldstein and the methods clearly outlined in *The Craft of Life* have my heartfelt appreciation! Becoming aware of the power of my unconscious beliefs and behaviors has been invaluable. Since bringing these "hidden" beliefs into conscious focus, I am grateful to experience a lasting personal transformation that allows me to have authentic and meaningful relationships with those I love and with myself. Thank You!"

—Christiane Stefanoff, acupuncturist, LAc

"When a person desires continuous improvement in any particular endeavor, a craft is required. In other words, a method that provides clear guidance, true principles, and a correct practice. By following such a method for an extended period of time and in a disciplined fashion, one acquires actual tools, skills, and strengths. In both my business career and in my athletic endeavors, this simple formula has been my pole star, and it has served me well. *The Craft of Life* provides everything one needs for genuine, continuous self-improvement. It shows you how to take control of your emotional reactivity by teaching you to recognize your unconscious patterns of behavior and the beliefs from which they come. While this effort does not result in the fulfillment of one's life fantasies (like finding your soul mate or getting rich quick); it has the effect of simply making life better by reducing fear, promoting balance, and encouraging authenticity with one's self and others. I highly recommend it."

—Gary Hooker, founder and CEO of Hooker Headers, SEMA Hall of Fame inductee

"*The Craft of Life* has had a huge, positive impact on my life and on my relationship with my husband. Its practical approach helped me to extricate myself from the many behaviors that interfered with living my life in a present, conscious, and joyful way."

—Nikki Winston, MBA, author of *Every Move You Make*

"*The Craft of Life* offers no pat answers. On the contrary, this method requires you to forgo any expectations of rescue from psychic pain and to find relief by moving toward it. Religion, meditation, and psychology all offered to make my life better, but they fell short because they didn't allow me to make sense of my own narrative. I also needed the fellowship of a group--other men seeking a way to build new chops for dealing with life's complexities. By teaching me to stay present with my perceptions and understand how they connect to my unconscious beliefs, masking behaviors, and emotional longings, *The Craft of Life* showed me how to make sense of life while overcoming the calcified beliefs that held me back from having healthy relationships and achieving my full potential."

—Don Chartrand, CEO, Ease Interactive

"There is an unconscious fear of disapproval behind every thought we have, every action we take. *The Craft of Life* not only guides us to discover this fear, but also gives us the tools to bring it into our awareness and move beyond its grip. This ability forever changes how we react to others and to ourselves. Through this work, my relationship with my own life has been completely altered. I am able to stop and mine my inner and outer conflicts for personal growth. Little gems are revealed every day. Thank you Robert Goldstein! You have given me something eternal."

—Raylene Rhodes, office manager

"As a primary care doctor, I work with patients who either want or need to make important, lifestyle changes for their health. *The Craft of Life* provides tools that empower people to care for themselves in a way that genuinely promotes consciousness and wellbeing. On a personal level, this process has helped me to overcome barriers that had frustrated and disappointed me for years. Through its practice, I have learned to engage in my personal and professional relationships in a new, healthier way."

—Mark Kalina, M.D.

"*The Craft of Life* has helped me enormously in my relationship with my 20-year-old son. Realizing how he triggers my wounding childhood beliefs has allowed me to recognize when I am responding from my past beliefs instead of present circumstances. In addition, I clearly recognize when he is responding from his own childhood beliefs and wounds. I now have the tools to approach him and communicate in a neutral manner. When he shuts me out and pushes me away, I see it for what it is—his own hurt—and not a reflection on me."

—Julie Howe, MBA

"I took up *The Craft of Life* after seeing changes in my husband and a good friend, both of whom were part of a group practicing this material. I'm no stranger to healing work, especially looking at past patterns, but the profound changes in these men made me curious. What I discovered is this method provides a template for uncovering the emotional longings we learned to bury during childhood and then helps us to see how we continue to keep them buried in our adult lives. It also offers clear guidance on how to transform our self-limiting beliefs and behaviors. Using these tools daily has allowed me to become a craftswoman in my own life and in my relationships, as I learned to discover and embrace my true self, my true longings, without masking or fearful hiding."

—Kim Chartrand, R.N.

"If you are truly ready to risk stepping out of your comfort zone and grow into a more authentic, happier, loving, and peaceful version of yourself, this is the book for you! As a single mom and a professional woman who is highly sensitive, the processes in *The Craft of Life* have become my go-to tools for resolving conflict, seeing past old beliefs that don't serve me, accessing my deep inner longings, and letting them be the navigators of my life choices. Among the most valuable tools is the concept of living symbols. Robert Goldstein's method guides us on how to gain insight and clarity about our beliefs by looking at the objects, relationships, and other living symbols we have surrounded ourselves with. If we aren't happy with what we see or feel, we can use *The Craft of Life's* "tools" to transform our self-limiting beliefs, insecurities, and judgments. When life feels daunting, overwhelming, or depressing, what better gift than to regain hope, knowing we have the ability to calm our reactivity and shape our lives from the inside out."

—Terry Sprague, Ph.D., professor, Art and Dance, California State University San Marcos

The Craft of Life

The Craft of Life

BUILDING CONSCIOUS, AUTHENTIC RELATIONSHIPS

Robert Goldstein

THE CRAFT OF LIFE PRESS

The Craft Of Life Press
P.O.Box 279
Cardiff-By-The-Sea, CA 92007
www.TheCraftOfLife.com

ISBN: 978-0-9982181-0-6
Library of Congress Control Number: 2017950881

Cover design and graphics by Tawn Babcock
Author photo by Rona Rundle, Psy.D.

For Amy and Emily

with all my love

The family. We were a strange little band of characters trudging through life sharing diseases and toothpaste, coveting one another's desserts, hiding shampoo, borrowing money, locking each other out of our rooms, inflicting pain and kissing to heal it in the same instant, loving, laughing, defending, and trying to figure out the common thread that bound us all together.

—Erma Bombeck

Author's Note:

I have used this method successfully to counsel women and men for over twenty-five years. It has been a slow, steady evolution as I have refined and adjusted the model again and again. I sincerely believe *The Craft of Life* has universal application for all adults. Whatever your race, sexual orientation, gender identification, religious beliefs, or socioeconomic status, this method will work for you. It will help you cultivate self-understanding, acceptance of yourself and others, and provide you with tangible skills to overcome fears and insecurities. I encourage you to learn the principles and skills that make up this craft, for they will serve you for the rest of your life. With the exception of one or two, the examples in this book are composite sketches of multiple people. Any direct description of a particular person is coincidental.

Contents

List of Charts

List of Forms

Foreword

The Craft of Life is an engaging, informative, and original book. It provides clear instructions on how to make constructive changes in one's beliefs, attitudes, and practices. Written to help people learn what they can do to experience happier, more fulfilling lives, Robert Goldstein's readers will discover many important things about themselves that began in childhood but continue to affect their current relationships. He provides a practical step-by-step approach for seeing one's past beliefs, behaviors, attitudes, and habits, and offers exercises on how to make lasting changes.

Everyone experiences conflict, confrontation, and fear of disapproval. How we respond to these and learn from them shape our identities and our futures. Readers will experience a great deal of insight and inner growth by utilizing the key concepts covered in this book, such as identity theory, the mechanics of transformation, and the accompanying charts.

For counselors, social workers, psychologists, or psychiatrists, the techniques in this book will help you to see your patients as wounded individuals. You will understand them without judgment and will accept their emotional deficiencies as ordinary expressions.

The Craft of Life contains many valuable lessons not found in other books, including how to strengthen the weaker, less developed side of one's identity. It also addresses how we can learn from our emotional wounds and unfulfilled longings in order to promote physical and emotional healing. Readers will engage in a journey of self-discovery and gain insight into their own stories, childhood beliefs, masking behaviors, and emotional yearnings—all in the pursuit of consciousness and authenticity.

The ultimate lesson from Robert Goldstein's book is that the only person you can change is yourself.

—Dr. Ann Webster, instructor, Harvard Medical School, and director, Benson-Henry Institute for Mind Body Medicine

Part One

Identity Theory—The Foundation

CHAPTER 1

Poppy's Story

Every object rightly seen unlocks a quality of the soul.

—Ralph Waldo Emerson

POPPY, MY GRANDFATHER, WAS a short, bald man with a round belly that I could never quite reach around when I hugged him. His tough, stoic nature was reflected in his workman's frame, powerful arms, and rough hands. He wore thick, black-rimmed glasses that sat prominently atop his oversized nose. Pop gave off a gruff, understated fierceness, which I recognized as more appearance than reality. Still, most people kept a safe distance from him—though it may have been the smelly, Dutch Master cigars he smoked continuously. He was pragmatic, said what was necessary and did what was necessary, no more, no less. He worked hard driving a big tanker truck during the week, delivering heating oil to apartment buildings in the Bronx. On the weekends, which I mostly spent with him, he worked around his house. There was always a project to do, and I followed on his heels like a puppy, trying with great enthusiasm to help. My main contribution, I quickly discovered, was getting in the way, and according to Pop, I had natural talent.

My grandfather regularly amazed me with his near magical ability to fix things—a broken toy, a stalled engine, a squeaky staircase. One time he did something that permanently changed the way I see the world. It was a Friday during summer, and a neighbor came over to borrow an extension cord. Mr. Tinnen was part of the maintenance staff at a nearby retirement community. He looked weary and upset, explaining that in the previous night's rain, the old auditorium building had leaked again, as it had for three years. Everyone was fed up. They had tried all manner of solutions—plastic tarps, caulk, cement, even a new roof. The demonic drip reappeared again and again. The damnedest thing was the leak often came in different locations or sometimes not at all. No one could figure it out and many experts had tried. My grandfather responded immediately. He told Mr. Tinnen that although he wouldn't guarantee anything, he expected he could find the leak. He didn't brag, but spoke matter-of-factly and with a sense of sureness that led me to believe he knew something no one else did. Finally, the three of us climbed into Mr. Tinnen's red Ford pickup and headed over to the auditorium. This was the equivalent of Gary Cooper in *High Noon* or Houdini saying he could get out of the straight jacket underwater.

Sitting in the front seat between the two men, I wondered how Poppy would do it and whether Mr. Tinnen was as excited as I was. I felt a low-voltage current pulse through my body. When we arrived at the site the maintenance crew was cleaning up water and preparing for another storm. Mr. Tinnen introduced my grandfather. Immediately there was a feeling of resistance. The head of the crew insisted that the leak could not be found and seemed irritated that my grandfather—a nonexpert—would even try. My grandfather simply asked Mr. Tinnen to show him the site of the leak.

We walked inside the building to the offices behind the auditorium. It was a mess: The ceiling was wet and the carpet was soaked, as was a side chair by the receptionist's desk. A pungent smell of mildew struck my nostrils and I winced. Poppy looked at every detail intensely, especially the length of one overhead beam. To me, he was Superman, using his X-ray vision to see inside the ceiling and walls. He asked the receptionist all sorts of questions about the leak—when and where and how much and at what time and is it always the same? He questioned Mr. Tinnen as well.

We went up and carefully checked the roof and gutters. Lastly, we took a slow walk around the perimeter of the auditorium. Pop asked Mr. Tinnen to bring a ladder and a long garden hose with a spray nozzle. I was fascinated, but hearing each succeeding person say that the leak could not be found I was admittedly inclined in their direction.

We took the ladder up to a second story balcony. Mr. Tinnen threw the end of the garden hose up. I leaned over the wrought iron railing to catch it. My grandfather called down to Mr. Tinnen to turn on the water and come up. Then he told Mr. Tinnen to stand on the ladder and spray the face of the wall just under the roof line. Mr. Tinnen immediately protested. This was ridiculous. The leak could not be in this spot. First off, it was on the side-face of the building, not the roof, and it was on the opposite side of the building from where the offices were—too far for a leak to travel. Plus, this was the particular spot that Mr. Tinnen and others had passed by, time and again, and assured themselves could not be the entry point for the leak. "This can't be the spot," said Mr. Tinnen. "Maybe not," Pop answered, "but I think it's here or one other place." Mr. Tinnen shook his head and then gave in.

My grandfather told him to stand on the ladder and spray a particular place until he was told to stop, adding he could count on about fifteen minutes. Downstairs, where the leak had last come out, Pop and I, now brothers in battle, sat down, side by side, in two worn red leather armchairs, and we waited for the mysterious leak to appear. I was beside myself with anticipation. Pop sat with remarkable calm. It didn't seem to matter to him whether it leaked or not, which I couldn't understand.

It was after 5 p.m. now; everyone had gone home, and the office was quiet. Minutes passed like long summer days. The whole thing was a mystery, and I was starting to get bored. I exhaled a great breath, sighed and sat and waited. Ten minutes passed and not a sign of water. We waited a bit longer, and then I suggested we might check that other spot he had in mind. "Not yet," Pop said. His two words struck my gut with blunt force; I understood that I should sit quietly and not ask further project-management questions. As my grandfather traced the ceiling line with his eyes, I began to wonder whether I might miss *Star Trek* because of this stupid leak, which couldn't be found anyway. We were deep into summer reruns and a particularly good episode was on that night. I envisioned a crew from the Enterprise beaming into the office with scanners and phasers, positive that either Scotty or Mr. Spock would find the leak while Captain Kirk and I went off on a real adventure.

The plock, plock, plock of dripping water interrupted my daydream. I looked up and saw what was now a steady stream of it, running along the big beam and spilling into a small puddle by the secretary's desk. My grandfather was talking to me, but I wasn't hearing him. "Butch, grab the trash can and put it under the water." I did and then ran up to tell Mr. Tinnen—with great pride—that we had found the leak. Mr. Tinnen was dumbfounded. It was as though he had just learned that the flat world is actually round. I could feel his sheer disbelief as he repeated this realization in his mind,

"Round . . .? How could it be round?"

To me, it was a great and astonishing magic trick, and now my grandfather was inviting Mr. Tinnen downstairs to see how it was done. He pointed to the exposed beam, "Look," he said. "The ceiling appears to be one continuous plane, but it isn't. That exposed beam dividing the ceiling down its center is pitched; it's on a downward slope. The ceiling is actually different heights on either side, but the beam disguises that fact." He led us into an adjoining storage room and pointed out that the ceiling joists ran perpendicular to the exposed beam out in the office, and, in fact, passed through the office ceiling and connected with that main beam. Mr. Tinnen didn't get it, and neither did I.

"In other words," my grandfather said, "the ceiling is higher over there on the far side of the building. Hidden from view, up inside the ceiling, there are wooden joists spanning from wall to wall. If water entered the building from the west over on the far side and traveled inside the ceiling, it would flow along the wooden joist's natural downward slope, eventually reaching the main beam in the center of the room. And, then, because the main beam continues on a downward slope, the water would make a left turn and run down hill along its path until it ran out of forward momentum. Then, lacking further forward movement, gravity would pull the water down to the floor. Water is entering the building and flowing downhill in logical sequence until it runs out of forward movement and then it leaks onto the floor. That's it—end of story."

Mr. Tinnen was more relaxed now, even happy, but it sounded too simple, too obvious to be true. My grandfather led us both upstairs to the balcony and continued with his explanation, "The new roof and gutters told me that the leak was most likely not coming from there. That leaves the sides of the building. For rain to enter the side of a building it would have to be blown in with force. If it drizzles, it won't leak, but if it pours and the wind blows, then it will leak. How badly would depend upon how strong the wind blew and how much rain there was. Last night we had a powerful storm from the west. The ceiling joists run west to east, which means water blown in would gather on a joist and flow downhill as I described before. When I checked the western wall here on the balcony, I discovered a number of cracks in the stucco just up from where the leak occurred. In our experiment, you sprayed water on the crack, letting in a steady trickle. This water flowed down the joist to its end, where it met the main beam. The water dribbled onto the main beam, which allowed the flow to continue, then traveled down that beam's slope before leaking onto the floor. Fill those cracks and any like them and your leak is solved."

Mr. Tinnen thanked my grandfather all the way home, lacing his gratitude with an equal measure of incredulity: "I can't believe it," he repeated, "I just can't believe it." I, on the other hand, believed it surely and completely, and I determined at that moment to learn to see everything the way my grandfather had seen that leak.

Finding the leak

Human beings have complex lives. We form innumerable relationships, from the most intimate to distant acquaintances. We fill our days at work or school. We create careers. We have pets and hobbies. We have children and grandchildren. Time passes and we age. We develop wellness problems—some physical, others emotional. Along the way, and many times, our perspective changes, our beliefs change, and what we want changes. At seventeen, we long for some boy or girl to love us. At thirty, we want something else. At fifty, it changes again—as it does at sixty-five. As we make our journey, we consistently move toward what we want. Sometimes it's a relationship, other times a car or a particular job. Time passes, we age, we build relationships, we move toward what we want; sometimes we get it, sometimes not. This is the ebb and flow of life.

As we make this journey, we try to make sense of life's enormous complexity. We talk to friends who think and see things as we do. Some settle on a religious perspective, others on one that is social or political; some focus on work or money, others on science, sports, or art; and for many, the focus of their lives is simply the struggle to survive. Years pass, we grow older and, as we do, we move toward what we believe in; sometimes we achieve it, sometimes not. This, too, is the ebb and flow of life.

As we make our journey, we may notice patterns in our lives, perhaps persisting over many years or even an entire lifetime. These patterns lead to natural questions: why can't I find the right partner, the one who will love and satisfy me? Why doesn't my partner see me or value me the way I want? Why can't I find my place in the world? Why can't I find my right job or be properly recognized by others? Why do I become angry over small things? Why do I let people overpower me? Why am I struggling financially? Why don't I feel supported or protected? And why do I keep so much of myself hidden from others? We all have many private questions about this great journey we're on.

But modern life is busy. We have to be at work or at school; we have to pick up the kids and take them to soccer; we have to meet so and so at this place; we have to make dinner, answer email, help with homework, and then watch the latest episode of our favorite show. We have so much to do and too little time for any of it, so our deeper life questions have to wait; mostly they go unasked, unexplored and, ultimately, unanswered. Yet their impact lives with us continuously, not only in our outer lives but also in our closest relationships, and mostly in our own hearts.

Then it happens: a twist of fate, an illness, a broken relationship, a loss of something or someone valuable and important to us. We stop, if only temporarily, to consider the meaning of life. We take time out and view things from this new and serious perspective. We feel the need to understand: we see a therapist; we take a workshop; we talk to a spiritual counselor; we sit quietly alone; we volunteer to help those less fortunate; and we take up some kind of **Inner Work**. We reach out to family and friends with a new measure of authenticity and vulnerability. We are searching for greater meaning and purpose beyond the living of everyday life.

Sooner or later, we all end up looking at our lives the way Mr. Tinnen looked at the auditorium. Here was a big, complex building leaking water from the outside in, causing all kinds of collateral damage. When this moment comes we realize that our own auditorium—that is, our lives—have been leaking a long time; we see that our relationships to others and to ourselves are not working. We recognize our own dissatisfaction, and it scares, saddens and even overwhelms us.

At this point, like Mr. Tinnen, we seek help. We hire professionals to assist us; we reach out to family or friends; we try to make logical changes in our behavior or attitudes. Typically, in the end, our personal leaks persist. We still can't seem to find just the right partner; we still aren't getting what we want from our current partner; we don't understand why this dissatisfaction keeps repeating itself; we only know it does, and we are left feeling discouraged or depressed at the sadness of it all. Some feel ashamed to have let it go on for so long. But standing before us, perhaps clearer than ever, is our leaky auditorium. We ask ourselves: how can we ever find the source of our leak? Where do we even start? How can we come to some genuine understanding when it all seems so big, so complex, so overwhelming?

The method in this book is about attaining greater consciousness and personal clarity. To accomplish this, we will learn to perceive the leaks in our lives—those things we believe are not working with others or ourselves—in the same way that my grandfather perceived the leak in the auditorium. He began from a simple premise: it is impossible *not* to find the leak. A leak must enter from a specific place, it must exit from a specific place, and these two locations must be connected. So, with this premise as his foundation, my grandfather demonstrated how to start, which is with openness and receptivity. There must be a willingness to look, and the looking should be undertaken with respect, care, and thoroughness. First, see the problem—which is what my grandfather taught me—and take the time to see things clearly before taking further action. He had quietly observed and let the auditorium show *him* the origin of the leak.

My grandfather was also a skilled craftsman who could envision the auditorium as a whole with an inner structure of joists and beams covered by an outer surface of ceilings and walls. He understood that both the inner and outer components were connected and must be seen as a whole. My grandfather perceived the problem in a way that allowed him to see the problem clearly and to solve it efficiently. Bear in mind this was a problem that numerous experts had tried to resolve, including engineers, builders, and other professionals. Although this problem had received a great investment of time and thousands of dollars, my grandfather resolved the issue in under an hour because he actually saw the problem and then considered it patiently and methodically.

My grandfather did not possess extraordinary skills or magical powers; what he had was an effective method for attaining clarity and solving problems where others didn't, and this proved to be the difference between reaching a permanent resolution or not.

Identity theory

The foundation of this book rests on one fundamental concept: **Identity**. Identity is the unseen, organizing principle that imparts form to all that we experience. It is like the die in an extrusion process, such as a cookie press. The amorphous dough represents the energy that animates life; the die (the cookie shape) at the end of the press is our personal identity. As the amorphous dough passes through, it becomes the form of the die at the end of the press. In this way, some of us become stars, others half-moons, others hearts, all arising from the same formless dough. It is identity's function to impart form by acting as the die for the energy that animates life. Change the die, even slightly, adjust one tip of the star or one edge of the half moon, and the cookie's shape will be different, must be different. Change your identity even slightly and your life and relationships, which are the outward expression of your identity, similarly will transform. They have no choice, for all life must obey the law of identity.

Yet, if a shift in identity brings about true personal transformation, the question then becomes, what must we do to change our identity?

Let's go back to where we all started: childhood. Growing up, most children collided with their parents over differing beliefs, and these collisions had the effect of changing a child's identity. Parents believed one thing; children believed another; the result was a painful collision. These collisions occurred countless times as we grew up. It is the natural course of things, as children rely on parents for everything from food and care to love and protection. A child's entire sense of safety and well-being comes from his or her parents, so when collisions occur, children eventually bow to their parent's greater strength and authority, because children ultimately fear their parent's disapproval and dread the potential rejection that follows. Our personal fear of disapproval and rejection form the foundation of our deepest, most abiding fears, and **Parent-Child Collisions** are their place of origin.

What exactly did our parents disapprove of? The answer to this enormously important question is not as straightforward as one might imagine, because the answer has more to do with how we perceived our parents than with what they actually said or did to us. Every child recognizes his or her parent's disapproval of specific behaviors or particular attitudes. We expected disapproval if we behaved in a certain way, said certain things, or simply were who they believed we shouldn't be. Receiving a parent's disapproval was painful, upsetting, and sometimes frightening. We learned to avoid this nastiness by hiding parts of ourselves. We learned at an early age to hide our true thoughts, our genuine feelings, but, more importantly, we learned who we should not be in front of our parents and what we should never ask of them.

What we hid were our deepest **Emotional Longings**. The things that would make us feel cared for and loved in the deepest, truest sense are what we surrendered in order to survive childhood. We believed our parents either could not or would not give these to us, so rather than ask, we simply hid them. We did not want to risk the pain of disapproval and rejection. Perhaps our father was harsh, so we learned not to ask him for gentleness and love. Perhaps our mother was an alcoholic, so we learned not to ask her for care and support. Perhaps our parents could not see or hear us, so we learned to withdraw quietly and never ask to be seen or heard. Perhaps our parents were gentle and loving but inadequate providers, so we learned never to ask for support because we did not want to hurt them. The list of unfulfilled emotional longings is long and deep. Every human being has them, but we keep them privately and secretly in the depths of our heart.

So we grow up and leave home to enter adulthood, but unbeknownst to us our unfulfilled longings and our **Childhood Beliefs About Disapproval** come with us. Through parent-child collisions, our identity changes on deep levels, though we don't yet realize how. We think we're leaving home to start a new, independent life. We believe we're moving away from what hurt us to find what we didn't get while growing up, but life is not so simple because life is based on identity. It doesn't matter what we think we might want or what we believe we should do, because we all create lives and relationships from the blueprints of our own identity. This is inescapable. Those blueprints were first formed in childhood with our parents and influenced greatly by the thousands of parent-child collisions.

Until we find a way to recognize and deal directly with our unfulfilled emotional longings, we will spend the rest of our lives avoiding them, not asking for them, and not acting on them, because we still fear disapproval and rejection for doing so. Not asking for what we deeply desire is how we block ourselves from getting the partner we want or getting what we want from the partner we already have. Allowing our fear of disapproval to control us by hiding our deepest emotional longings is the norm in relationships, and the direct result for most is ongoing dissatisfaction, feeling unseen, and misunderstood. This causes emotional disconnection in our primary relationships, especially with ourselves, which leads to additional problems, such as physical illness, emotional imbalance, economic struggles, and seemingly endless career or life obstacles—all of which represent the leaks in our personal lives.

It is important to note that parents are not to blame; they must be themselves, and they must teach their children how to be in the world the best way they can. They are struggling with their own unfulfilled emotional longings and fears of disapproval, which they also acquired in childhood. Blame is not the point. Locating the origin of our emotional wounding is the point, and parents do represent the source of our emotional wounds, which are the deepest leaks in our identity. Disapproval is a universal and unavoidable childhood experience. All parents subject their children to it—mostly in ways they are unaware—and all children learn to dread and fear it—with greater awareness and sensitivity than parents might imagine.

Unfulfilled emotional longings fueled by fear of disapproval remain the beating heart of our wounded identities—that is, until we identify our emotional longings, own them, and act on them directly. This is how we can heal ourselves and reclaim the power that we surrendered as children to our parents. Learning exactly how to do this is the craft of life. Learned well and practiced often, this craft will teach us how to conquer our fears of disapproval so we can build a relationship of authenticity with ourselves and with others. *The Craft of Life* offers a true and effective process for profound personal transformation.

Inner work as craftsmanship

Let's stop a moment and consider the term inner work, which is the psychological and spiritual effort one makes within versus the outer effort one makes at the gym or at our job. After several decades of self-exploration, I'm convinced that inner work is a true craft. In times past, whether making furniture, baking bread, or weaving rugs, a novice would spend years with a master craftsman, learning the trade. The process was straightforward: start at the beginning, learn and practice each basic skill, and repeat over and over, until the novice could demonstrate proficiency. At this point, he became a journeyman who was on his way to becoming a master craftsman. Mr. Tinnen and I were the novices; my grandfather was the master craftsman. Even as a boy, I recognized the distance between our understanding and abilities, and his. This experience set me on a general path of devotion to craftsmanship that continues to this day.

There is a crucial place in mainstream society that craftsmanship is rarely seen and that is within our relationships. How does one go about intentionally building a conscious, satisfying, and authentic relationship? How does one go about resolving the innumerable leaks that vex us all? We have no mainstream social organizations that teach these particular skills. A person can learn the intricacies of computer programming or how to play the piano, but where does one learn the equivalent in building healthy, satisfying relationships? Parents do not intentionally teach their children how to build quality relationships; they simply model their own, which is typically fraught with all kinds of unconscious behavior and unintended results.

Living symbols

Unwinding all of this would seem to be a daunting, perhaps impossible task. Actually, this is not the case because we have **Living Symbols** as our great ally. All of the outer forms that compose our lives are what I call living symbols because they represent our inner beliefs and inner identity. Most of us experience the outer details of our lives and take them more or less at face value. Our car is what we drive. Our job is what we do to earn money. Our spouse is the person whom we married. Apart from their practical and emotional value, the outer details of our lives do not seem to have additional meaning, but nothing could be further from the truth. From the nearly unlimited possibilities that life presents, each of us chooses to wear specific clothes in a distinctive way, eat particular food, work at a specific job, make relationships with particular people, and express attitudes and values that represent who we are. The tens of thousands of details that each of us has chosen reflect our self-image and make us different from anyone else. Seeing these details as expressions of our personal beliefs is to see life as living symbols. If we took the time to note the outer details in our lives, we would begin to see a picture of a specific person along with a belief system. We would begin to see our own unique identity reflected back to us. If we penetrated into the deeper meaning of these details, we would discover the root cause of our own identity, and we would begin to understand our relationships and ourselves with great clarity.

One can trace any leak from where it exits, which is easy to find because of the puddles and water stains, and follow its trail back to its entry point. This is the craft we are about to learn. Our focus, however, will be on the leaks in our lives: the unfulfilled emotional longings in our current relationships, the cracks in our self-esteem, and the repeating dissatisfactions produced by our fear of disapproval. These particular living symbols represent our puddles and water stains. They are all clearly visible; we know them well, so we all know where our journey begins. There is a place in our lives where they first entered, which were our parent-child collisions; there is a place where they now manifest, which is in our current life and relationships, and these two points—past and present—are connected as plainly as they were in that physical auditorium. By having the willingness to look at the outer details of our lives and our relationships in a new way, by learning about identity's inner structure and the natural laws by which it is bound, we can bring clarity to life issues that have plagued us for years. We can solve the unsolvable mysteries we gave up on long ago: our sure guide will be the living symbols around us.

CHAPTER 2

Perception and Belief

Man is made by his belief. As he believes, so he is.

—Goethe

PERCEPTION IS WHERE OUR consciousness begins. We receive the world through our senses, then perceptions naturally follow. Perceptions are mostly autonomic; we don't have to do anything but receive them. Let's stop for a moment and perceive consciously. Don't think or edit, just sit quietly and observe the sights, sounds, and smells around you. Sitting in my chair, I see the walls and ceiling of this room. I hear a dog barking in the distance. I smell lemon furniture wax. The world is composed of trillions of things to perceive and all we need is to be alive and present to receive them. Perception is the first step; it is the foundation of human consciousness.

But perceptions are only raw data. To make sense of them, we must introduce meaning. From the earliest age, we begin the process of enculturation, learning about the myriad concepts that we perceive from the cultural perspectives into which we were born. We learn that a doorway is something we walk through, a chair is to sit on, an apple is food to eat. Billions of concepts, thousands of words—all of which we learn about and store in memory. With meanings now attached, we can understand the things that we perceive. But to build a personal life, we need a way to rapidly organize our perceptions into a functional scheme. To do this we ask ourselves a specific question, and that one question answered carries the transformative power of alchemy. One question, one answer, fantastic power. We ask ourselves, does this perception appear to be real or true?

Imagine someone gently tosses a softball at you. You respond by raising your hands and catching the ball. What does your reaction mean? You perceived the ball coming toward you, and you understood the concept of a softball striking your body and potentially causing you pain. Your perception of the ball coming toward you appeared to be true. You believed what you saw, so you raised your hands to catch the ball. Incoming softball (perception) appears real (belief is formed), so you decide (choice preceding action) to raise your hands to catch the ball (action based on belief). Perception, belief, decision, action. So, when our answer is, "Yes, this appears to be real or true," our perception instantly transforms into a personal belief and we respond accordingly. When our answer is no, our perception disappears like smoke in the wind.

A perception that appears to be real or true becomes a belief. In this simple, black and white fashion, this clear on-or-off binary way, we convert all of our raw perceptions into personal beliefs—or not. However, once we throw that switch and create a belief, we have formed the basis from which we will make our decisions and then take our actions, because decisions and actions are always based on what we believe. This means that perception, belief, decision, and action are linked sequentially to form the foundation of our lives.

Let's replay our example, only this time imagine someone tosses you a bowling ball instead. You perceive the ball coming toward you; you understand the concept of a heavy ball striking your foot, potentially causing you severe harm. Your perception appears true, so you believe what you perceive, and you decide not to raise your hands but to step aside to avoid the ball entirely. In this case, there's a bigger, heavier ball—different perception, different belief—and, as a result, a different decision and action. The point is that action is always based on what you believe, and belief is always based on what you perceive to be real or true.

Let's replay this scene one more time. Imagine that you are tossing a softball to E.T. the extraterrestrial. He perceives the ball coming toward him but has no concept of what it is. There are no softballs on his planet. To him the softball is unknown, but he trusts you not to hurt him, so he does not raise his hands. Thunk, the ball strikes him on the head. "Ouch, E.T. hurt," he says. His perception of the incoming softball was not associated with pain, so he did not raise his hands or try to catch the ball. His action was based on what he believed. Next time E.T. will raise his hands because his perception and his beliefs have changed. E.T. is no dummy.

Whenever we perceive something that appears to be real or true, one of two things happens: a new belief is created or an existing belief is reinforced. This process happens automatically: new beliefs join our inventory of existing beliefs, while reinforced beliefs simply get stronger. We carry our entire belief system in our memory wherever we go, so it is always readily available. It is our belief system that creates our experience of reality.

Let's note that perceptions can be actual or imagined; both have exactly the same power. Here are some examples of actual perceptions: I see my keys on the table; this perception appears to be true so I believe my keys are on the table. I smell bread baking; this perception appears to be real, so I believe bread is baking. I hear my neighbor singing; I feel the heat of the fire; all these perceptions appear to be real or true, so I believe them. This concept applies equally to an imagined perception, which could be any of the above but happening only in mind through a memory, dream, daydream, hallucination, and so on. This is why the illusion of 3D movies works. We perceive the boulder coming out of the screen is heading straight for us, so we duck because it appears real. After, when we realize it was just a film image, we laugh at how real it seemed. The same concept applies to the keys we saw on the table. As we get closer, we realize that what we thought were keys was actually loose change. From a distance we believed one thing (keys), but when we got closer our belief changed (loose change). *A perception that appears to be real or true becomes a belief.*

An early personal experiment exploring beliefs

When I was eight, I did one of those dumb, impulsive things kids do. I prefer to dignify it as one of my earliest sociological experiments. For whatever reason, I thought it would be interesting to pretend to throw a spitball at the kid sitting three chairs in front of me. My thinking was that the music teacher, seeing my very real-looking actions, would believe that I actually threw it, when, in fact, I did not. Why on earth I would do this I cannot say, but I did it. I waited until my teacher was watching. I cocked my arm like I was throwing a baseball and then hurled nothing at the kid three seats in front of me. The teacher immediately demanded to know why I threw a spit ball. I told her, "I didn't throw anything." "I saw you throw it," she said. "No, I only pretended to throw it." "I *saw* you throw it." she said angrily. "No," I insisted, "I only *pretended* to throw it." Needless to say, I didn't win this argument. Though I tried to explain my insanity, in the end, she showed no appreciation for science or empirical testing, and I ended up in the principal's office. After this episode, she forever believed that I was a liar—a perception that appeared to be true—and I never again gained any further ground with my music teacher. Did I mention the experiment was a success?

She perceived me throwing something at the other kid, so she believed it was true, and nothing I said could alter her perception. This is commonly the case, she, like the rest of us, believed unshakably in what she perceived as true. This is both the power and trap of our personal beliefs: we accept our beliefs with something close to certainty, so when we are wrong, it is hard to see and almost impossible to believe. As human beings we relate to each other not based on a factual reality, but on our perception of reality. And our perception is often wrong by a lot. This is important when you consider that our perceptions form the basis for our decisions and actions.

You will choose your spouse and your occupation based on what you believe. You will decide how to raise your children, who to vote for president, and what to eat for breakfast—all based on what you believe. In fact, everything you will ever do will be based on what you believe and not on what you think or feel. I can say without hesitation that belief is literally the bedrock of human life. I can also say it makes enormous sense that we begin to understand our own beliefs because they are the essence of our identity, and they hold the true explanation for all that is not working in our lives. Every one of our private dissatisfactions is rooted in our perceptions and beliefs.

The meaning of beliefs

To most of us, a table is just a table—a mass of solid matter—but to a physicist the same table is the *appearance* of solid matter composed of tiny building blocks or atoms. These are two different perceptions of the same thing. The physicist might continue further and tell us that the atoms themselves are composed of even smaller units called protons, neutrons, and electrons or subatomic particles. The fact is that a table exists as solid matter, as a cluster of atoms, as subatomic particles, and as energy—all at the same time. This represents a complex view of the same thing. However, when most of us look at a table, we see solid wood and don't consider anything further. We can choose to use a table simply to eat dinner on, or we can choose to use the same table to understand the atomic construction of the universe.

Our lives are like that dinner table. We can perceive them as nothing more exotic than us going about our daily living, or we can choose to look more deeply and learn to perceive the beliefs from which our lives are constructed. Beliefs are the fundamental building blocks of who we are. They are the atoms and subatomic particles of our existence. While it is not necessary for most of us to understand the construction of the universe, it would benefit all of us to understand the architecture of our personal identity. So we have a choice: to perceive our lives and relationships just as they appear—to accept them at face value—or to look more deeply and see our lives as a complex constellation of beliefs. If we choose to understand and use beliefs in this manner, extraordinary self-understanding becomes possible.

Beliefs: The imperceptible key to understanding

Little in mainstream society asks us to identify or explain what we believe. It is culturally sufficient that we simply express our opinions, and it would appear the more forcefully the better. The result is that few of us realize how our beliefs directly affect the emotional quality of our lives and personal relationships. Our culture does not ask us to undertake this deeper investigation, so it is likely that we have not done so. There are issues that are highly emotional, such as politics and religion, but even then, we know and express our beliefs mainly at the surface but not necessarily at the root. What beliefs lie at the foundation of your identity? From which beliefs do you decide and then act from? Which beliefs do you hold that cause the repeating patterns of dissatisfaction that you have lived with for years? These are the important questions, because it is only on the level of perception and belief that change is truly possible.

Today, like everyday, you will perceive the world around you, and you will determine which perceptions appear real or true, and by doing so you will form your personal belief system, which will shape your identity. From your beliefs you will make decisions and take actions and all of your actions will produce results, the sum of which becomes your life. Perception, belief, decision, action and, finally, result occur together in linked sequence—but they all derive from belief. At the end of the day, your life literally is what it is because of your beliefs.

Summary

Belief formation is the origin for all of our actions, because it precedes any mental or physical activity we might make: we must have a belief before we can decide or act. A belief is a perception that appears to be real or true. My entire belief system is with me wherever I am, and I use it to choose my possessions, friends, partner, occupation, or breakfast. Everything I am, everything I do, is a direct expression of what I believe, and I cannot change anything without first changing the perception and belief from which it came. All transformation, large and small, comes from a shift in peception and belief. In the chapters ahead, we will delve deeply into your personal belief system, especially your beliefs about fear of disapproval, which are the most important beliefs of all.

Chart 1
BELIEF FORMATION

Belief formation is the source and origin of all other actions; it is the event that precedes all mental or physical activity. Therefore, it is always the first action that we take.

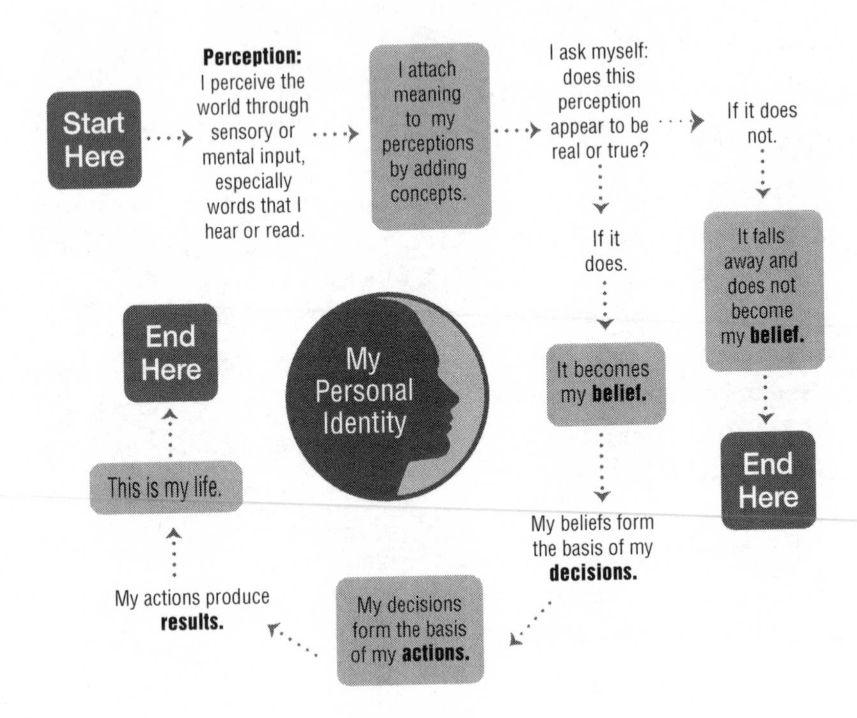

A full-page, color version of this chart is available for free download at TheCraftOfLife.com.

Exercises and group work

Throughout the book are exercises designed to reinforce the concepts you are learning. They will give you the opportunity to develop identity theory as a craft. One option, which I strongly recommend, is to form a small study group. I belive that a study group is the best way to work with this material. If you are interested, please see my second book, *The Craft of Life: Workbook for Study Groups*. It is a complete, easy-to-use guide that supplies the same direction and exercises I use in my own study groups. If you are working alone or with a partner, I would still recommend the workbook, because many suggestions will apply to you as well, and it will all but guarantee that you are getting the most from this process by undertaking it as it was designed.

Exercise 1: "The Monsters are Due on Maple Street"

Go online and find a copy of television producer and narrator Rod Serling's "The Monsters are Due on Maple Street." This was an old episode from the original Twilight Zone television series from 1960. You can find it on YouTube, Netflix, Amazon, or a similar website. It may be posted in three parts. View the original from 1960 instead of the remake from 2003.

Growing up, I was a huge fan of Rod Serling. If you have never seen this old black and white show, it will, to a certain degree, seem somewhat dated. No matter. It serves our purposes perfectly. You will probably need to watch it twice. The first time just to enjoy the show. The second time to see and understand belief formation underlying the actions of the characters. Belief formation is our point of focus with this exercise.

Following your viewing, answer/discuss these questions as an individual or as part of a group:

1. What is a belief?
2. In practical terms, how do you use your personal beliefs? Explain.

3. Can you think of any decision that you have ever made that was not based on your personal beliefs?
4. Can you think of any action that you have ever taken (apart from autonomic ones) that was not based on your personal beliefs?
5. Could you observe the belief-formation process in action as you watched the show? Give some examples.
6. Choose a character and an action from the show and answer the questions below. Be sure to give descriptions.
   a. What does this character perceive?
   b. Does this perception appear true to him/her?
   c. Does this perception become a personal belief?
   d. Does this character make a decision because of this belief?
   e. Does this character take action because of this belief?
   f. Can you clearly see that the result of this character's action came initially from what he/she believed?
7. Can you see how perceptions that appear to be real or true to a given character become personal beliefs? Give two examples of a perception appearing real or true to a specific character.
8. At the end, the aliens conclude that it will not be difficult to take over our planet because our beliefs can be easily manipulated. Is this just an old idea or are there examples of this going on today in our society? If so, name one and explain.
9. Does advertising take advantage of the belief-formation process? If so, give an example and explain.
10. Does our electoral process take advantage of the belief-formation process? If so, give an example and explain.
11. Have you ever used the belief-formation process to influence someone else? If so, give an example and explain.

CHAPTER 3

Personal Identity

And remember, no matter where you go, there you are.

—Confucius

IF WE TOOK ALL of the beliefs that we hold about ourselves—I believe I am tall, I believe I have brown hair, I believe I am a bad dancer, I believe I am a good husband, and so on—and mathematically added them up as though they were numbers, the sum total would form a self image. In other words, we would have a unique conglomeration of beliefs. This unique collection of beliefs represents our **Personal Identity**. It is who we believe we are. It is not who we are; it is who we *believe* we are.

Imagine a white moving van as it backs slowly into a warehouse loading dock. The van stops. A short, muscular man wearing white coveralls and a white cap gets out. He walks around and opens the rear doors, exposing a cargo hold packed from floor to ceiling with cartons. Each one contains thousands of sheets of paper. Typed on each sheet, line by line, are your personal beliefs. The man unloads each carton onto a moving conveyor that carries them into the warehouse and into the waiting mouth of a large, box-shaped machine.The machine works steadily, chugging and vibrating as it swallows each carton. Suddenly, it stops.

A tall door rises and out steps a unique human being who represents the sum of the beliefs that were fed into the machine. Personal Identity is the self image produced by the sum of our beliefs.

I believe I am a male. *I believe I have brown hair.* *I believe I have brown eyes.* *I believe I am 5' 11".* *I believe I am married.* *I believe I have two daughters.* *I believe I live in Washington.* *I believe I was born in Boston.* *I believe I love nature.* *I believe I love the ocean.* *I believe I like kayaking.* *I believe I have to work for a living.* *I believe I am a member of my family.* *I believe I am a member of my community.* *I believe I am an American.* *I believe I am a human being.* *All the rest of my beliefs.*	**Add this column**
ME (MY PERSONAL IDENTITY)	**Equals total**

Although the beliefs I hold about myself are close to infinite, if I could list each one and add them up as if they were numbers (see example above), the total would represent my personal identity. Put another way, if your self image were a picture on a computer screen, then the pixels comprising the image would be your individual beliefs. When examined close up and magnified, you can actually see and name each individual belief, but as you move away from the screen, the individual beliefs blur and blend into a single picture of you.

As you might guess, no two lives appear exactly alike, because no two people perceive things in exactly the same way. Throughout history and at any point in time, we are each a completely unique being because of our beliefs. No one like us has come before or will come thereafter—it simply isn't possible. Even twins who look alike are different people with different lives because their perceptions and, ultimately, their beliefs, are different.

Identity defined

If someone tells us we are smart and this appears to be true, then it becomes one of our beliefs. If we also perceive ourselves as strong and responsible, these beliefs combine to produce a self image of someone who is smart, strong, and responsible. In addition, if we try to sing but only produce an unpleasant, off-key sound, we believe we cannot sing. These four beliefs constellate with our other beliefs to create a single self image or personal identity.

Again, for a perception to become a belief it must *appear* to be real or true. If you sing off key but hear it as sweet melody because you are tone deaf, you will believe you can sing, and you will join your family around the candlelit cake and belt out "Happy Birthday" with gusto. As long as it appears to you that you have a good voice, you will believe it. However, perhaps you are singing and your cousin Jane remarks, "Good God! Is that noise coming from you?" And your brother adds, "I've never said it, but you sound terrible." If these comments or perceptions sound true to you, they will change your previously held belief that you have a fine singing voice and replace it with the new belief that you cannot sing. Old beliefs fall away when they are replaced by new, apparently truer perceptions of the same thing.

Referencing the earlier mathematical example, when we change even a single belief about ourselves, the total number representing all our beliefs also changes. This indicates of shift in identity, which is true regardless of how small or large the change might be. Identity transforms whenever we add a new belief or revise an old one: this is the definition of personal transformation and the natural method by which change happens.

Perception generates belief & belief shapes identity

It is during childhood development that our identity forms and emerges. As children, we interact with our world, discovering ourselves daily. Let's imagine a boy who is particularly coordinated. He walks early, runs nimbly, can balance on sofa arms; he is able to catch and throw a ball beyond his years. Each time that he performs some physical feat with his inherent agility, he develops or strengthens his beliefs about his natural coordination. Eventually, he comes to believe that he is highly coordinated because he perceives this about himself daily. As days and years pass and these experiences and perceptions compile, his unique identity becomes ever more pronounced, especially as he participates successfully in increasingly complex activities—from walking and jumping, to climbing on furniture, to throwing things, to climbing in trees, to successfully aiming a basketball or a baseball, to riding a skateboard, to skiing and surfing. The boy repeats the same developmental process thousands of times and his earlier experiences continue to inform the direction that he takes: he physically interacts with his world, perceives his ability, and believes in what he perceives because it appears to be true. Again and again he experiences himself as physically able—more than most. All of these beliefs concerning his physical prowess constellate and a significant part of his identity emerges for him and for all to see. Then he makes choices and decisions based on his beliefs. He joins teams and plays sports. He dreams about becoming a professional athlete and starts preparing himself for this inevitability because he sees himself as a better athelete than those around him. This process is so completely organic as to be invisible, but, as we can see, his perceptions continue to generate beliefs, and his beliefs continue to stockpile and drive his decision. His life becomes a living expression of what he already believes. We are the sum of our beliefs, and our external lives are a direct expression of what we already believe.

It is reasonable to take a different perspective and argue that this boy had natural ability from the start, which had nothing at all to do with what he believed or didn't believe. He was from birth a highly coordinated and a talented athlete and no belief was going to change that. While it is true that his natural ability is inherent, it is equally true that the emotional quality of his life and the use of his natural talent are directly affected by what he believes.

I had a client named Drew who was like the boy described above. He was strong and graceful in his movements. But instead of being interested in athletics, Drew wanted to be a ballet dancer. His father, a blue-collar factory worker, made it clear that dancing was for "fags" and no son of his was going to embarrass the family by doing it. Instead, because Drew was a natural athlete, his father pushed him into sports. Starting with Little League, Drew played baseball, then ran track and later excelled as a tennis player. But he was never happy or fulfilled, and he felt continual anxiety from the ceaseless pressure of competition. He came to believe that his natural talent was a curse that kept him trapped in a life he did not want because it did not express who he believed himself to be. Growing up, Drew's perceptions, based on *his* natural agility, generated opposite beliefs from the boy above. Drew perceived that having special athletic talent was a curse that led to his oppression, and, as a result, his life became an expression of these beliefs instead. Ultimately, he moved as far away as he could from sports and activities requiring physical prowess. Perception, belief, decision, action, and result always occur in a locked sequence. Natural talent or looks will always be affected by the beliefs we form as a result of our relationships, especially with our parents. In the end, belief trumps everything, including reality. I cannot think of a stronger statement to make about the power of beliefs and their effect upon our lives.

Summary

In the previous chapter, I mentioned two reasons why belief is the most important of all principles. We can modify this understanding; there are actually three reasons:

First, all of our decisions and actions are rooted in what we believe.

Second, all changes, great or small, come from a change in our beliefs. In order to transform ourselves, we must change what we believe.

Third, we are the sum of our beliefs. What we do, who we are, what we own—all of it is a direct result of what we believe. *Identity is the self-image produced by the sum of our beliefs.*

We choose a spouse based on what we believe. We raise a family based on what we believe. We interact with others based on what we believe. The entire emotional quality of our existence comes from us making decisions and taking actions based on what we believe. Our life, our identity, our ability to change ourselves—all are based on belief and the **Belief-Formation Process**. This is why belief is the most important of all principles; it is to our greatest advantage to take the time to learn this concept well, because when we come to understand our beliefs, to truly understand them at their roots, we finally come to understand ourselves.

Final note

This book will put forth ideas in stages or layers. There will be a first exposure, followed later by a second, which will be deeper and fuller, than later a third, which will be even more comprehensive. Each succeeding layer will be built upon previous ones. Think of the task of repainting your living room, which also progresses in stages. First, you move the furniture to the center of the room; then you scrape and clean the walls, spackle the holes and cracks; then you apply a coat of primer, a coat of paint, and you paint the molding and trim; and, finally, you clean up and move all of your furniture back into place. Different stages. Many layers. We are only at the beginning of this material: we are scraping and cleaning the walls. We will progress forward through other stages, but not until the end will you be able to sit on your sofa and appreciate your freshly painted room. In this work, you are undertaking the renovation of yourself, and this process asks for patience and stamina to move from beginning to middle to end. If you have ever repainted a room, you already know that afterwards, sitting on your sofa, looking at the fruit of your labor, it was well worth the effort.

Identity is the self-image produced by my beliefs

In this exercise, your objective is to see the connection between your identity and your beliefs. I imagine that some of the questions may make you somewhat uncomfortable. I am aware of this and included them intentionally. Our work together will be based on serious self-exploration for the purpose of genuine personal transformation. You are going to list numerous things about yourself, and then, like the machine in the warehouse, you are going to add them up and see what identity they produce.

If you are working with a study group, as with all the exercises, do it together. Put the names of the group members into a hat and have everyone pick a name. If you get your own name, put it back and choose again. In this exercise, explore in question-and-answer fashion. One person is the interviewer and asks the person whose name they have received the questions below and then that person answers aloud to the group. This is the group's first chance to create an open emotional space conducive to personal sharing. Be careful not to judge or criticize anyone for anything—that is not your role. Support one another in revealing and investigating personal truths. Mostly group members serve as witnesses. This is a skill that everyone must learn and practice again and again. And we will use this skill of conscious support throughout our entire journey.

Often in a group, there is someone who feels compelled to be right. The group must regulate this person immediately by bringing the issue directly out into the open and dealing with it as a group, otherwise the purpose of the group will be undermined. At first, this will be uncomfortable because confrontation brings feelings of disapproval. As the group exists to help all members dismantle their fears of disapproval, someone will have to be brave and speak up. Just say it out loud. Talk openly about your fear of disapproval and ask the group for their support; you will almost certainly get it. Now, it will be up to someone else to be brave and offer you support. There will be a confrontation and, surprisingly, everyone will benefit from it. Be careful not to politicize a conflict, which occurs when one member meets privately with another to form an alliance. Be bold. Put your issue in front of the group and let the group handle it together. You will likely be surprised at the support you receive. If you are doing this alone, write your answers down so you can clearly see them and have them to reflect upon later.

Exercise 2: Identity is the self-image produced by my beliefs

1. Explain how your car represents your beliefs?
2. Explain how what you are wearing represents your beliefs?
    a. Shirt/Top:
    b. Shoes:
    c. Accessories (scarf, tie, etc.):

d. Slacks, pants, skirt, dress:

3. Explain how your physical appearance represents your beliefs?

   a. Weight (thin, normal, overweight):

   b. Hair (long, short, dyed, curly, straight, neat, messy):

   c. Degree of physical fitness (fit, super fit, out of shape):

4. Explain how your expression of anger, or lack of expression, represents your beliefs?

Now in your mind, combine your responses to the four questions from this exercise to form a composite image. Can you recognize your own reflection from your self image? Can you see how your beliefs compose your personal identity? Briefly explain what you learned from doing this exercise.

CHAPTER 4

Personal Living Symbols

And you may find yourself
behind the wheel of a large automobile
And you may find yourself
in a beautiful house, with a beautiful wife
And you may ask yourself
Well . . . how did I get here?
—David Byrne and Brian Eno

LET'S BRIEFLY TOUR THE outer details of your life. First, look at the outside of your home—your house, your apartment building, wherever you live. Take note of the structure's type, condition, and specific appearance, such as color and style. Now go inside and look at your living room—your sofa, chairs, TV, and tables. Walk into other rooms and notice how the furniture is arranged. Open closets and medicine cabinets; look carefully at what's inside. As we have seen in earlier chapters, what you observe is a unique expression of yourself. No other human being will have the same home or objects kept in the same way. Your life, which you have populated with specific items and keep in a specific way, is a direct reflection of your identity and your beliefs.

It is the same with your personal relationships. In your imagination, see yourself with a good friend. What does it look like when you're visiting with each other? What do you talk about? What is the general feeling between you both? Where do you go? What do you do? Again, what you see is unique to you. No other person has friendships like yours. Your life, your home, your relationships all reflect with great specificity what you believe.

You perceive the world through your senses. Perceptions that appear to be real or true become your beliefs. The sum of your beliefs produces your personal identity. Once your identity is formed, you embrace possessions, activities, relationships, ideas, and values that represent what you already believe. All of these populate your life and become your personal **Living Symbols.** *Living* because they are alive right now. *Symbols* because they represent something more than what they appear to be; they represent your beliefs. Living symbols are your beliefs made manifest and personal beliefs are the source of our individuality.

Living symbols—a closer look

If you believe Mrs. Smith, whom you see at church each week, is a kind, charming elderly lady, but you believe your neighbor's blue-haired daughter, a politcally-active teenager, whom you rarely see, is irritating and disturbing, then Mrs. Smith is one of your living symbols who represents attitudes you approve of, while your neighbor's daughter is one of your living symbols who represents attitudes you disapprove of. There is no good or bad, only your different beliefs represented by two different people, who become two specific living symbols in your life. In this simple and direct way, your living symbols (Mrs. Smith and the teenage girl) represent what you believe.

If you believe being physically fit is important, then you might have a drawer full of vitamins and supplements, a refrigerator stocked with organic foods, a membership to a local gym, and workout clothes hanging in your closet. You would not likely have a cabinet full of junk food or a refrigerator loaded with highly-processed foods or be sixty pounds overweight. Eating well and staying physically fit are living symbols that represent what you believe about your health and body. The source or origin of your beliefs are also important to consider. You may eat well and stay physically fit because your mother criticized you when you were growing up if you gained weight or became unfit. Your obsession with eating well and staying fit then are living symbols that represent your fear of your mother's disapproval. In this simple and direct way, your living symbols represent two different levels of your personal beliefs.

Perhaps you are married and for years your spouse does not give you what you emotionally long for, which is to be seen and valued. Not getting what you emotionally long for from your partner becomes a living symbol that represents your fear of owning and asking for your own emotional longings. It is likely that you have never asked your partner to see and value you because you believe that doing so would bring disapproval and rejection. This results in tension and disconnection within your relationship, all of which are living symbols that represent your fear of embracing and communicating your own emotional longings. In this simple and direct way, your living symbols of ongoing dissatisfaction in your relationship represent your hidden beliefs.

When you believe something, it manifests in your life and appears in a form that accurately represents it. This cause and effect relationship between our inner beliefs and their outer manifestation is what makes living symbols so valuable; they are a true way to see and understand ourselves—our inner beliefs—by examining what is outside of ourselves. Thus, our outer life reflects our inner beliefs.

There are no exceptions to this principle. If something is in your life, whether it is a physical object, a relationship, a value, or a behavior, it is because it represents your beliefs. Perception generates belief; belief forms identity; identity makes or chooses that which expresses what it already believes, and all of these are living symbols, which are identity's beliefs made manifest. This is called the law of identity. All visible forms comprise a living language that communicate who we believe we are. From this perspective, life is a three-dimensional mirror, and, wherever we look, we see our own beliefs, our own identity, reflected back to us in symbolic form.

The power and beauty of living symbols is that they are 100 percent accurate because they are bound by the natural law of identity, which is always present and active like the laws of gravity and motion. Although not recognized as a scientific principle, I believe one day it will be, because the law of identity represents cause and effect at its most fundamental level. Living symbols cannot lie, conceal, or camouflage; they must accurately represent belief. It is possible to look at the living symbols in any person's life, and regardless of language, age, gender, education, mental, or emotional condition, those living symbols will reveal conclusively who that person believes him or herself to be.

Your personal living symbols reveal where you are currently emotionally wounded, how you were first wounded, what you are afraid of, how you hide your fear, and what you need to do to heal yourself. As we move forward, we will work with our own living symbols for they will guide us safely and accurately along our way. The greater issue lies in your ability to accept your own living symbols and what they reflect about you and your beliefs, because arguing with living symbols is like arguing with a mirror.

The organic nature of living symbols

In all of the above examples, the living symbols are self-created or chosen, but what about those forms that are not, such as physical diseases, mental illness, or sexual orientation? And what about naturally occurring events like twists of fate or accidents? We don't choose diabetes as though it were a pair of new shoes, and we don't intentionally seek out a car accident like we would a new job. Nonetheless, all observable forms, including illness, addiction, natural disasters, and so forth are living symbols that strictly conform to the law of identity. These living symbols manifest from a deeper, unconscious part of identity. In later chapters, we will delve into the seen and hidden selves and these other organic forms of living symbols. We will explore the process by which they enter our lives, as well as constructive methods for managing their painful presence.

The idea that life occurs in a specific cause and effect relationship, especially when applied to those who appear to be innocent, can be disturbing. How could being born with a cleft palate or some other challenging medical condition be a living symbol, representing a belief? Most people believe in genetics: the principle that physical traits are carried forward from generation to generation. It is widely known that genetics includes a propensity for passing along specific diseases. My grandfather and father both had diabetes, so it was not a surprise when I was diagnosed with the illness, which can pass from generation to generation. Is it such a great leap to include belief in this equation? Is it such a stretch of imagination to consider there is not only a genetics of biology but also a genetics of consciousness? Beliefs are passed down from generation to generation, and these beliefs comprise a family lineage as surely as facial features, body shape, or specific talent. We believe we are individuals when in fact we have generations living inside us. We are born into a family shaped by beliefs from relatives in times and places long past. There is nothing random in life, only the continuation of beliefs from generation to generation and, unfortunately, many of these beliefs were hurtful, lacking in consciousness, and out of balance. All this really means is that life is based on collective responsibility. We must take ownership of ourselves, our world, and each other, which doesn't strike me as a particularly outlandish notion.

Chart 2
THE LAW OF IDENTITY

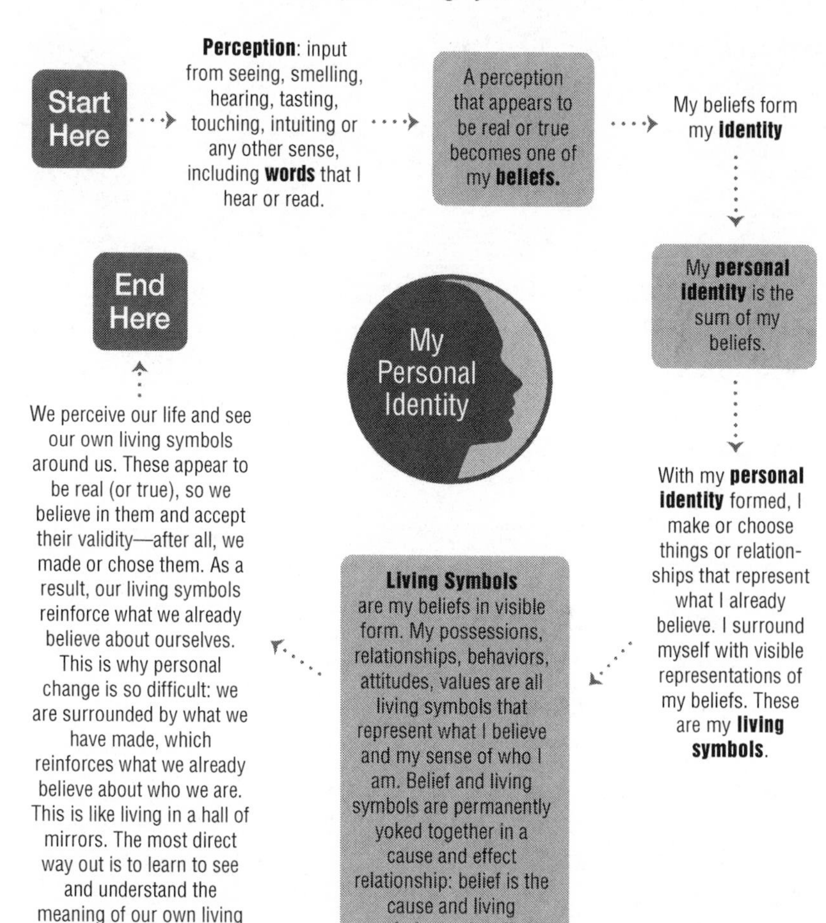

A full-page, color version of this chart is available for free download at TheCraftOfLife.com.

Exercise 3: How living symbols represent my beliefs

From this point forward, continue on as described in previous chapters with group exercises or individual work. Everyone should arrive prepared to discuss the questions at the bottom of this page. For groups, put everyone's name back into a bag and pick names. If you get your own, choose again. Start with members who have not had the chance to speak much. The person who has chosen your name should act as interviewer and ask the following questions. Interviewer: do not be rigid. If you have related questions that will help the person flesh out a fuller response, ask them. Use the questions below as a starting point. The rest of the group should listen attentively and may ask supporting questions, too. It is not necessary to have every member speak. All will benefit from hearing the responses from others. Further, the group may choose to carry a particular exercise over to the next meeting. You are looking for a rich mental and emotional experience.

1. Name one object in your life that you use regularly and explain how it represents your beliefs.
2. Name one activity in your life that you regularly do and explain how it represents your beliefs.
3. Name one personal value that you use regularly in your life and explain how it represents your beliefs.
4. Name one relationship in your life that causes you pain and explain how it represents your beliefs about being hurt. Talk about the feeling(s) that you experience with this person.
5. Name one relationship in your life that makes you feel loved and explain how it represents your beliefs about being loved. Talk about the feeling(s) that you experience with this person.
6. The above list contains the following living symbols: objects, activities, relationships, and values. Do you agree

that by looking at these visible manifestations, it is possible to see into your personal belief system and your identity? Review the list and explain.

7. Briefly explain what you learned from this exercise.

1. The gym. It creates a stability I've never had before.
2. My calendar on my wall. It helps me stay consistent and accountable w/ how I fill my days
3. Be self-sufficient & independent. No one else will show up for you.
4. My relationship w/ my parents. They're more secretitive than truthful. It really made me value honesty.
5. My older sister. We've been through so much together and a part. And I can say now we really do understand each-other.
6. It really just tells me how much I value growth. The action of taking accountability and applying disipline in your lifestyle.
7. This exercise helps you take a step back and reflect on everything that is objectively important to you.

CHAPTER 5

Summary: The Law of Identity

Systems thinking is a discipline for seeing wholes. It is a framework for seeing interrelationships rather than things, for seeing patterns of change rather than static 'snapshots.'

—Peter Senge

IN PART ONE, WE explored the foundation of identity theory—perception, belief, identity, and living symbols—to understand, at a deeper level, the mechanics of personal transformation. Let's have a quick review.

We stand at the center of our world with our senses open, automatically perceiving life around us. Perceptions that appear real or true become our beliefs; this is the belief-formation process. The sum of our beliefs becomes our identity. We then make choices based on the beliefs we have formed. Our choices (our relationships, behaviors, attitudes, possessions, activities) are living symbols, which are our beliefs made manifest. From the perspective of living symbols, life is a three-dimensional mirror, and, wherever we look, we see our own beliefs in symbolic form. More specifically, we see our own identity, our own story, reflected back to us, and we immediately recognize ourselves in what we have created, so we accept it as true. This entire process of perception creating belief and belief shaping identity, which then chooses or makes forms that represent itself, is the law of identity in action. This also can be called story creation.

To change ourselves, we must somehow change our story by changing the beliefs that compose it. This means we must be willing to see our beliefs in a new way, because shifting perception and changing beliefs are the only way true transformation occurs. This is the most fundamental principle of identity theory. Once we form a belief, either consciously or unconsciously, we are constrained by the law of identity, and that belief must appear in our lives in some tangible form.

The beauty of living symbols is that they are 100 percent accurate because they must adhere to the law of identity, just as our planet must obey the laws of gravity and motion. If you took the time to note the outer details of your life, such as the specific people, possessions, and activities, you would begin to see a picture of a unique person who has made unique choices. You would begin to see your own identity reflected back by these details. Why did you choose this interest over that one, this activity over another, this friend over someone else? If you penetrated into the deeper meaning of these details, you would discover the root beliefs that compose your own identity, and you would begin to understand the hidden motivation behind much of your behavior, especially your emotional reactivity.

If we can learn to see our lives in a way that is factually correct, we can begin to understand who we are, what we believe, and what we really want. Then, we can apply our new understanding to resolve personal issues that have vexed us for years, even decades. However, until we can see ourselves, our lives, with this degree of clarity, we cannot understand these issues and cannot take control of our lives or solve problems in a direct and efficient manner. We must first see a problem before we can solve it.

In Chapter 1, I told the story of my grandfather perceiving, understanding, and solving the unsolvable leak in the auditorium building. In conclusion, I wrote: "*By looking at the outer details of our lives and our relationships, by learning about the structure of identity and the natural laws by which it is bound, we can bring clarity to life issues that have plagued us for years. We can solve the unsolvable mysteries we gave up on long ago: our sure guide will be the living symbols all around us.*"

We began with a first look at foundational concepts: belief formation and the law of identity. Now that we have an abstract sense of these concepts, it is time to expand and deepen their meaning by looking at how we personalize them within our own lives. In Part One, we have seen the skeleton on which identity theory rests. In Part Two, we will add flesh and blood and see how the skeleton comes to life. We will see how these abstract principles are operating right now in our lives and relationships.

Part Two

Understanding Conflict and Wounding

CHAPTER 6

Childhood Beliefs about Disapproval and Emotional Longings

The monsters of our childhood do not fade away, neither are they ever wholly monstrous.

—John le Carré

THERE ARE FOUR MAJOR factors that influence how we perceive the world at any given moment. The first is our unique individuality, which begins at birth. The second is our current age. The third is our family's beliefs, which we were immersed in throughout childhood. And the fourth is our emotional wounds, which contain our deepest fears and emotional longings. It is a combination of these four factors that determines how we perceive the world and how we form beliefs. However, it is our emotional wounds that have the greatest influence.

Imagine a ten-year-old boy horsing around in his backyard. Suddenly, he trips, falls hard, and breaks his ankle. The boy is taken to a hospital, where he is diagnosed with a severe injury to the bones in his ankle. The doctor tells his parents he will walk with a limp for the rest of his life. The boy, now physically wounded, perceives his new situation, and his beliefs about himself begin to change.

His original belief	His new belief
I'm like everyone else.	*I'm different now.*
I can do anything other kids can do.	*I can't do what other kids can do.*
I do not stand out.	*Everyone can see that something is wrong with me.*
I have nothing to hide.	*I have to hide my injured leg.*

His new perceptions create new beliefs. The new beliefs change his identity, which changes the basis of his decisions, which means his life will change course. Perhaps he will choose to drop out of Little League; maybe he will become increasingly distraught over his limp; perhaps he will develop a quick temper when other kids make fun of the way he walks. Prior to the accident he was physically fit, and he perceived himself as normal. Now he has a physical impairment, so he perceives himself as injured, different, less than, and this perception will dramatically alter his life. While most of us do not suffer from serious physical injuries, which is used here as metaphor, we all have emotional wounds that are equally affecting. These emotional wounds leave us feeling injured, different, less than.

We are born individuals, and we perceive the world according to our age and our family's beliefs. The final piece to the identity equation is our parents. This is because all parents, consciously or unconsciously, intentionally or unintentionally, wound their children emotionally. These parental wounds alter children's beliefs, which transforms their identity and changes the way their lives manifest. By this measure, parenting is the most significant of all jobs, because parents shape the world through the emotional wounds they unknowingly pass on to their children.

The formation of childhood beliefs about disapproval

I saw a television show[1] once that ended with the following scene: A young couple just had a visit from the wife's parents. They both feel like a tornado has passed through. The wife is lying in bed with a cold cloth on her forehead. She's exhausted and has a massive headache. Her husband, also exhausted, is leaning in the doorway. She says to him:

—"It's so strange. I'm thirty years old. I'm married. I have a home. I have a job. How come my parents can still push all my buttons?"

—"That's easy," replies her husband. "They installed them."

Parents establish the beliefs by which they expect their family to live. They communicate these through their words, behaviors, attitudes, possessions, and, most of all, how they handle conflict. Honesty is a virtue; hard work is essential; sex should be kept private; children should be seen but not heard. Let's use *hard work is essential* as an example. Parents will teach this belief with their words ("If you want people to respect you, work hard and do a good job."); their behavior (By working long hours, working at home at night, and working on weekends); their attitudes ("No wonder my brother-in-law can't afford a new car, he spends every weekend playing softball and drinking beer."); and their possessions (a spare room with the equipment necessary to work at home). Children exposed to these various living symbols, words, behaviors, attitudes, and possessions, will realize that working hard is important to their parents and conforming to this belief is expected, while failing to will bring disapproval. Modeling one's beliefs and values is a natural and inherent part of parenting, but it sets the stage for a series of future parent-

1 *Mad About You, "Paul in the Family." Episode s01 e05* NBC, (1992-1999; Burbank, CA), TV sitcom.

child collisions that will become traumatic events that will eventually wound the child.

Obviously, parents and children have differing perceptions and, as a result, differing beliefs. When a child fails to conform to a parent's beliefs, the parent feels personally rejected, hurt, and angry. Typically the parent will push back and emotionally overpower the child in an attempt to right the situation. On the other hand, when a parent rejects a belief important to a child, it is the child who feels invalidated. Then the child becomes hurt and angry and will push back against the parent, usually yelling something like "That's not fair" or "I hate you." While this may appear as an arrangement of equals, it is not. This dynamic begins in infancy and continues throughout childhood. During this period children are vulnerable and immature and cannot possibly stand up to their parent's greater strength. In fact, children want and need their parent's strength to assist entry into the world. They are dependent upon their parents for everything, especially love, protection, and mature guidance. But parents, not young children, hold the power and influence in the relationship.

Once these initial collisions over differing beliefs occur, a dynamic is born in which young children begin to feel a consistent pressure to uphold specific parental beliefs. If children do, they learn their parents will not disapprove of them. If children fail, however, they learn to expect disapproval and possibly rejection, which is painful and threatening. Children just want to be themselves—temper tantrums, bad habits, and resistant attitudes intact—and they want their parents' love, acceptance, and support, so parent-child collisions and threats of rejection are deeply disturbing. To young children, they're like powerful, psychic jolts. At first, they struggle to believe their parents would disapprove of them in such a hurtful way. A small child might think, "Hey, I'm just being me." But after the impact and pain from the first few parent-child collisions, the child relinquishes this naive belief, because he or she comes to understand the parent is completely serious.

Now the child is in emotional purgatory: trapped between fear of parental disapproval and the desire to be himself or herself openly. On some level, by some inner thought, the child realizes: "I have to be me. I can't *not* be me. But there are beliefs, behaviors, and attitudes that my parents disapprove of. I display some of those. I *am* some of those. I want some of those. This means I can't be completely myself in front of my parents anymore, or they will disapprove of and reject me. What do I do?" I am highly exaggerating all of this to make visible what occurs in private moments, almost imperceptibly during the course of normal, daily living and from the earliest age. Although I do not know the precise language by which a small child comes to these deeper understandings and realizations, I only know that they do. Often when I look at some innocent four year old, I reflect on the thoughts that went through my mind when I was four and I wonder, "How could I have thought that when I was four?" While children don't seem at all sophisticated, four year olds often perceive desires and emotions to a degree that would startle most adults.

The small child, faced with painful parental disapproval, is left completely alone to figure out this all-important question: "How can I avoid my parent's disapproval?" Regardless of race, gender, religion, or nationality, the universal answer is to hide. So we hide whatever it is we believe our parents don't want to see or hear from us. We hide our genuine thoughts, our true feelings, our sexuality, our anger. We hide whatever we believe might bring disapproval or rejection from our parents; most important of all, we hide our deepest emotional longings, because we believe with near certainty that our parents can't or won't give them to us. We so much want our parents to meet us with an open heart and mind, to accept us for who we are, to love and protect us no matter what. Instead, we perceive our parents, at certain times, as being unable or unwilling to meet us in these ways. Perhaps they are angry or disinterested, drunk or depressed, absent or busy. Any one of these situations, or a thousand more like them, creates deep, unfulfilled emotional longings because children perceive they can never ask for or have what they long for most.

For children wrestling with this heaviness, hiding their deepest emotional longings becomes the simplest and most direct answer—the most straightforward of coping mechanisms. So we give up our longing to be seen, understood, loved, or cared for or whatever it is that we long for most. You have done this and so have I, and this hiding creates an emotional wound that seals the direction a child's life will take. This profound event, this realization that we cannot have what we want most, which occurs in even the best of family situations, is traumatic. Like the boy who injured himself in his backyard, this is when our ankle snaps.

The decision to hide those deep emotional longings causes a change in beliefs, which spontaneously initiates a profound personal transformation. The child literally becomes a different person. At one point the child believed she could be herself openly and have all of her emotional needs met, but after a series of parent-child collisions she no longer believes this. Previously, she did not fear being overpowered by her parents, but now she does. She did not fear disapproval for displaying certain beliefs, behaviors, or attitudes, but now she does. She did not fear disapproval for asking her parents for love, comfort, protection, respect, or whatever it is that she longs for, but now she does. From now on she will work to avoid her parent's disapproval by hiding her deepest emotional longings from them. She resigns herself and accepts her decision as necessary for her own emotional survival. She does not want to risk the horror of rejection or abandonment.

This entire dynamic, as dark and disturbing as it sounds, is a normal part of our enculturation process. It happens to every child in every country throughout the world and across time. It is a universal experience. Growing up, every one of us chooses to avoid the pain of disapproval. This activity is pivotal. While it would seem that the opposite—seeking approval—would be a logical counterpoint, in fact, identity theory has nothing to do with seeking approval. Our emotional wounds are based on avoidance of disapproval and rejection, and this repetitive activity of hiding to accomplish that will be our ongoing point of focus.

It is valuable to visualize all of this as part of our family lineage. Parents spend their lives unconsciously doing the same thing with their own parents. Grandparents did the same with their parents, and great-grandparents did the same with their parents. Each succeeding generation fits neatly inside the previous one like a series of nesting dolls. From the toughest man to the gentlest child, an entire family lineage is built in this fashion, until one member successfully challenges the family's historical wounding beliefs, freeing everyone else to do the same. A Native American proverb says, "He who heals himself, heals his family seven generations forward and seven generations back." There is a deeper truth to this statement than one might believe.

Parent-child collisions—a closer look

Parent-child collisions over differing beliefs occur in two general ways: the first is a direct collision. This occurs when a child literally violates a parent's belief and collides with that parent directly. If *being neat is essential*, the child has defied this belief by dressing sloppily or by doing a poor job of cleaning their bedroom. When a mother sees that her child has violated one of her firmly held beliefs, she feels the impact from collision and reacts by reinforcing the belief to her child—usually with strong disapproval.

Here is an example of a direct collision in which Sarah's mother directly states her belief and upholds it by threatening fierce disapproval:

> "My mom was a neat freak. Everything needed to be put away and in its place or she came undone. At first I resisted and left dishes in the sink or clothes on the floor in my room, but she hammered on me relentlessly. Eventually I gave in and started keeping everything neat and clean. After awhile I realized that I was keeping things pretty much the way she wanted—although I still slipped up a couple of times a week and she let me have it. I don't know how old I was when I realized that I was actually afraid to leave things messy. I could feel my mom's disapproval hanging over me when I thought about leaving dishes in the sink or not putting something away. I love my mom, but she made me fearful and neurotic." *Sarah L.*

The second type of collision is indirect, and it is far more common and prolific. This occurs when a child, in his own mind, believes he has violated a key parental belief and anticipates disapproval for doing so. This collision is more powerful and formative because it relies solely on the child's own perceptions and beliefs. For example, a boy longs to spend time with his father to receive his loving affection, but he sees that his father is an angry, unapproachable alcoholic. The boy wants to connect with his father, but fears his disapproval and rejection should he ask. So he doesn't ask as a way of avoiding disapproval. A child will not ask for an emotional longing when he anticipates disapproval or painful rejection in response. All children are emotionally aware, and they learn at an early age exactly what they should *not* ask for.

William's story is a good example of indirect collision.

> "My father was an alcoholic. He worked his ass off in a car factory and came home every night and drank a six-pack . . . or more. I saw him slap my mother around many times. The thought of asking him to stop because his behavior scared the shit out of my sisters and me was out of the question. I knew from my earliest memories that he was like a pile of oily rags that could go up in flames at any time. The main thing my father taught me was to stay the fuck away from him and to not ask for anything—especially emotional caring—and his disapproval came as cold, mean words or a slap in the face." *William B.*

By repeatedly watching his father's behavior, William formed the belief that if he were to ask for emotional caring, his father would respond with angry, violent disapproval by physically attacking him. His father never directly said this to him, but William culled it from his own perceptions and beliefs.

Whether a parent or child is right or wrong, good or bad has little to do with any of this. How a child perceives the situation is what matters. In both of the examples above, the child feels threatened and hides what he or she emotionally longs for as a practical way to avoid disapproval. In the direct collision case, young Sarah thinks but never says, "Mom, I don't want to clean my room. I want to leave it messy. Will you stop being so angry about it? Will you stop judging and criticizing me? It hurts when you disapprove of me for being myself." In the indirect collision, William thinks but never says, "Dad, will you stop drinking so much and spend more time with me? Will you be gentler and more affectionate and take care of us? I want to feel loved and protected by you." Again, I am using words that are obviously too direct and sophisticated for a child, but they represent the true understanding that even a small child possesses.

From the earliest age, children learn to hide behaviors, attitudes, and beliefs, and they learn not to ask for anything that might bring painful disapproval. Things not to ask for becomes a short mental list that all children know well and bring with them into adult relationships. These are the specific things that a child truly longs for but is afraid to request. In the future, this list of what-not-to-ask-for becomes exactly what the adult child wants from his or her partner or spouse but doesn't get until he or she is able to ask for them directly. The words must pass her lips; she must learn to say them. In relationships, we don't get what we want until we learn to ask repeatedly for it in the most direct way. However, asking directly is nearly impossible when we believe that doing so will bring painful, humiliating disapproval and rejection, which is precisely what we all believe.

> I was raised by a single father who spent the majority of his time working to take care of his three kids. By the time I was five, I clearly understood that I should not ask my father for love, affection, or emotional support. He did not have these things to give me. More important, he did not want me to ask for them. He worked all the time. He was often angry, and he had no more energy or time to give me. That is what I saw and firmly believed. Asking him would have made him feel bad or angry and then attracted a terrifying and painful response. So, over the years, I became skillful at swallowing my emotional needs and not asking for love, affection, or emotional support. In fact, it felt unmanly to do so. I got through my childhood but then found to my horror that I became an adult who still could not ask for these things. I am now in my second marriage and am trying to undo my fear by asking my wife directly for what I want most. It's a struggle that hasn't gone completely away and it often leaves me feeling humiliated." *James G.*

When a parent overpowers a child with fear-inducing disapproval, that parent takes strength away from that child, or, more accurately, forces the child to surrender a portion of his or her power. The child must become weaker to avoid further disapproval. The child must subordinate himself or herself to a parent in order to prevent conflict and disapproval escalating into rejection or, worse, abandonment. This is what all children come to believe. Since the whole point is to avoid further disapproval, the surrendering of strength is necessary: we must make ourselves weaker and subordinate to survive emotionally. We must let our parents win the conflict. Essentially, we learned to escape these parent-child collisions by simply letting go of what we authentically think and feel.

What then becomes of our strength? It does not just evaporate like water in the sun. The answer, which we will delve into deeply in Chapters Eight and Nine, is that we hide our strength within the unconscious part of our identity. Thankfully, it is still there. In an oyster, we may find a pearl; in our unconscious, we will find our lost strength because that is where we put it. The strength we need to face disapproval and not be overpowered by it, but remain true to ourselves, is still within us, safe and intact, but hidden. It lives at the center of our unconscious like the pearl in an oyster.

Childhood beliefs about disapproval—our core emotional wounds

So what might children believe when they feel forced to hide specific feelings, behaviors, and attitudes? What might they believe when they feel too afraid to ask for what they emotionally long for? How do these beliefs affect their identity or influence their choices and actions in their daily lives, especially in their closest relationships? What living symbols might their beliefs manifest? Below is a brief list of beliefs that three children—now adults—carry with them. All are ordinary people who came from typical American homes. Each represents one of their actual childhood beliefs about disapproval, learned from direct and/or indirect collisions with their parents during childhood. They each give insight into how deeply their childhood beliefs about disapproval affected their adult lives. You and I have our own childhood beliefs about disapproval, which affects our current lives and relationships in much the same way.

1) *I should not ask my parents (or their proxies) to understand me. If I do, I will be disapproved of.* This individual grew up believing that neither her mother nor her father understood her, which caused great emotional pain. She believed that if she asked her parents to understand her, they would take it as criticism and judgment, and then she would receive their angry disapproval. She learned to hide her deep emotional longing to be understood. When she finally left home and began an independent life as a young adult, she took this wounding belief with her. Whenever she became involved in an intimate relationship, this belief came to the fore because it was part of her identity. The direct result was, first, she consistently chose partners who were proxies for her parents and who did not understand her and, second, she could not bring herself to ask her partners for the understanding she craved. Just as an orange will come forth from an orange tree, being misunderstood in her relationships is the living symbol that is the fruit of her wounding belief. This causes her significant pain, but she will neither express it to her partner nor express her deep anger, because she still fears disapproval for doing so. Her ability to be strong and to voice her pain when feeling misunderstood is precisely what she believes her parents asked her to hide a long time ago. So she continues to repeatedly hide her hurt and anger and her desire to be understood. This behavior now feels natural to her, for she has enacted it thousands of times. Although she has many strengths and talents, she is unable to voice her hurt or anger when she feels misunderstood. This wound, left unattended, will determine the emotional quality of her intimate relationships for the rest of her life.

2) *I should not ask my parents (or their proxies) for help, care, or support because they will not give them to me. If I do, I will be disapproved of, rejected, and abandoned.* This individual grew up believing that neither his mother, who

died young, nor his father, would help, care for, or support him, and as a result he felt great emotional pain. He also believed that if he asked his father for support, he would receive angry, even violent, disapproval for making his father feel criticized and judged. So he learned to hide his deepest emotional longings. When he left his father's home and began life as a young, independent adult, he took this wounding belief with him. This belief was now part of his identity. Whenever he became involved in an intimate relationship, this wounding belief came to the fore. As a result, he not only consistently chose partners who were unsupportive, but he could not bring himself to ask his partners for the care and support that he craved. Not to be cared for or supported became the living symbols of his wounding belief. This causes him significant pain, but he will not express his feelings about it because he still fears disapproval for doing so. His ability to be strong and voice his pain when not receiving help or support is precisely what he believes his parents asked him to hide so long ago. So he does as he believes he should, hiding his hurt and anger along with his desire for help, care, and support. It feels natural for him because he has done it many times before. Although he has many strengths and talents, he is unable to voice his hurt or anger when he does not receive emotional support. This wound, left unattended, will determine the quality of his intimate relationships for the rest of his life.

3) *I should not connect authentically or emotionally with my parents (or their proxies). If I do, I will be disapproved of.* This person grew up believing her parents disapproved of both emotional authenticity and emotional connection. She also feared that if she asked to discuss this issue openly with her parents, they would be hurt or disapprove. So she learned to hide her genuine thoughts and deepest emotional desires. When she finally left home and began her life as a young adult, she took these wounding beliefs

> with her, for these beliefs were now part of her identity. Whenever she became involved in an intimate relationship, these beliefs came to the surface. The direct result was that she consistently attracted partners who could not give her an authentic emotional connection, and she feared asking her partners for the emotional intimacy that she craved. Not being emotionally authentic or able to achieve an emotional connection in her relationships became the living symbols of her wounding beliefs. This causes her deep pain, but she will not express her ongoing frustration and loneliness about it because she still fears disapproval for doing so. Her ability to be strong and voice her pain when feeling emotionally inauthentic or disconnected is precisely what she believes her parents asked her to hide so long ago. So she does as she believes she should—repeatedly hiding her frustration and loneliness along with her desire for emotional authenticity. It feels natural; she has done it a thousand times before. She, too, has many strengths and abilities, but she is unable to voice her frustration or loneliness when she feels emotionally disconnected. This wound, if left unattended, will determine the quality of her intimate relationships for the rest of her life.

In all three examples, a belief manifests within a real relationship and becomes a living symbol made visible by the wounded identity that chose it. Our lives are always a representation of what we believe, and belief will always be the fuel for the manifestation of life.

Side note: *A childhood belief about disapproval is the result of multiple collisions between parent and child over differing beliefs. However, only collisions that instill a fear of disapproval become a childhood belief about disapproval. The absence of the fear of disapproval means that whatever the disagreement between parent and child, it is nothing more than a disagreement; it does not create a wound. A childhood belief about disapproval occurs when we believe we must keep some emotional longing hidden from our parents to avoid their disapproval and rejection.*

Summary

One day we will reclaim and inhabit our true strength—this is a goal of the *Craft of Life*. And then we will be able to ask for what we emotionally long for from our parents or their proxies. Our wound happened in childhood when we perceived ourselves being overpowered by our parents with disapproval. As a result we capitulated. We accepted their beliefs. We accepted the legitimacy of their disapproval, and, in so doing, we had to reject our genuine feelings and deepest emotional longings. Then we went further and sacrificed some of our personal strength—strength that we believed would be offensive to our parents because it would allow us to stand up to them and not be overpowered. But we *were* overpowered. We were frightened to death by disapproval and rejection, so we acquiesced. What else could we do? We had to survive. Are parents the bad guys? Absolutely not, for they were once children too. Being a child is one of the few things that all human beings have in common. Regardless of race, gender, religion, education, class, wealth, or age, all of us were once children, which means every human being experiences some version of what I am describing in this chapter. We know each other's pain, so it is no cliché that at our root we are all brothers and sisters.

Exercise 4: Things I learned not to ask for as a child

When you were a child, you learned not to ask your parents for certain types of emotional support, because you believed that if you did they would be hurt, would not understand, or would reject your request and respond with disapproval, anger, rejection, or abandonment. So you didn't ask. Over time these unasked for things became your secret emotional longings that live to this day in the depths of your heart. This exercise is about perceiving your pain from these unrequited emotional longings and the wound from which they first came.

Mother

1. Name the emotional expression that you desired most or wanted more of from your mother, but did not or could not ask for.

   ____

   ____

2. What do you believe her response would have been if you had asked her directly for this?

   ____

   ____

   ____

3. In your current or most recent relationship, do you receive a sufficient amount of this emotional expression from your partner?

   ____

4. Do you directly ask your partner for this?

   ____

5. Explain why:

   ____

   ____

   ____

6. Can you see a link between the wound (the source) that you received in childhood when your mother failed to give you this emotional expression and the pain or symptom that you experience now with your current partner? Explain:

____

____

____

Father

1. Name the emotional expression that you desired most or wanted more of from your father, but did not or could not ask for.

____

____

2. What do you believe his response would have been if you had asked him directly for this?

____

____

____

3. In your current or most recent relationship, do you receive a sufficient amount of this emotional expression from your partner?

____

4. Do you directly ask your partner for this?

____

5. Explain why:

____

____

____

6. Can you see a link between the wound (the source) that you received in childhood when your father failed to give

you this emotional expression and the pain or symptom that you experience now with your current partner?

____

____

____

Questions

1) By doing this exercise, were you able to see the root of your emotional longing(s)? Explain.
2) Were you able to recognize your deeper emotional wound and see it as the source of your current emotional pain? Explain.
3) Explain the connection—as you now see it—between your oldest emotional wounds and your current emotional pain or dissatisfaction.
4) Do you now believe the emotional wounds you sustained in childhood are still present and active within you and affecting your current relationships? Explain.
5) Do you believe it is worth doing the work to heal this wound? Explain.

Group Instruction

Each member of the group should do this exercise, then come together and exchange insights and experiences.

CHAPTER 7

Masking Behaviors and Emotional Longings

The only normal people are the one's you don't know very well.

—Alfred Adler

EVERY PERSON HAS A unique identity. Living symbols represent this through our individual face, voice, body, personality, and belief system. No two people are ever the same. It follows, then, that no two parents convey their beliefs in exactly the same way, and no two children receive them in the same way, which is why siblings have a different experience growing up in the same household, with the same parents, even when circumstances and conditions are comparable.

Faced with a parent-child collision, all children will adopt specific behaviors to avoid and manage their fear of disapproval. These behaviors form a mask we don to hide our immediate genuine feelings and our deeper emotional longings. As children, whenever we felt hurt by our parents, we experienced genuine feelings, but we believed that if we expressed them, we would face disapproval, rejection, or abandonment, which became our worst fears. So we adapted in order to survive; we learned to use specific masking behaviors as a practical way to avoid our private horror of disapproval and rejection. Once this pattern begins, we continue to use masking behaviors throughout our lives until they become conditioned and unconscious.

We all know the feeling. Suddenly, we look up and see big headlights in the distance. Disapproval is coming straight at us like a train speeding down its tracks. We feel its shake and thunder in our bellies as it nears, and we tremble in fear of what we expect to happen next: personal annihilation through disapproval. We're about to die, so escape is all we can think of. So we adapt. We enact a particular behavior to hide our genuine feelings and emotional longings and, just like that, the roaring train suddenly disappears. Our father is angry and fierce, so we hold our tongue, hide our true feelings from him, withdraw within ourselves, and go emotionally numb. These are masking behaviors. Or we go away and lose ourselves in a book or work. These are also masking behaviors. Or we go away, ask for nothing, and become depressed. Or we go away and get high or drunk. Or we don't go away and instead attack back, trying to overpower with greater fierceness. Or we stand firm and resist stoically like a tree withstanding a storm. All of these and thousands more like them are masking behaviors in that the behavior we finally present is a mask that hides our genuine feelings and our deepest emotional longings.

An example of how individual all this is may be seen in twins. Each twin (let's call them John and Jim) has his own personality. Over many years, their father has demonstrated that *hard work is absolutely essential for success and respect*. As boys they are given the chore to clean the bathroom. They do a quick, sloppy job and then go off to play with friends. When their father sees the poor job they've done, he becomes angry because they've crossed one of his principal beliefs. He takes this personally as a gesture of disrespect. He confronts both boys and demands an explanation. After hearing their story, he reprimands them angrily and stresses the importance of working hard, of doing a good job in order to succeed in life. John feels hurt and overwhelmed by his father's searing disapproval. He promises never to do a bad job again. Jim feels angry that his father cares more about a clean bathroom than about him as a person. He shrugs off his father's talk as hollow pontificating. Since another one of their father's beliefs is that expression of feelings is unacceptable, both boys hide their hurt and anger and say nothing.

If their father persists in communicating these two beliefs—hard work is essential and expression of hurt or anger is unacceptable—John will end up consistently working hard and doing a good job, because unconsciously he has learned that this masking behavior is what he must do to avoid his father's disapproval. He will work hard his whole life whether he wants to or not, whether it is appropriate or not, whether it makes sense or not, whether his father is alive or not. To avoid his father's disapproval, which he has internalized as self-disapproval, he will always work hard at school, at his job, at his marriage and family life. He will work hard without any conscious understanding as to why; he will only feel driven. Society may brand him a success, but within he will feel unfulfilled. John has learned the following childhood beliefs about disapproval: *I should not expect anyone to see or understand me, nor should I express my genuine feelings, especially anger. If I do, I will be disapproved of.* John's learned masking behavior is to work hard, which allows him to keep his genuine feelings hidden and deeper emotional longings unconscious, so he never has to deal with his childhood beliefs about disapproval. John is emotionally wounded and out of balance, and he will spend the rest of his life trying to sort out his masking behaviors and childhood beliefs about disapproval and the effects they have on his life and relationships.

His twin brother, Jim, will have a different experience. He will be unwilling to work hard or do a good job, because doing so will stimulate the wound that he carries from his father.

Jim will likely fail because he will resent feeling pressed to work hard or work well. He will spend too much time with friends, so his schoolwork will suffer. He will not fulfill the potential that his teachers see in him. In fact, he will likely have "an attitude." All of these are living symbols of his inner wound. He will not do well in his occupation, because he will be continually chastised for his sloppy work or avoidance of work altogether and, because of his built-in resentment, he will not respond by working harder. He will be more interested in having fun or escaping. He may fail at marriage, because this too is hard work. He will spend his life waiting for his father to come to his senses and stop disapproving of him, but this disapproval now lives inside of him and has little to do with his father anymore. Yet, he will wait for this fatherly approval, even after his father has died. It is unlikely that he will succeed at much because he will resent and resist having to focus and work hard, and he will not have a conscious understanding as to why. He will remain angry and unfulfilled at being misunderstood and wrongly judged: I should not expect anyone to really see or understand me. If I do, I will be disapproved of. *I should not become vulnerable nor express my pain or deep sadness within. If I do, I will be disapproved of.*

Jim's masking behavior is to slack off, avoid working hard, and play. By not working hard he keeps his genuine feelings hidden and his deeper emotional longings unconscious, and he never has to deal with his childhood beliefs about disapproval. Jim is emotionally wounded and out of balance, and he will spend the rest of his life trying to sort out his masking behavior and childhood beliefs about disapproval, and the effects they've had on his life and relationships.

Please note the specificity of childhood beliefs about disapproval and masking behaviors. It is nearly impossible to make simplistic generalizations, such as my mother is meticulously neat/I am not/ therefore my mother will disapprove of me if I am not neat. Or, my father is afraid to compete in the world/I am not/therefore my father will disapprove of me if I appear competitive. You cannot simply transfer a parental belief over to yourself wholesale. The critical questions to ask yourself are, which of your parents' beliefs actually wounded you and which denied you emotional comfort and nourishment? In other words, where do *you* fear disapproval?

Side note: I have been told by some clients that my emphasis on pain, wounds, and disapproval can feel negative at times, especially in the early stages of this exploratory process. I understand how someone could experience this material in that way. However, I believe a major societal problem today is that few have real clarity about themselves, their lives, or their relationships, and this lack of clarity prevents many from finding true healing within and emotional fulfillment in their relationships. In order to gain this clarity and heal our emotional wounds, we must be willing to confront our fear of disapproval. Willingness to do so is a prerequisite for genuine self-discovery and personal transformation.

As it was for my grandfather, the first step is to find the leak, which means to find our emotional pain and to see it clearly—its origins and present effects on our lives. We cannot heal what we cannot see. We cannot understand what we cannot perceive. Therefore, seeing clearly will always be the first step. This is no different from visiting a physician whose first effort is to accurately diagnose your pain or problem. Each one of us must confront avoidance and denial because we all use both regularly to manage our lives. From my point of view, this is not a good way to live, because nothing constructive comes from it—especially in rearing children. So, on our journey together we will delve into the depths of our pain and wounding, but only for the purpose of seeing clearly, so that in the end we may understand ourselves and begin to work effectively toward our own healing. This will make us more conscious, stronger, and far better partners and parents in our relationships. In Part Three, we will focus exclusively on the very positive act of self-healing.

Group support can also be a tremendous balance for the fear and discomfort that can arise in the initial stages of our journey. We learn we are not alone in our wounding or our struggle to understand ourselves.

Summary: Childhood beliefs about disapproval and masking behaviors

A child is born into a family. Growing up she encounters her parents' living symbols: their words, ideas, feelings, possessions, occupations, friends, interests and non-interests, as well as their personal problems, strengths, and weaknesses, including how they handle conflict, and so much more. It is through these that she repeatedly perceives her parents' beliefs. Some she accepts, because they fit with what she believes; others she rejects because they are not true for her. When she rejects one of her parent's key beliefs, there is a parent-child collision and a painful confrontation. The child's rejection of her parent's belief is natural because it is an expression of her own identity. She is being true to herself. So, for example, she hates to eat peas or to keep her room neat and clean; her mother hates that she won't eat her peas or that her room is always a mess, so she disapproves. As a result, the child either A) accepts her mother's domination and eats her peas and cleans her room to avoid disapproval, thus triggering a childhood belief about disapproval, or B) she rejects her mother's belief and refuses to eat her peas or clean her room as a form of resistance, again triggering a childhood belief about disapproval. With each choice, she adapts by exchanging her original belief for a different one, a natural behavior for an unnatural one. She adapts in order to cope with the disapproval she feels, which deepens her wound because her final choice is a distortion of her natural self, which becomes hidden behind her masking behaviors.

We all go through life with childhood beliefs about disapproval. They are wounding because they make us believe we must hide our genuine feelings and deepest longings to avoid the pain of disapproval, rejection, and abandonment. We first learned this as children through countless parent-child collisions, and it was then that our emotional wounds were created. We carry these old wounds into adulthood as beliefs that influence our perception and compel our actions in the form of masking behaviors. As a result, the emotional quality of our closest relationships is determined by our childhood beliefs about disapproval. Now, as craftsmen and craftswomen, we must work to see, understand, and heal each one of these distorted beliefs, which is what we are undertaking together, right now.

Disapproval comes in many forms

Disapproval comes in a myriad of forms—too many to actually list. Yet, whether you receive it physically as a slap in the face or emotionally as neglect, abuse, or rejection, whether it is screamed at you in fiery rage or comes through icy silence, whether it is spoken matter-of-factly or with corrosive words that cut and burn, all are forms of disapproval. We recognize disapproval as a feeling in our bodies. There are distinct sensations that all of us experience when we feel it. Learn to recognize these feelings of upset and sensations of disturbance; learn to recognize the location in your body where they appear and then come to know them simply as disapproval. For in the end, that is what they are.

Chart 3
WORDS AND PHRASES THAT MEAN DISAPPROVAL

Angry at	frowned upon	**Point a finger at**
abandoned	frustrated with	put down
abused		prejudice
admonished	**Gossiped about**	
accused	guilt	**Racism**
attacked, verbally		rebuked
attacked, emotionally	**Hated**	rejected
attacked, physically	homophobia	repelled
	hurt	resisted
Blamed		reviled
belittled	**Invalidated**	reprimanded
bullied	ignored	ridiculed
Chastised	**Judged**	**Sarcasm**
compared		should or shouldn't, told
condescended to	**Lambasted**	scorned
condemned	looked down upon	sexism
criticized		shamed
	Made fun of	silent treatment, given
Disappointed in	mocked	
disconnected from	misandry	**Teased**
disdained	misogyny	transphobia
disgusted with		
disliked	**Neglected**	**Withdrawn**
dismissed	not good enough	
disrespected		**Yelled at**
	Overpowered	
Found fault with	overlooked	**Unloved**

A full-page, color version of this chart is available for free download at TheCraftOfLife.com.

Exercise 5: Identifying my masking behaviors

In this exercise, you will identify some of your masking behaviors by keeping a *Masking Behaviors' Journal.* Please take a full week to complete this task or, better still, two weeks. It isn't worth rushing or feeling pressured to get it done, because, hopefully, you will be using the upcoming exercise for years to come, so take your time.

You will be on the look out for emotional pain, no matter how slight. Emotional pain precedes the appearance of masking behaviors. We feel pain, so we react with masking behaviors. That is their relationship. Please visit the list of feelings at the end of Chapter 15 called "Follow Your Pain & Discover Yourself." All of these represent some form of pain. If you acquaint yourself with these, you will be well prepared to do this preliminary exercise.

A simple, direct way to know you are in emotional pain is to recognize it in your body. This varies from person to person, but everyone can sense emotional pain in the body as tension radiating from a particular location, such as the stomach, heart, or throat. If you can identify emotional pain as a specific body sensation, you have a shortcut to knowing when you are in pain.

Whenever you feel emotional pain, write it down in your journal, then note your reaction to it, and write that down as well. Your reaction is your masking behavior. For example, I felt fear (a form of pain), so I judged the other person as stupid and incompetent (my masking behavior), or I felt shame (another form of pain), so I became silent and withdrew into myself (my masking behavior). It is also common to have positive or seemingly constructive masking behaviors. I felt emasculated, so I went to church and worked at the soup kitchen, or I felt angry, so I went off and read a book. If your reaction hides your genuine feelings then it is a masking behavior.

This is where group members can help each other. The reason is simple: while we can't always identify our own masking behaviors, it is usually easy for others to do so. Our masking behaviors are obvious to everyone but ourselves. You will need to bring an open mind and heart as you invite help from the other group members to identify and confirm your masking behaviors. Work together and try to list four to eight masking behaviors for each member. We will use these extensively in our work ahead.

Form 1
MASKING BEHAVIORS JOURNAL

Day	Date	Write a Brief Description of Your Confrontation	Name the Emotional Pain You Felt	Write Down Your Reaction ***(your reaction is your masking behavior)***
		Examples		
Thurs	*2/25*	*My husband told me not to be late again.*	*I felt judged, angry, and insulted.*	*I became enraged and lashed out at him.*
Sat	*2/27*	*My girlfriend told me my clothes were not good enough for the restaurant we were going to.*	*I felt shamed and embarrassed, as if I'd failed.*	*I became silent and withdrew.*

This form is available at the back of this book and as a full-page, editable version for free download at TheCraftOfLife.com

CHAPTER 8

Our Seen and Hidden Selves: A Divided Identity

Reconciliation is to understand both sides; to go to one side and describe the suffering being endured by the other side, and then to go to the other side and describe the suffering being endured by the first side.

—Thich Nhat Hanh

WHEN WE CHOOSE TO hide specific parts of ourselves—for example, particular thoughts, feelings, or behaviors—we are actually hiding the underlying beliefs that give rise to our thoughts, feelings, or behaviors. However, beliefs are neither physical nor material; they are not something to be put under our mattress or behind a box in our closet. A belief is a thought, an intangible component of the mind. So where do we hide this abstraction? And what happens when we do?

Previously, I wrote that children react to disapproval by hiding. They understand that if they hide whatever attracts disapproval, the disapproval goes away. It's a commonsense solution to a practical problem. "Who broke the button on the TV?" Mom asks. "Not me," says the five-year-old. Denial is a powerful form of hiding. "That guy is so gay—it's disgusting," says the father.

"How can he act that way?" replies his closeted, gay son. Avoidance, too, is an effective method of hiding. But the gay son may not realize his father's reaction is based on his father's own fear of disapproval from his parents. We all fear disapproval when asking for what we long for, for being who we are, so we all have something to hide. To accommodate this need, identity had to make an evolutionary change and restructure and divide itself into two sections: one to remain wholly or partially visible—known as our seen self; the other to be absolutely removed from sight or wholly concealed—known as our hidden self.

In a broad or general sense, the seen self represents the conscious part of identity, the hidden self the unconscious part. The concept of the conscious and unconscious come from the great body of work by Sigmund Freud, Carl Jung, and other depth psychologists. My concepts build upon the foundation laid by these other men and women; however, my use of the terms seen and hidden selves, while bearing relationship to other definitions of the conscious and unconscious, are specific in both their meaning and their place within my model of identity theory.

As you might imagine, our two halves of identity have very different purposes. *The seen self's function is to maintain a self-image that avoids disapproval by never asking for what we long for emotionally*. So we dress, speak, behave, and even think in a certain way to accomplish this. Our seen self acts instinctively and compulsively, aligning itself with our childhood beliefs about disapproval, which, unfortunately, leaves us with a boatload of unfulfilled emotional longings. It's easy to understand why the seen self requires a hiding place.

The seen self buries our emotional longings in the dark, unconscious hidden self. Our seen self believed it needed a place to hide parts of ourselves, so the hidden self came into existence based on this belief: *The hidden self is literally the perfect hiding place. It serves as the secret repository for our unexpressed emotional longings and sacrificed personal power.*

While it sounds like our seen and hidden selves maintain a harmonious relationship in which one helps the other in a form of symbiosis, the opposite is the case. The relationship between the seen and hidden selves is organically adversarial because both are diametrically opposed in what they want. Both parts of identity function in service to disapproval, but they do so in opposite ways. The seen self accepts and fears disapproval and responds to it by hiding, but to the hidden self disapproval does not appear to be real or true, so it cannot form any beliefs about it, meaning the hidden self literally does not believe in disapproval; to the hidden self, disapproval has no validity whatsoever, so it views seen self's beliefs about disapproval as meaningless because to hidden self they are non-existent. The hidden self wants us to stop hiding and respond by being true to who we are and expressive of what we genuinely feel. These are opposite perspectives, opposite beliefs, opposite agendas. As a result, these two fundamental parts of identity live in a state of constant tension, which means *we* live in a state of constant tension, because these two divided parts of self make up our one identity.

I believe that any system of inner work must teach people to see and work with the unconscious part of the mind in an effective, practical manner. If we cannot see our unconsciousness in some indirect way, then we are ignorant of half of who we are and literally cannot resolve our inner conflicts effectively or efficiently. This is something that all people doing inner work should look for and insist on. It must be a cornerstone of any genuine healing practice or little healing will take place.

Whenever you look in a mirror, you typically see one person, one identity staring back at you. From this moment forward, look harder, look deeper, and you will see two. Your seen self is easy to spot—it's the you looking back brushing your hair, tweezing your eyebrows, or shaving your beard; but hidden self is there in the background, mostly invisible, but waiting to be recognized. Let's start this new effort right now. Throughout this book, we will be examining and discussing the seen and hidden selves as though they were two different parts. Yet, in fact, they are one temporarily divided whole.

Following World War II, Germany was divided into two sections: communist east and democratic west. The capital city of the one unified Germany was Berlin, which was situated in communist East Germany, but it, too, was divided into communist east and democratic west sections. On August 16, 1961, in the middle of the night, communist East Germany erected the original Berlin Wall. The barbed wire wall surrounded the entire democratic portion of the city, effectively cutting it off from the free world and instantly turning West Berlin into a city island stranded within the borders of East Germany. This is an apt metaphor for the hidden self, which exists within the territory of the seen self, and is now surrounded by the equivalent of the Berlin Wall. Everything in it remains cut off and segregated from the outside world. The Berlin Wall stood for nearly three decades, and during that time it appeared as if there were two Germanys, two Berlins—east and west. In truth, there was always only one. When the wall finally came down in 1989, Germany reunited and became whole again. The celebration of the reunification in 1990 was felt around the world. One day all of us will experience this joy when we take down our inner wall and reunite our separated selves. On that day, our seen and hidden selves will integrate fully and become one.

Confrontation and the dynamics of the seen and hidden selves

This section will show you how the seen and hidden selves function together. Confrontation occurs. A parent-child collision happens in real time with proxies for our mother or father—for example, a friend, a co-worker, or customer service agent on the phone. We experience confrontation, emotional pain, and then fear. We believe we have failed and feel disapproval from ourselves or others. This sequence is universal; it reoccurs every time in the same way. All we need do is watch it during moments of confrontation to see it happen. This is good because its sheer consistency permits us to work with it in a highly-effective manner. When you know the train always comes on schedule, you know exactly where you have to be to catch the train on time. Confrontation, pain, fear, disapproval, and finally, hiding is the sequence that we will be watching for and working with. And, just like the train, they always come on schedule, every time.

Let's say your mother is a highly emotional person who consistently responds to your weaknesses by verbally shaming you. One day a bully knocks you down at school and humiliates you. You return home with your pants torn and dirty. Your mother asks, "What happened to you?" Her words and tone of voice set off a feeling of confrontation. You believe her disapproval is coming because you acted in a way that you think she will perceive as weak. You respond with the universal kid answer, "Nothing." Your seen self is aware of the confrontation and is actively hiding your genuine thoughts and feelings from your mother. Of course, this is all unconscious behavior; you have no awareness of what is taking place. While your mother is highly emotional, she is not stupid, so she presses further, "Something happened. Your pants are torn. What happened?" Within you, the confrontation escalates. You feel pain in your stomach and fear is washing over you like a fourteen-foot wave. You are standing in the spotlight. You believe you have failed and are being disapproved of. Your seen self shifts into survival mode. It adopts your childhood beliefs about disapproval, enacts your masking behaviors and hides your emotional longings as practical ways to avoid the impending disapproval. This all occurs in less than a second. So, you become silent, and you hide your genuine feelings with a lie: "I was playing at lunch and fell down." Your mother says, "Do you know how expensive those pants are? You can pay for the next pair out of your allowance and work money." You go off to your room. The confrontation ends. The pain and fear subside, but, still, you feel terrible, because what you truly long for emotionally is what you believe you cannot have. You cannot tell your mother that what you want is to be vulnerable, yet still be understood, loved, and respected by her. You cannot ask your mother for her help or emotional support because your childhood beliefs about disapproval tell you that these are not possible. This is what your seen self firmly believes.

We can see how the seen self reacted to the above confrontation. It responded to disapproval in all the expected ways, but what of our hidden self. What role did it play? Well, it was our hidden self that co-manifested the entire situation. It does this all the time to give us the opportunity to reconsider and choose again. Our hidden self lives in the unlit portion of our identity, voiceless and silent, while calmly and patiently waiting for us to awaken, to become conscious and to choose a different reaction when faced with disapproval. Our hidden self wants us *not* to hide our genuine feelings but to express them, *not* to hide our emotional longings but to ask for them, *not* to shrink in the face of disapproval, but to stand strong and be authentic in the moment. Our hidden self exists in our unconscious as part of our mind, and to reach through to the material world it manifests opportunities for new choices. These always come in the form of conflict or confrontation, because everything that hidden self represents is a battle cry for our seen self to defend itself from attack and annihilation.

Our hidden self perceives the seen self's fearful beliefs and attitudes, but these do not appear real or true, so they never become part of hidden self's beliefs. This means that hidden self literally has nothing to defend or protect us against because it sees seen self's fear, which is our fear, as false; actually it sees our beliefs and attitudes about fear as non-existent. Because of this, it is impossible for hidden self to take an active role in defense as does seen self. This would be like fighting windmills. Hidden self is confined to the power of identity, which means it may only manifest that which it believes. So it remains eternally silent but in full possession of our deepest truth, which is that fear of disapproval is an artificial creation that accomplishes nothing, because it is based on nothing real or true; it is the product of our own projection. And, so, hidden self repeatedly manifests situations that offer us the possibility of choosing again–choosing to see past our fear of disapproval, choosing to move toward balance and wholeness, choosing to act is such a way as to promote our own healing and awakening. All conflict and confrontation come from deep within our hidden selves. Each one is a call to awaken and to honor our genuine feelings, our deepest emotional longings—in other words, our truth. It is a choice we can make. Our problems in life are less outside ourselves than we believe, because their root causes are always deep within us. Whatever outer manifestation we are struggling with—a broken marriage, a bad job, a financial woe, or a chronic illness–all are living symbols. They are physical expressions of long-held beliefs that live deep within us. From this perspective, it makes greater sense for us to focus our effort within and to worry less with what is outward. This is why true inner work is so effective, while outer work, such as a mere behavioral change, often is not.

If we learn to recognize our hidden self when living symbols appear, and if we can learn to understand these powerful communications from the depths of our own identity, we will see indirectly into our own unconscious. This means we can now see what we normally don't, which will allow us to act in ways we normally can't. Inner work at this level is profound; it is what we will be focusing on together as our work progresses.

Calvin

Calvin, a former client, grew up as an only child under his mother's care. His father had abandoned the family when he was two years old. Though he grew into an extremely intelligent and able-bodied man, Calvin appeared as weak and pouty in intimate relationships. His mother never got angry at him when he was a boy, but she regularly let him know that she was disappointed in him when he did anything she believed was wrong. His mother's disappointment made him feel small and ashamed. If he raised his voice to her or tried to protest angrily, she became visibly pained. This made Calvin feel worse. With no healthy father figure to intervene, Calvin learned to hide much of his masculine strength when in his mother's presence. Displays of anger or independence caused his mother upset and brought immediate disapproval, so he hid these expressions. As a result, his seen self became easily frightened, dependent, and submissive in relationship to women (or people who reminded him of his mother). Conversely, he concealed his emotional longings within his hidden self—the beliefs that he could be emotionally strong and independent and express his anger openly.

Two of Calvin's childhood beliefs about disapproval were: *1) I should avoid confrontation. If I don't, I will be disapproved of;* and *2) I should not express anger. If I do, I will be disapproved of.*

Three of his masking behaviors were: *1) Give in and comply; 2) Apologize and do what the other person wants;* and *3) Retreat and pout like a hurt boy.*

This meant that whenever Calvin experienced confrontation, his knee-jerk response was to hide his genuine feelings of anger and to go off and pout, or give in and do what the other person wanted. This meant Calvin habitually hid what he longed for emotionally, which was to own his strength as a man and express his anger directly.

The beginning of healing

Calvin's seen self believed his mother disapproved of displays of manly strength, so instead he often presented himself as compliant and dependent when in front of her. Calvin's seen self believed that if he appeared this way, he could avoid confrontation and disapproval. This is a simple, logical conclusion. In our own lives, we make parallel observations and conclusions concerning our own fears of disapproval, then adapt in similar ways with masking behaviors and attitudes of our own.

When Calvin first came for counseling, he had little sense of his potential strength. His focus was outside of himself on the repeated failures that he experienced in his relationship to women. Whenever he tried to act with self-confidence, he became timid, anxious, and incapacitated. This is a prime example of how our seen self will direct our lives based on its fear of disapproval while remaining ignorant of other parts of ourselves or other options of behavior.

> Keep in mind the most fundamental principle of belief formation: you must first perceive something in order to initiate belief formation. If you cannot perceive something, it may as well not exist, because you cannot consciously form any beliefs about it.

Your seen self tries to create an image of who it believes you should be (in order to avoid parental disapproval); your hidden self contains the rejected truth of who you are. But it is these hidden parts of self that we need in order to restore balance and wholeness to our identity. When the seen self experiences emotional pain, it will typically seek a way out of that pain by the fastest, easiest method possible, which means enacting masking behaviors and hiding emotional longings. However, if the pain continues long enough and hurts deeply enough, the seen self will finally seek a more permanent solution, which can only come through awareness and understanding—in other words, consciousness. This desire is the beginning of healing because it marks the start of an authentic relationship between our seen and hidden selves, which is the basis for all true healing.

After Calvin's repeated weak and woeful behavior with women in numerous relationships over the years, of which most ended in disapproval and rejection, he began to seek understanding and healing. This usually doesn't occur until most other temporary solutions have been tried and exhausted, such as another new relationship or losing oneself in work, sex, drugs, alcohol, food, shopping, meditation, and so on. If the seen self has exhausted enough failed solutions, or, finally, if it just wants a way out of pain, it will choose to begin some form of genuine inner work. This may be psychotherapy, counseling, meditation, artistic expression, contemplation, active imagination, dream work, or some other form of self-exploration. *Simply defined, true inner work is when our seen self reverses its position and chooses to work intentionally to understand and integrate our hidden self.* When we seek to understand and accept those parts of ourselves that we have habitually rejected and avoided, we are then engaged in a genuine process of personal transformation. Unless some version of this deeper process is undertaken, a person can engage in self-help for years and accomplish little to nothing. On the other hand, if this is one's aim, then understanding and healing can begin in earnest and transformation can progress effectively.

When we began our work together, Calvin's seen self believed that strong, independent behavior, which included expressions of anger, had to be hidden because they led to disapproval and rejection. As we penetrated this issue together and looked at it in new ways from new perspectives, Calvin's seen self came to believe that hiding anger and strength was actually worse than expressing it. In our work, Calvin's seen self began looking at parts of himself that he had never seen before. This seeing with new eyes is what allowed him to form new beliefs. Calvin could not see these parts of himself before because they were unconscious to him.

So our work together represented a shift in perception that led to a change of beliefs. Calvin eventually came to the realization that continued hiding of his genuine feelings did not represent what he believed anymore, nor would it give him what he wanted emotionally. He began to see that this behavior had doomed him to a never-ending series of painful, unsatisfying relationships that always ended badly.

Personal transformation is not accomplished through a great act of will, like a deprivation diet. Using our will to stop a behavior is mostly a waste of time that in the end fails, not unlike yo-yo dieting. No one can suddenly stop believing something that he or she currently believes in, in the same way that no one can escape the force of gravity and suddenly fly. We must learn to understand and respect the unbendable power of belief formation and the law of identity. Transformation is accomplished spontaneously through a steady, gradual change in perception, which creates a steady, gradual change in beliefs, which then creates a steady, gradual change in identity. This is the natural flow of true healing.

We can use our will and choose to look at our fear of disapproval differently. This is the right use of will. According to the *Random House Dictionary of the English Language*, will is defined as "the power of control the mind has over its own actions; the power of choosing one's own actions." This is an effective way to work. Calvin could not will himself to express anger, but he could use his will to observe the detrimental effects of not expressing his anger, which he did over a period of time. This caused a shift in his beliefs. Once a belief shifts, so does identity—that is the law of identity. So, once Calvin's seen self agreed with and accepted this new belief about expressing vs. suppressing anger, his relationship to anger and strong, independent behavior began to change. He began to believe that owning and expressing anger and standing up for himself in his relationships were necessary for his own well-being. He also realized that to finally stand up *for* these women, to protect and support them, he would first need to learn to do this for himself. Slowly, and with extreme caution, Calvin's seen self began owning the anger and masculine strength that it had previously hidden and began to express it to others, including his mother and her proxies, or those who reminded him of her. When Calvin began to speak and act from his genuine feelings, he had less to hide, and, as a result, those parts of his hidden self became part of his seen self. This is the alchemy of healing. Several parts of Calvin escaped over his inner Berlin Wall, which separates the two parts of his one identity.

At this point, Calvin's emotional life reversed direction from unconsciousness toward consciousness, from continuous wounding to slow, progressive healing. The evidence of Calvin's change of beliefs were the emergence of new living symbols in his life: dramatically improved relationships, expressing anger when appropriate, standing up for his desires and needs, and finding relief from chronic back pain that he had lived with for years. As an unexpected benefit, when his mother reached the end of her life, Calvin was able to broach these issues with her directly. He no longer feared her disapproval, so could speak with her from a place of strength and solidity. This cleared much pain for him, allowing him to live even freer, and allowed their love to intensify and come to the fore. It also helped his mother pass into death with greater understanding, emotional connection, and peace.

Further notes on the journey ahead

How we deal with frightening confrontation and fear of disapproval contains the full story of our personal emotional wounds, which will become the focus of our work. Confrontation, pain, fear, disapproval, hiding—this is the sequence we will be working with, but frightening confrontation is the trigger. Meeting confrontation in a new way is the essential work of the craft of life; it is where our real effort begins.

A quick sketch of my seen and hidden selves

Within the context of our work together, the following exercise will give you a first glimpse into your own psychological makeup. Bring an open mind, a courageous heart, and a willingness to explore as these are requisites, because from this point forward you will be trying to see the two parts of your identity.

Exercise 6

Part 1: A sketch of my seen self

If you cannot answer a question, leave it blank. If a question specifies partner/boyfriend/girlfriend, you may use current or past relationships, or you may substitute your parents during childhood.

1. I openly eat or drink the following item(s) in front of others without any fear of disapproval:

   Anything lols
   ____

2. I openly do the following activity in front of others without any fear of disapproval:

   Cook
   ____

3. I openly display the following two personal possessions to my partner/boyfriend/girlfriend without any fear of disapproval:

   ____
   ____

4. I openly express the following two feelings to my partner/boyfriend/girlfriend without any fear of disapproval:

   Joy, meloncoly
   ____

Your seen self's function is to maintain a self-image that avoids childhood beliefs about disapproval, which means we dress, speak, act, even think in a certain way to accomplish this. The above exercise is a small sketch of the self-image that you are comfortable presenting to others without any fear of disapproval.

Part 2: A sketch of my hidden self

If you cannot answer a question, leave it blank. If a question specifies partner/boyfriend/girlfriend, you may use current or past relationships, or you may substitute your parents during childhood.

1. I hide eating or drinking the following item(s) from others because I fear their disapproval should they see me consume these:

   ____

   ____

2. I hide the following activity from my partner/boyfriend/girlfriend because I fear their disapproval should they see me engage in it:

   ____

   ____

3. I hide the following two personal possessions from my partner/boyfriend/girlfriend because I fear their disapproval should they see them:

   ____

   ____

4. I hide the following two feelings from my partner/boyfriend/girlfriend because I fear their disapproval should I express them:

   Sadness

   ____

The above is a small sketch of six living symbols that you prefer to keep hidden. Each is rooted to deeper emotional longings concealed in the dark unconsciousness of your hidden self.

The hidden self's main function is to be the container for our secret emotional longings. The hidden self wants its contents to be revealed and integrated with our seen self so that our identity becomes whole and open, and we become receptive and vulnerable because this represents our highest truth.

speaking up to anything I'm not okay with.

CHAPTER 9

Looking into the Abyss: Our Hidden Self

And if you gaze long into an abyss, the abyss also gazes into you.

—Friedrich Nietzsche

WE HAVE JUST READ about the seen and hidden selves, which are two fundamental parts of divided identity. These two selves can be seen at work in the film, *Black Swan*, which was nominated for an Academy Award for Best Picture in 2011. Although the film has strong sexual content and some disturbing images, it offers us clear, visual examples of the seen and hidden selves. By watching this film, you can gain a deeper understanding of the concepts presented up to this point. It also offers you the opportunity to experience what it feels like to look directly at something disturbing or unpleasant. You might consider this a preliminary exercise in facing one's fears, which is a necessary strength in the development of our craft.

If you have never seen this film, you may have to watch it twice—once to experience the movie, which is powerful, and again to see the concepts we've been exploring. Here is the storyline: Nina, a dancer in a major New York City ballet company, lives with her mother, a former ballerina, who treats Nina like a child and controls her to the point of suffocation. The director of the company, Thomas, is preparing to put on *Swan Lake*, which requires the lead ballerina to dance the parts of both the white and black swans. The white swan embodies innocence and grace, while the black swan demonstrates guile and seduction. Thomas chooses young Nina to play the lead role. Nina is a natural fit for the white swan, but she struggles mightily to express the sensuality and sexuality of the black Swan. To complicate things further, a new dancer, Lily, joins the troop. She catches Thomas' eye as well because Lilly personifies the black swan. As Thomas presses Nina to own her darker, unexplored side, she is simultaneously pressured by her mother to avoid these same feelings, and she starts to unravel.

In the beginning, Thomas talks about *Swan Lake*, the first production of the new dance season:

"This is about a virgin girl, pure and sweet, trapped in the body of a swan. She desires freedom, but only true love can break the spell. Her wish is nearly granted in the form of a prince, but, before he declares his love, the lustful twin, the black swan, tricks and seduces him. Devastated, the white swan leaps off a cliff, killing herself and in death finds freedom . . . We are going to strip it down, make it visceral and real. Which of you can play both the white AND black swans?"

This short monologue tells us what the movie will be about right from the start. It is a classic tragedy. There will not be a happy ending, but why? The answer may be found in the title of the film *Black Swan*. The black swan or the hidden self is the central theme of the film. In the story, the innocent girl (seen self) is asked to play both the white and black swans, something she is wholly unprepared for because she is disconnected from and terrified of her hidden self (black swan). As a result, pain, suffering, and tragedy ensue. Apart from all else, this is a cautionary tale of what happens when we are relentlessly driven by our childhood fears about disapproval to reject our hidden self and then find ourselves unprepared when our hidden self suddenly pushes its desire for integration straight into our face. Just as Thomas said, this is going to be visceral and real.

In the film, watch Nina as she works tirelessly to maintain a self-image that avoids her mother's disapproval. Her seen self embraces the white swan because it is aligned with its beliefs, and her seen self rejects the black swan because embodying it will bring disapproval, rejection, and inner conflict. As the white swan, on stage and in real life, Nina avoids her mother's disapproval; as the black swan, on stage and in real life, Nina attracts her mother's disapproval. The director wants her to embrace her inner black swan, which represents her passion, sensuality, and sexuality, but, at the same time, Nina's mother and her own seen self want Nina to reject the black swan and all that it represents.

Nina's hidden self does not accept any of her seen self's beliefs about disapproval; it wants her repressed passion, sensuality, and sexuality revealed and integrated. But Nina's seen self fights to maintain its separation from hidden self. These two equal parts of her identity remain divided and diametrically opposed in what they want. As a result, they appear to be in a pitched battle, fighting for dominion over Nina's life. This is what *Black Swan* is about. To fully grasp the content in this chapter, please stop here and watch the film. As you do, observe Nina's seen self as the white swan and her hidden self as the black swan. Watch her white swan work to avoid her mother's disapproval; watch her black swan press for recognition and validation. And, most of all, watch Nina, wholly unaware of this strained dynamic, struggle to maintain control of her life and herself in the face of these two great inner forces. Watch her use masking behaviors to hide both her authentic feelings and her deep, disowned emotional longings.

(Begin Here After Watching *Black Swan*)

The hidden self: A deeper look

Why would I ask you to watch a film with so many disturbing scenes? Let's take a deeper look at the hidden self. In the end, I think, you will be surprised.

I had a client named Beverly who had a recurring nightmare for decades. It began in her childhood and continued through the time I met her in her late 40s. Here is a typical iteration of her dream:

She is alone in a house. She goes out back through an oversized, heavy steel door. She sees a hideous figure hiding among the trees at the back of the yard. He has scars upon scars on his face. He is dark, repulsive, and terrifying. He looks at her. She feels a frantic fear in her chest and throat—like strangulation. He steps out from the trees. Her fear heightens. He says, "Do you see that this tree is dying?" She does not respond. She is too afraid. He repeats, "Do you see that this tree is dying?" She turns and runs toward the house. He pursues her. She runs, her heart pounding. She hears his foot falls behind her. Her fear escalates into panic. She reaches the door and enters the house gasping for breath. She is absolutely terrified. She slams the iron door shut and lets out a great sigh of relief. She is safe. She tries to turn the lock on the door, but it's stuck. Suddenly, she realizes there is a smaller door nearby, and it's open. The scarred man is running toward her, nearly reaching the door by now. She slams the small door shut and pulls the key out, and it becomes a sword. End of dream.

In our work together, we came to refer to the terrifying figure as the scarred man. The questions arose immediately: Who is he? What does he represent? The short answer was that he represented a part of Beverly's hidden self. When we disapprove of and reject a part of ourselves due to fear of disapproval, we abandon that part and it becomes a component of our hidden self. As time passes, we reject and hide that same part over and over, again and again. In our own perception, this part becomes associated with a deep sense of fear—something we must avoid at all cost. In our imagination it becomes a monster. But it is not actually a monster; it only appears that way because we are so afraid of it ever getting out and being seen by anyone else, which would cause unimaginable disapproval.

Biography work is the foundation of the counseling portion of identity theory. Beverly told her story. She had grown up on a farm in the Midwest as part of a large family. Her father was an upstanding member of the community and the church, but, within his family, in his home, he was an all-powerful, tyrannical patriarch. He ruled the family with power and fear, and everyone was terrified of him. As would be expected, her mother was obedient and subservient to her father. Beverly's father was also an alcoholic, so when he was not carrying out the rigors of farm work, he was often drunk and enraged. Whenever Beverly had moments of free time, she would take refuge in a grove of trees at the far end of the property. It was the only place she could find that was private and safe. However, one time, when Beverly was a young girl, she went up to the hayloft in their barn. A hired man, who was working during a harvest, followed her. He sexually assaulted her. During this horrific act, she turned her head and saw a small kitten staring back at her. Since Beverly was a talented artist, I asked her to do a painting of all of this—not from a literal or realistic perspective—but as an abstract expression of her feelings.

As we worked through her biography, we also engaged in a Jungian technique called Active Imagination in which one can take an inner part of self—for example, a part of a dream—and dialogue with it directly. If done correctly, the result is something like a waking dream. The part of self we wanted to dialogue with was the scarred man in her recurring dream. But this prospect terrified Beverly. After all, she had spent decades avoiding him, and now I was asking her to speak to him directly. Our pace was slow, conservative, and careful. We moved only as fast as she was comfortable. Over the course of our time together, Beverly progressed from first glancing at him, to direct eye contact, to stepping toward him, to approaching him up close and examining his scars, to finally speaking with him directly. Over time, Beverly was steadily building a relationship with the scarred man. Her seen and hidden selves were finally collaborating.

In Beverly's final Active Imagination process she opens the iron door. She goes outside into the yard. The scarred man is there. He is yelling that the trees are dying, but, instead of running away, she walks toward him, trying to recognize who he is. As she approaches, she clearly sees that he is grotesque. She asks him, "Who are you?" and he replies, "The way you see yourself." She asks him if there is any way she can stop the nightmares. He replies, "Maybe I could come inside." She walks back to the house, toward the steel doors. She is afraid but not terrified. She opens the small door for him. He walks into the house, but, as he crosses the threshold, he transforms. Suddenly, he is strong and beautiful. He turns and carries her into the house, where she realizes he is her true self.

As for the painting Beverly had made earlier, she brought it to a session, and we looked at it together. It is common for me to look at abstract art from multiple perspectives. In this case, I turned the painting first on its side and then fully upside down; it was then that the painting jumped out and came to life. Suddenly, there at the center appeared a child sitting in a tree with a sword through its heart. Scattered on the canvas were images reminiscent of wounded fallopian tubes. On one side of the painting was the scarred man, and off in a corner, as plain as though she had intended to paint it, was the face of a kitten. None of this was visible until the painting was turned upside down. Beverly had unconsciously painted her emotional wounds—all perfectly composed in one picture. More to the point, her hidden self, which Beverly was reaching toward, had expressed itself through her painting, albeit upside down. When Beverly saw this, she was shocked. Because we fearfully avoid our own hidden self, unconscious manifestation is often the only way it communicates with us.

Think of identity as extremely fertile soil. The seeds that we sow into it are beliefs. Once planted, our beliefs sprout and grow; they must take form and manifest into something born of that seed and whatever grows will be a living symbol of our own identity. This happens organically and spontaneously. This is the law of identity in action. We construct our lives from our beliefs, and every belief that we hold is an expression of our seen and hidden selves. Your seen self fears disapproval and works ceaselessly to avoid it, so it asks you to create a life based on these beliefs; your hidden self does not recognize fear or disapproval, and it contains your genuine feelings and deepest emotional longings. The hidden self is composed of everything you believe you should not ask for, everything you believe you must keep hidden, so when the hidden self does become visible, it appears as something that triggers your deepest fears, and it always manifests as something broken or not working. The pain and negativity of this occurrence—a lost job, a broken relationship, or an illness, for example—hides the more important fact that your hidden self is trying to communicate your yearning to express your genuine feelings and desires in order to have your emotional longings fulfilled. Yet, it is you who must recognize this and choose to do so. All the hidden self can do is manifest these deeper, hidden beliefs so that you recognize them and act upon them, thus healing your seen self and freeing your hidden self at the same time. Every conflict, every confrontation, simultaneously presents us with both our masking behaviors and our emotional longings. Do we want to hang on to our fear of disapproval, or do we want to reach for the emotional connection that will heal our deepest longings?

If your seen self fears asking for help and support because you believe this will cause disapproval, then your desire for help and support will become part of your hidden self. To bring your secret, unconscious fear to your attention, your hidden self might manifest a situation, such as a medical or financial problem, in which you really do need help and support. Through this manifestation, your hidden self asks you to consider your fear-based beliefs and choose again, with the hope that you will awaken and decide to ask for assistance instead of denying that you want and need it. This is the ongoing struggle between the seen and hidden selves—the two parts of our one, divided identity. It is the battle between our deep fear of disapproval and, paradoxically, our equally deep desire to have our emotional longings fulfilled.

Beverly perceived her parent's beliefs: their harsh practicality, their lack of gentility, kindness, or love, and their constant focus on finishing chores and ignoring feelings, communication, or relationships. Beverly's perceptions led her to believe she wasn't good enough, didn't fit in, and was unworthy of love and understanding. She could never directly ask her father for gentleness, protection, or understanding, nor ask her mother for care and love. She believed, and rightly so, that asking for these deep emotional longings would have led directly to her parent's disapproval and attack, so instead she learned to hide them from everyone, including herself. Because of her childhood beliefs about disapproval, which she accepted as true, Beverly came to view part of herself as scarred, defective, and frightening.

This explains why the first appearance of the hidden self is typically in the form of a monster or frightening creature because that type of image is what represents, in our own minds, our current fearful beliefs about the hidden parts of ourselves. I do not subscribe to the idea of good vs. evil. I believe there is only consciousness vs. unconsciousness. Our interior monsters pursue us, scare us, and injure us, but, in the end, they are only parts of ourselves that we have rejected and abandoned—parts of ourselves that we have kept undernourished and unloved. They are our emotional wounds left unattended for too long.

For all of these reasons, the deep emotional longings that Beverly hid as a child morphed into the scarred man living inside her and as the top-most layer of her hidden self. Only he knew her inner truth: that her tree—her one place of safety where she was free to be herself—was dying, and the gentle femininity that the tree represented was dying as well. The scarred man was pursuing her, not because he wanted to hurt her but because he was trying to save her. But she ran from him as fast as she could, because it was she who projected her fears onto that part of herself, just as we all do.

This brings us back to the black swan. The black swan, as it lives in Nina, is not a horrible monster, but rather Nina's sexuality, her womanhood, and her deep desire to be loved and protected, all of which she has disapproved of and abandoned in her hidden self because of childhood beliefs about disapproval learned from interacting with her parents. If Nina were able to approach her black swan, as Beverly had approached her scarred man, it is likely that she would have experienced the beginning of healing and integration instead of the madness that consumed her.

And what of the ongoing battle between the white and black swan? This represents the same ongoing battle in you and me with our own rejected emotional longings, or those things that we so deeply desire but still fear owning or asking for. In the privacy of our mind, hidden from all other human beings, we sense an ugly, deformed part of ourselves, an unlikeable, unlovable being. We all have some version of the scarred man or black swan living within us, which represents our deep but rejected emotional longings.

Expect the seen and hidden selves to tussle, for they both believe they are pressing for their own existence. The seen self believes it will die if the hidden self is seen by anyone. The hidden self knows it cannot die, but it also knows that it must remain trapped forever until seen self allows it to come out and be recognized. At times, both will fight for their beliefs in a pitched battle. When they do, we hear a horrible cacophony in our head, and we feel overwhelmed by panic, confusion, and anxiety, just as Beverly and Nina did. At these times, we can slow everything down and listen for the two distinct voices of the seen and hidden selves and restore sanity during these moments of madness. We will do exercises later in the book to develop this all-important skill.

I carry eternal gratitude for my hidden self, because I would be lost without it. I would be wholly at the mercy of my seen self, which is perpetually terrified and closed-minded. In fact, all of us would be lost. Our hidden self contains the truth of who we are, and it works ceaselessly for the full restoration of our identity. This means we will live in a state of inner conflict until our seen self finally allows connection and integration with our hidden self. We can expedite this process by developing the practical skills required to see and understand our hidden self and to build a new relationship with it. This is what the work of identity theory is about and what we are doing together right now. It is worth revisiting two of the quotes that appeared earlier on, which will carry more meaning for you:

"The monsters of our childhood do not fade away,
neither are they ever wholly monstrous."

—John le Carré

Reconciliation is to understand both sides; to go to one side and describe the suffering being endured by the other side, and then go to the other side and describe the suffering being endured by the first side.

—Thich Nhat Hanh

The two sides are the seen and hidden selves. Both need our understanding. Both need our validation. It is only we who can consciously begin this profound process of reconciliation. Instead of an exercise, here is a review to discuss in the group or to reflect upon if you are working alone.

Exercise 7: Review questions for group or individual

1. Describe some of the behaviors and attitudes that Nina's seen self believes she must display to avoid her mother's disapproval.
2. Describe some of the behaviors and attitudes that Nina's hidden self believes she must hide to avoid her mother's disapproval.
3. Discuss how Nina uses "hiding" as an emotional survival technique.
4. Discuss the effect this hiding has on Nina's life and the emotional quality of her relationships. Name some decisions and actions that Nina takes as a result of this hiding.
5. Name two specific confrontations that Nina experienced, and try to see if this sequence occurred as expected. Confrontation, pain, fear, disapproval, and hiding—this is the sequence we will be looking for and working with.
6. How does the white swan embody and represent Nina's seen self?
7. How does the black swan embody and represent Nina's hidden self?
8. Is the hidden self bad or evil? If yes, explain. If no, explain.
9. What does Nina believe might happen if she owned her sexuality?
10. Do you have a better understanding of your own seen and hidden selves? Explain.

CHAPTER 10

Why We Can't See Ourselves with Clarity

We all have a blind spot and it's shaped exactly like us.

—Junot Díaz

WE'RE DRIVING AND NEED to change lanes, so we look into our side view mirror. No one is there; we put on our turn signal and move into the next lane only to be shocked by a blaring horn. Startled, we pull back into our original lane and look again. There actually had been another car next to us and we almost crashed into it! We had checked and no car had been visible. We had signaled appropriately, but, still, we almost crashed. The other car was in our blind spot. All cars have side view mirrors and yet there's always a blind spot.

A blind spot is an area you can't see from *your point of view*. The last phrase in this definition is especially important. Whatever is in your blind spot can, in fact, be seen, just not from your current vantage point. To see what is in your blind spot, you must change your perspective. Just as with a car, our emotional blind spot is a permanent mechanical problem that is part of our human condition. We will always have a blind spot, so we must have a way to change our perspective to overcome it.

Following our near crash, we go to an auto parts store to see if they have something that might help. The clerk directs us to a pack of small, circular convex mirrors. We adhere these to our side view mirrors, and our blind spot is now visible. We have successfully altered our point of view. With this ridiculously simple step, we have changed our perspective by expanding our field of vision.

As I've mentioned earlier, if you cannot see a problem, you cannot solve it effectively. When we feel fear of disapproval, we react with a masking behavior to keep our authentic feelings hidden.This is the precise moment when we fall into our blind spot and lose sight. This means it is crucial that we learn to recognize our masking behaviors. In the counseling portion of identity theory, a person is asked to share their biography so that we may discover their childhood beliefs about disapproval, masking behaviors, and emotional longings. All of this information ends up on a single sheet of paper called the *Responses to Disapproval Form*.

Once a person has this sheet of information, they have the equivalent of a small, round convex mirror. Confrontation occurs, they respond, but they are able to compare their actual response to the information on their *Responses to Disapproval Form*. Now, they can see their own blind spot. In the beginning, this is uncomfortable and cumbersome; it requires effort. Nonetheless, a person eventually develops the ability to see themselves falling into their blind spot. This is a milestone. It is a remarkable achievement to be able to observe oneself fall from consciousness into unconsciousness. This allows a person to develop the ability to not enter into their blind spot—in other words, to choose not to act out their masking behaviors, but instead to speak their authentic feelings and ask directly for their emotional longings. None of this powerful transformational work could be done effectively without their *Responses to Disapproval Form*—their little, round convex mirror.

In *There's a Hole in My Sidewalk: The Romance of Self-Discovery,* author Portia Nelson includes her wonderful poem "Autobiography in Five Short Chapters." In chapter one, she describes falling into a hole in the sidewalk. She tells us it isn't her fault, but it still takes her forever to find her way out. In chapter two, she walks down that same street, pretends not to see the hole, but somehow it finds her, and she again falls in. She tells us once more that it isn't her fault, but it still takes a long time for her to get out. In chapter three, she writes:

I walk down the same street.

There is a deep hole in the sidewalk.

I see it there.

I still fall in . . . it's a habit . . . but,

my eyes are open.

I know where I am.

It is my fault.

I get out immediately.

In chapter four, she finally walks *around* the hole and by chapter five she walks down another street entirely. Nelson's deceptively simple poem tells the story of a progression of consciousness that all human beings eventually go through. We do not change until we take ownership of the holes that we habitually fall into in our lives. And not just one or two holes but all of them. Filling in the *Responses to Disapproval Form* lays the groundwork for a profound shift that will allow us to own our blind spots and eventually avoid them all together. This represents a major change in consciousness. Finally, responsibility is in the right place and we are now in a position to take control of our lives in a new way. But if we continue to blame others for our reactions, we will remain stuck in our blind spot, for our reactions are our masking behaviors.

Pat

To illustrate, here is an example of a client who used his *Responses to Disapproval Form* to overcome a blind spot. Pat is a sixty-something man with a wife and two grown children. He is a warm, intelligent, and genuine person who has always lived on the fringe of society rather than as a member of the mainstream. He remains a part of the New Age movement, emphasizing feelings and relationships, and the importance of a healthy lifestyle. His interests are inner work, self-improvement, organic gardening, meditation, and Tai Chi.

Pat's father, however, was the complete opposite. His father grew up in a large Catholic family during the Great Depression and worked ferociously to get ahead. He was a successful, competitive athlete and later a soldier in World War II. He worked and went to college, the first in his family to do so. Eventually, he became a teacher, then a vice principal, and eventually a principal at a local high school—all while raising a family of five. For all of his remarkable achievements, Pat saw his father as dissatisfied with his life, his marriage, even his occupation. When home, he appeared to Pat like a king, albeit an unhappy one. At the dinner table, he never asked for something to be passed to him; instead, he silently pointed with the expectation of service. The household ran exactly as he wanted and expected. If not, his explosive temper took over, which was backed by a barber strap hanging behind a door. He never asked nor cared what anyone around him was thinking or feeling; instead, he commanded obedience and order.

When Pat was a boy, he tried to live up to his father's expectations, but the consistent pressure was just too great, and, in his heart, his father's beliefs were not his own. This became the basis for thousands of parent-child collisions throughout Pat's childhood.

During college, Pat began to find his own voice. He studied psychology instead of business and, for the first time, went in his own direction. Eventually, the strain between upholding his father's constrictive values and following his own impulse to explore a spiritual lifestyle became overwhelming, so Pat left school to start a new life.

Pat always believed his father loved him, but he also believed his father disapproved of him for choosing an alternative lifestyle and not building a solid career that provided a consistent income for his family. Before Pat's father died in his late 80s, he verbally gave Pat his full love and approval. This is not uncommon. Parents, when older and gentler, will often give these precious gifts to their children, making the end of life a richer, more intimate experience. Unfortunately, this brief occurrence cannot erase a lifetime of painful parent-child collisions, so we still hold on to our childhood beliefs about disapproval, and, we, ourselves, become our own greatest source of disapproval. Once learned and adopted, our childhood beliefs about disapproval remain intact within us as *our* beliefs and have little to do anymore with our parents. It is worth remembering that external disapproval is common, but self-disapproval is constant.

A confrontation

Pat went home to visit his family. He has a long history of conflict with his older brother, who is a proxy for his father. His older brother consistently disapproves of Pat for the same reasons that his father did earlier in his life. In order to foster peaceful relations, Pat asked if he might accompany his brother when he next went to work out, which was something his brother did regularly. When they were at the gym, some of his brother's friends joined them. All were men in their 60s. One man thought he remembered Pat, but was actually confusing him for a younger brother. That's when Pat's older brother said, "You're thinking that if this was my younger brother he looks terrible." "Yeah," said the man, "That's what I was thinking." This set off a series of mocking comments from the various people in the room about Pat's thin physical appearance. In the moment, Pat responded to these disrespectful comments by becoming one of the guys and going along with the joking.

Pat's reaction was a masking behavior designed to help him avoid further disapproval from his brother and his friends by disconnecting himself from his genuine feelings and emotional longings. Because Pat's reaction was immediate and felt so natural, he didn't notice any of this, which is exactly what happens to all of us. We feel the threat of disapproval, and, in the blink of an eye, we are in our blind spot—unable to see clearly and to own our genuine feelings.

When I asked Pat, now, after the fact, how he felt about all of this, he said, "Angry. I wanted to slap them all in the head." Pat and I then took out his *Responses to Disapproval Form* and reviewed the entire episode together. Here is Pat's form:

Responses to Disapproval Form

Pat

When I feel fear or emotional upset in my body, it means I'm having a confrontation in the moment, amplified by parent-child collisions from the past. This tells me that BOTH my childhood beliefs about disapproval AND my emotional longings have become activated, and my seen and hidden selves are in conflict. My seen self presses me to obey my fear of disapproval, while my hidden self reminds me to own and act on what I truly want. They represent opposite beliefs, opposite agendas. Now, I must choose to follow one or the other.

These are my childhood beliefs about disapproval:

1) I should give my power away to my father (and his proxies), or I will be disapproved of.
2) I should not challenge or question authority, or I will be disapproved of.
3) I should fear angry outbursts, and I should never challenge them when they happen, or I will be disapproved of and emasculated.
4) I should accept being with others who feel unhappy, tense or trapped, and say nothing, or I will be disapproved of.
5) I should not expect others to care for me with warmth or loving kindness, or I will be disapproved of.
6) I should fulfill my father's (or his proxy's) vision of my life, or I will be disapproved of.

These are the GENUINE FEELINGS I typically hide:

1) Anger
2) Hurt
3) Sadness
4) Fear
5) Loneliness
6) Shame
7) Frustration
8) Anxiety

These are my MASKING BEHAVIORS, which lead me to my BLIND SPOT:

1) Yield and then withdraw
2) Become quiet and inward
3) Close down emotionally
4) Be obedient and comply (be a good boy)
5) Go away, read, or do my work

These are my EMOTIONAL LONGINGS and what I want:

1) To be protected and supported emotionally and financially
2) To receive heartfelt warmth and nurturing (especially from women)

3) To be considered and cared for
4) To voice my genuine thoughts and feelings and to receive a reasonable, rational response in return
5) To own and express my anger
6) To feel as strong as the other strong people in the world and not be overpowered
7) To be heard, understood, and validated

At first, Pat disassociated from most of his emotional pain, because his tendency is to accept the authority of others. Further, Pat did not initially see being mocked by his brother and the others as a form of disapproval. But when we looked more closely at the situation, Pat agreed his brother and his friends had disapproved of him. Based on their derogatory comments, Pat felt he was not good enough. He was a failure in their eyes, so he yielded to this group of mocking men and withdrew inwardly; he became quiet, compliant, and obedient. As this unconscious response overtook him, Pat lost the ability to recognize or express his anger or to ask directly for what he truly wanted, which was to be received in a reasonable, respectful way. Further, he wanted to be heard, understood, and, at an even deeper level, to be supported and protected. Ultimately, he longed to feel as strong as the other men in the room and not to feel overpowered by them, which could not happen until Pat became aware of these patterns and began to meet confrontation with new understanding.

Pat had felt fear and pain, and his reaction was to embrace his childhood beliefs about disapproval, enact his masking behaviors, and hide his emotional longings. Using his *Responses to Disapproval Form*, he could see clearly into his blind spot for the first time. "I have definitely gained greater insight into my reaction. Before I didn't see that I was being disapproved of by my brother or his friends; now I can see it clearly. I can also begin to see and understand my unconscious response. I can see that if I stick with this [process], it will help me make much better, more honest relations. And it will keep me in touch with what I really want from people in terms of feelings."

This was the beginning for Pat as he undertook the work, the craft, of seeing into his blind spot. The key to being conscious is knowing when you aren't. At first, Pat didn't know when he wasn't being conscious; now, he does. Our blind spot occurs when we react unconsciously from fear of disapproval with masking behaviors, and, then, it prevents us from knowing that we have become unconscious. It is our blind spot that prevents all of us from change, growth, and healing. It is what keeps us stuck. This means that overcoming our blind spot is the key to self-healing.

This is by far the most important issue you will confront in any form of self-improvement or inner work. Without exception, all of us fall into our blind spot on a regular basis. This is yet another practical argument for group work and development of inner work as a craft. The primary purpose of a group should be to help you see yourself when you are stuck in your blind spot.

The simple elegance of identity theory is that it provides a tangible device—the *Responses to Disapproval Form*—which, like that small, round mirror, allows you to see yourself when you have fallen into your blind spot. This tool converts inner work from a mysterious, incomprehensible process into a practical craft. Learned well and applied often, this craft will take you to the depths of your identity and the heights of consciousness as its practice strips away your deepest fears of disapproval and frees you to be your authentic self.

As we progress, you will have the opportunity to assemble your own *Responses to Disapproal Form*.

Exercise 8: Observing my blind spot

I have long wrestled with the following question: Is it possible to awaken someone who is *currently* stuck in his or her blind spot? I don't have a conclusive answer. Sometimes it is, but mostly it isn't. However, there are some things I can say with certainty:

1) When someone is in an emotionally reactive state—their blind spot—it is a waste of time to reason with them.They are in too much pain and have temporarily lost any rational perspective. Their beliefs have swallowed them whole. Talking or arguing will only make things worse. If you try, expect to be misunderstood and attacked. If you try harder, expect to be attacked with even greater anger and force.
2) Like tea that is too hot to drink, it is best to wait for the other person to cool down. This may be minutes, hours, or days. The duration depends on the person and the depth of their pain. More to the point, the issue is how deeply they're emotionally wounded, which is the source of their pain.
3) Although it may be impossible for someone to awaken us to our blind spot, it is certainly possible for us to awaken ourselves.

True inner work requires developing the skill of awakening from our own blind spot. The following exercise is the first step in that difficult process. We are going to spend some time observing our own emotional reactivity by catching ourselves when we fall into our blind spot. All that we really control in any confrontation is our reaction and to do that we must first see our own reactivity.

STEP 1: Someone says or does something that causes you pain and emotional upset. It can be anything, however small, so long as it causes you pain. The pain and emotional upset you're feeling will alert you that confrontation is happening. As I have said, our most common point of focus during confrontation is on the confrontation itself—who is right or who is wrong–and we get swept up in the emotional exchange and then defend our position because we feel under attack. Different people respond differently to confrontation. Some get angry, others fume and become defensive, and a few remain stoic. Although there are too many responses to name, the common ground in all instances is to get sucked into and lost in the pure emotion of the conflagration. It is like being in a building that is on fire; the only thing that seems worth focusing on is the fire itself and how to escape. Remember, confrontation is fraught with disapproval, and disapproval is the equivalent of emotional death or personal annihilation, so expect to find yourself running for your life in a figurative building with smoke, flames, and heat.

Our practice requires shifting our focus away from the confrontation and focusing on our reaction instead. For one week, I suggest carrying the following form around with you and fill it out when appropriate. It is a Confrontation Diary.

During parent-child collisions, the following four responses always occur in the same sequence. Please memorize them as you will be using them for a long time to come. The triggering event is a parent-child collision happening in the present moment.

1) Someone says or does something that causes you pain or emotional upset.
2) You feel attacked and disapproved of by the other and/or yourself.
3) You become emotionally reactive.
4) You fall into your blind spot.

At some point, you will find yourself in emotional pain: someone cuts you off on the freeway, someone says or does something hurtful to you, etc. Your first job is to locate and write down the confrontation in your diary. Keep track of every confrontation for one week.

1. Day:

___

2. Time:

___

3. Place:

___

4. Confrontation with whom:

___

5. Description of confrontation:

___

___

6. Did someone say or do something that caused you pain? If yes, name the person and the pain:

___

___

7. Did you feel hurt and/or angry? If yes, explain:

___

___

___

8. Did you feel attacked? If yes, describe this:

___

___

___

9. Did you feel disapproved of by the other and/or yourself? If yes, explain how:

___

___

___

10. Did you become emotionally reactive? If yes, please describe your reaction:

___

___

___

11. Did you fall into your blind spot following your emotional reaction? If yes, what did you see:

    ____

    ____

    ____

Repeat the above exercise several times during the week.

The group should meet and all members should bring in several attempts at the exercise. Pay particular attention to the four responses. Test the consistency that I am forecasting and discuss these as a group. Do they hold? What was your experience? How reliable a model does this pattern of response present? Go around the room and let individuals read their responses. Discuss and investigate together. Support one another with real understanding and kindness. If some members are struggling to see all of this clearly, stop and find a way to help.

CHAPTER 11

The Receptive and the Active: A Relationship of Balance

What goes up must come down.

—Proverb

WE ALL LIVE OUT-OF-BALANCE lives, but, for the most part, we don't perceive this about ourselves. We move through our day, fully engaged in our usual responsibilities or interests, and react to circumstances as we normally do. We go to work; we pick up the kids from school; we shake our fist at the guy who cut us off on the freeway; and in the evening, we have a beer or a glass of wine and watch TV. We have no reason to question our typical behaviors as out of balance because they feel natural to us. This deceptive sense of naturalness causes us to lose both perspective and clarity. As a result, we rarely see our own imbalance. To understand what this means, we first need a working definition of balance, so that we may recognize and assess it within ourselves.

I think it's fair to say that culturally we lack a clear concept of social or psychological balance. We have a sense of what it means to be normal, but not what it means to be balanced. Perhaps the closest we come is the general concept provided by rules or laws. Each tells us if we cross a specific line, we have gone too far. The crossing of the line, for example stealing, represents going too far. Religion is similar. If you have an affair with your neighbor's spouse, you have gone too far. Likewise with family rules, if you speak disrespectfully to your parents, you have crossed a line and should expect consequences. With physical health, if you continue to overeat and not exercise, you will develop illness or disease because you've gone too far. But none of these scenarios specifically addresses the issue of balance.The concept of excess is similar. We recognize when someone is out of balance because of something they do too much. They work too much, watch sports too much, drink or eat too much, or talk too much. Perhaps they are too closed and defensive or too submissive or angry. In these anecdotal ways, "too much" becomes the visible trait we use to identify what we think of as out of balance. But again, this does not provide a clear definition, only a way to recognize imbalance when we see it.

Balance is often defined as a state of equilibrium or an equal distribution of weight, but when it comes to our beliefs and behaviors, equilibrium between what? What are the two sides that are supposed to exist harmoniously so as to produce a state of emotional balance? The questions remain: What is balance? How can we learn to recognize it in ourselves?

Have you ever asked yourself, "Are my behaviors balanced?" "Are my words balanced?" Not many of us have ever done so. Balance will always be a vitally important concept, because it is the most fundamental indicator of mental and emotional well-being; in other words, visible beliefs and behaviors that evince a healthy, conscious person. Learning to recognize and understand balance and use it as a tool for consciousness is something that would benefit all. Let's take a closer look.

The receptive and active: A relationship of balance

The receptive and active represent the universal principle of balance. They are like the pans of an old-fashioned balance scale that appear to be two but are actually one. A balance scale has two pans but is only one scale.

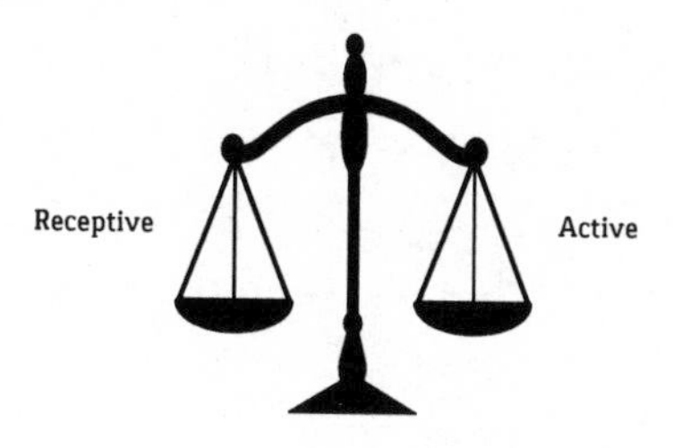

The two pans represent the receptive and active parts of any belief or behavior, but the one scale represents the entirety, because it is an expression of the *relationship* between these two components. Since the two pans are joined, their relationship is such that when one rises, the other falls proportionally. In this way, they represent balance. If one rises twelve degrees, its opposite falls twelve degrees. We can see by simply favoring one we automatically create an imbalance, because balance is a natural, self-regulating dynamic: when one side goes up, the other must go down.

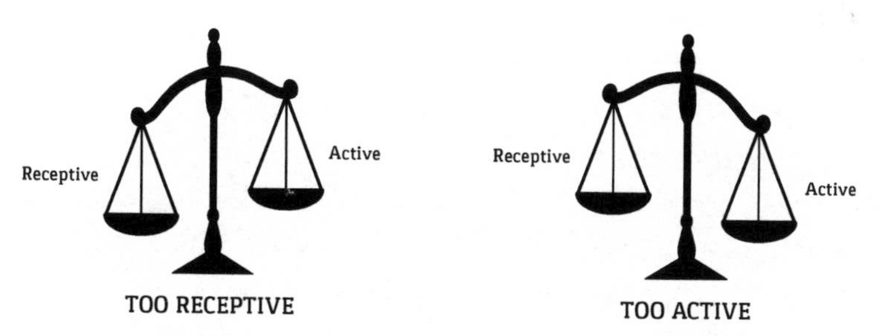

The receptive and active perform a basic, identity-sustaining function. Together, they literally control the formation of beliefs, which is the fundamental, life-directing activity for all human beings. The **receptive opens** in order to receive perceptions; the **active thinks** about perceptions received. These are their two functions: to open and to think. If they were a pumping heart, one would relax the pump to allow a new cycle of circulation to begin (the receptive), while the other would pump blood out, promoting circulation (the active)—two activities but only one heart. The receptive comes first because opening readies us to receive. The active follows the receptive the way the second runner in a relay race receives the baton from the first and continues on. Once we open, we receive perceptions, and then we must ask ourselves whether these appear real or true. In other words, we must think about perceptions received in order to convert them into beliefs (or not). Opening to receive, followed by thinking, makes for one integrated action (even though it appears to be two separate actions). This introduces the concept of balance, that is, openness and thinking in equal measure or equal value, which resembles the two sides of a scale when balanced.

The simplest definition of imbalance is that some of us are too open and think too little (receptive), while others are too closed and think too much (active). In the most direct terms, this is what creates and defines imbalance.

As we identify our beliefs, we simultaneously establish our personal imbalance–the two go hand in hand. This means that all aspects of who we are must become part of either our seen or hidden selves—the two parts of our one identity. When characteristics of either the receptive or the active remain noticeably absent, when they are not visible living symbols in our lives, it means they are an unconscious part of our hidden self. They remain hidden because we fear disapproval and rejection for displaying them. The moment we hide either, we immediately fall out of balance to one side or the other. The characteristics on open display become part of our seen self and these become the dominant tilt in our lives. The characteristics we reject and disown due to fear of disapproval for showing them become part of our hidden self and these become the subordinate tilt in our lives. Whichever characteristic we show becomes part of our seen self; whichever characteristic we conceal becomes part of our hidden self. This is the practical link between the receptive and active and the seen and hidden selves.

Transforming a definition into a tool

Now that we have a definition of balance, we need to convert it from the abstract into a practical tool, which will help us understand our own personal imbalance. If we want to take our temperature, we need a thermometer. If we want to know our weight, we need a scale. If we want to understand our own imbalance, we need a tool that will allow us to see it clearly.

It is identity's function to impart form to beliefs, so our identity takes our beliefs and turns them into the car we drive; the clothes we wear; the job we have; the size, shape, and health of our body; the way we relate to people and things; our attitudes and behaviors and so on. All of these are visible living symbols that represent our personal beliefs. To recognize the relationship between our receptive and active we must learn to see our own living symbols in a whole new way: this new perception becomes the tool we will use to see and understand our own internal imbalance.

We'll begin crafting this tool by taking a survey of the major living symbols in our lives, which we will do in an exercise at the end of this chapter. You are going to look at your life; note your living symbols, and identify them as receptive or active. You will determine which ones you display more of? Whichever you see more of, you will call dominant; the remaining half, the ones that are less visible, you will call subordinate. A dominant/subordinate binary presents a plain, workable picture of imbalance—too much of one, not enough of the other. This is clear and comprehensible. You have now taken an invisible, inner condition, a state of mind, and made it tangible and visible. With relatively small effort, you have made the unseen seen and the unknown known. This is extraordinarily powerful.

The next step is to assign meaning to these receptive and active living symbols. What exactly do they reveal? Growing up we had thousands of parent-child collisions and from these we learned to hide specific parts of our identity, while accentuating or exaggerating others. It all depended upon our perception of parental disapproval. If we feared disapproval for showing receptive characteristics, we hid those. If we feared disapproval for displaying active traits, then we hid those instead. In hiding, we unintentionally created imbalance deep within our identity. We began to hide more of one and less of the other; we began to show more of one and less of the other—again, all based on our personal perception of parental disapproval. So, we went out of balance to either the receptive or the active.

Living symbols are a physical manifestation of our beliefs. If we believe we have to keep our receptive side hidden, then we will manifest an overabundance of active living symbols throughout our lives. If we believe we have to keep our active side hidden, then we will manifest an overabundance of receptive living symbols throughout our lives. Whichever it is, we are either too receptive or too active and either will be clearly visible through the living symbols in our lives in that one will always be dominant. Whichever is dominant means we *do not* fear disapproval for showing those particular traits; whichever is subordinate means we *do*. Fear of parental disapproval compelled us to hide, which spontaneously created inner and outer imbalance, all of which is revealed with absolute certainty by the living symbols that make up our lives. By looking at our living symbols as a visible relationship between our internal receptive and active, we may quickly see into our deepest emotional wounds and begin to perceive our personal imbalance. As a result, we come to understand that our inner childhood beliefs about disapproval and our outer physical reality perfectly mirror each other. This is the true meaning of seeing life as living symbols, of seeing life from the inside out.

Taking this one step further, there are particular living symbols that are especially valuable because they reveal our personal imbalance definitively. These are the things that stand out sharply about us. These are the behaviors, attitudes, and circumstances that are easy to see simply because they are so big or exaggerated, or so small or understated. They stand out because they are so much more or less than the norm. A great mountain stands out against a landscape of flat plains; a huge, harvest moon stands out from a typical night sky; a very rich man stands out from those who have regular incomes; a great singer with wide range and gorgeous tone stands out from other singers; an authority figure who wields power and fear stands out from the majority who do not relate this way. These living symbols represent more than the norm, more than what is standard. They represent, in some form or another, excess and intensity, or that which is enlarged or amplified.

The opposite also stands out. A long drought stands out against a standard pattern of normal rainfall; a sudden, serious illness stands out against years of good health; significant personal loss and failure stand out against long term stability; continually being bullied or overpowered stands out when compared to what most experience; a painfully shy person stands out against others who are not. All of these living symbols represent less than the norm, less than the standard. In some form or another, they represent insufficiency, not having enough or coming up short when compared to others.

This is similar to the practice a doctor employs when diagnosing an illness. She looks at your body and compares it to a standard, healthy human body, which represents the norm and has been thoroughly documented with weights, measurements, dimensions, and so on. Your blood pressure is this; your cholesterol is that; your heart does this; your eyes show that. When your doctor finds something about you that differs from that of a healthy body, it will be visible to her because you are more than or less than the standard in some area. Your weight is too high (more than); your blood pressure is too low (less than); your heart rate is too fast (more than); your blood count is too low (less than). So, you receive a diagnosis of illness. Comparison to a standard version of a healthy human being is the primary way a doctor diagnoses illness. While I use the phrases more than and less than, excessive or insufficient, these should not be taken as judgments or criticisms; they are descriptive of a condition and nothing more, and the state of imbalance, which they describe, is one we all suffer. We are going to look at the living symbols in our lives that stand out because we see them as more than or less than when compared to the norm—not good or bad, not right or wrong—only too much or not enough.

In order to begin using this new tool, we must expand our understanding of what it means to be too receptive or too active. Learning to identify living symbols as predominantly one versus the other is our next step. Let's begin with a short list of visible, identifying traits for each. Please note that the receptive and active do not represent opposites, but rather two different sides of one thing. This makes their relationship more subtle and nuanced.

The receptive's main characteristic is openness—of heart and mind. In order to receive anything, one must first be open. In general, anything that relies predominantly on openness is an expression of the receptive. The active's main characteristic is thinking—thinking about ideas, concepts, feelings, and most importantly about perceptions. In general, anything that relies on thinking is an expression of the active. Here is a short list identifying traits associated with both:

RECEPTIVE	ACTIVE
1. Open	1. Thinks
2. Receptive, receives	2. Analyzes
3. Emotional	3. Man-made
4. Natural, organic	4. Mechanical
5. Plants and nature	5. Machines, science
6. Appears without power	6. Supportive
7. Follows	7. Protective
8. Feels, expresses feeling	8. Disciplined
9. Senses, shows sensation	9. Strategizes
10. Intuits	10. Organizes
11. Listens	11. Plans
12. Yields	12. Demonstrates power
13. Excuses	13. Judges
14. Forgives	14. Fixes
15. Spontaneous	15. Explains
16. Subordinate	16. Dominates
17. Soft or delicate	17. Hard, tough
18. Surrenders	18. Resists
19. Vulnerable	19. Calculates
20. Shows faith	20. Works, earns

If you look at the world, everything you see will have fundamental characteristics of receptive or active. A tree represents the receptive; it is natural. A car represents the active; it is mechanical. A tomato represents the receptive; it is a plant. A computer or telephone are man-made machines that represent the active. A person who consistently yields or subordinates himself displays receptive traits; a person who consistently resists, pushes back, and overpowers displays active traits. A follower represents receptive traits; a leader represents active traits. A corporation, for example, represents the active, because it is based on thinking, analysis, and strategizing. It is also man-made and relies on mechanical devices and so on. A forest represents the receptive, as it is open, natural, organic, and native. However, trees planted as part of the landscaping within a housing development transform and become a living symbol of the active because they are part of a man-made creation. A natural lake is a living symbol of the receptive, but a reservoir, which is man-made, is a living symbol of the active because it is the product of planning, building, thinking, and so on. These last two examples speak to the subtlety I referred to earlier, because they represent not a fixed concept but a dynamic relationship between the receptive and the active.

Continuing in this vein, here is a short list of activities that lean more in one direction or the other:

RECEPTIVE	ACTIVE
1. Fine art	1. Craft
2. Religion, prayer	2. Sports
3. Meditation	3. Business
4. Dance	4. Science
5. Music	5. Finance
6. Silence	6. Construction
7. Nature	7. Medicine
8. Gardens/gardening	8. Technology
9. Healer	9. Law
10. Psychic, intuitive	10. War

It is not possible to create a defined black and white list identifying everything as either receptive or active. Meaning will always be a reflection of the relationship between the two (including the list above). This is the very essence of balance, because balance, by definition, must be fluid and changeable. Living symbols are dynamic because identity is continually shifting due to various factors, including age, perspective, and even whom you're with in the moment. This is why I call them "living" symbols. Such symbols are as alive as anything I can think of and their meaning will always be a representation of the current relationship between our receptive and active. In this way, they offer a clear picture of our personal state of balance or imbalance and, as a result, the required direction for our personal healing. If we are truly healing, then we are transforming, and the relationship between our receptive and active traits will show this through a noticeable change in our living symbols: our dominant part of self will become less so, while our subordinate part will become increasingly present and visible.

Using the character of Ebenezer Scrooge from Charles Dickens' *A Christmas Carol*, we see that he is focused on making money and maintaining order through rules. His beliefs are closed and fixed, and he relates to others not as people with feelings but as objects to be used efficiently and effectively. Scrooge is out of balance to the active, which we recognize from the excess of active living symbols in his life, and all of the expressions of his imbalance are part of his seen self. In other words, Scrooge believes he must be this way or else he will be disapproved of by his parents (or their proxies). Conversely, all of his warmth, care, and kindness are absent. These unseen identity traits are part of his hidden self and define his subordinate imbalance. Scrooge is clearly too active and insufficiently receptive.

In examining my own life, I have many receptive traits. I am an excellent listener, and I have a strong intuitive sense. I can be warm, gentle, and forgiving. I am usually open and receptive. However, if I were to make a movie of my life for one week and then watched the footage, the *visible* behavior I would see dominating my actions, possessions, attitudes, and values would be active. Visible is the key word. What I see when I take the time to look is that I spend the majority of my time thinking, organizing, planning, analyzing, and working. I communicate first and foremost from my thoughts versus my feelings or intuition. I use many machines and mechanical devices. I regularly spend time fixing, building, and maintaining things. Far less of my time is spent listening, feeling, and being receptive with clients, students, family, and friends. I love flowers and growing things, so I spend time gardening. I love the ocean and nature, so I spend time on these more receptive activities, but the bottom line assessment as reflected by my personal living symbols is that I spend the vast majority of my time being active. This is clearly visible. This is what stands out, so this is my dominant trait. I spend far less time being receptive. This, too, stands out. Because my subordinate is less visible, it means it is hidden and more unconscious within my identity. I am out of balance because I am too active, which automatically means I am insufficiently receptive, which means more of my receptive traits are hidden. Simply put, I think too much but am not sufficiently open or vulnerable, and this is clearly evidenced by the living symbols in my life.

Because I know and accept my story, I can certainly see why. I grew up without a mother. My father was absent and did not provide support or protection, either emotionally or financially. Hence, I had no model for receptive behavior. I was too busy surviving using active behaviors. My father did not value my feelings or emotions. He taught me to hide them or else I would receive his angry disapproval. What I believed he wanted was for me to take care of myself, to be active and to not bother him, which is what I did. Again, it is easy to see how I became dominant active and subordinate receptive.

Further, my father was out of balance to the receptive. He was emotional, reactive, undisciplined; he was unable to earn, protect, and provide. He lacked power in any meaningful sense of the word and relied almost completely on his natural talents and abilities, most of which had to do with being charming and flirtatious. Left unprotected and uncared for, I was unintentionally forced to overcompensate for my father's lack of active ability, which is exactly what I did.

My father did not "do" this to me. Like the rest of us, he was only being himself and parented me accordingly. I also believe I was born with a natural bent toward the active. For this reason, my organic responses to disapproval and rejection—my coping mechanisms—were all expressions of the active. Parents are not the cause of our patterns, but they do reveal them to us.

Since life is about restoring balance, we can see where I have my work cut out. In general terms, I need to begin a practice of intentionally developing my underdeveloped receptive side while simultaneously underutilizing my overdeveloped active side. I need to practice openness, think less, and remain emotionally connected, while strategizing, analyzing, and arguing less.

All of my emotional wounds from childhood press me daily to live and relate from my active while avoiding and undervaluing my receptive. I feel completely comfortable living from my active side. Conversely, I feel uncomfortable and unnatural living from my receptive side. Ask me to solve a problem. Easy. Ask me to be open, vulnerable, and express my feelings. Hard. Ask me to organize and plan an event. Easy. Ask me to go with the flow and spontaneously let things happen. Hard. Ask me to discuss things rationally. Easy. Ask me to engage in an emotionally charged confrontation, while expressing my own raw emotions. Hard. Ask me to organize a disorganized area. Easy. Ask me *not* to organize a disorganized area. Hard. I can look at my own life and clearly see my own imbalance. I recognize what it is and where it comes from, and, most important, I know what I need to do to heal myself. Whether I do or don't is not the point, for I can do neither without first seeing what I am describing here. Seeing clearly remains the first step and the true foundation for all self-healing and the raising of consciousness.

If we look at our most noticeable outer behaviors, we will clearly see a tilt to either receptive or active. Do we spend more time thinking, analyzing, earning, strategizing, planning, explaining, organizing, and fixing? This is how someone with a dominant active would behave. Do we spend more time being open, responding to life from our feelings and intuitions, surrendering to what life brings, waiting to see what happens, going with the flow, being vulnerable or subordinate, and yielding? This is how someone with a dominant receptive would behave.

The value and meaning in seeing life through living symbols is that in every visible manifestation, in every object, attitude, and behavior, in every decision, action, and reaction, we may see visible expressions of our internal beliefs and, therefore, our own imbalance. This simple diagnostic tool offers profound value to those seeking self-transformation as it offers an objective way to understand one's self. Our living symbols offer us an immediate view into the depths of our psyche, which provides us with a fast track to do accurate inner work and manifest true self-healing.

By understanding the concepts of receptive and active, we are now able to see an outer picture of our inner imbalance. We are able to recognize, describe, and understand what it means. Through our efforts, we have zeroed in on behaviors usually unnoticed, typically undefined, mostly unconscious, and brought them directly into the light of day. By doing so, we have become more conscious human beings with far greater awareness of ourselves.

The practical value of seeing our own imbalance

One place that I apply my understanding of the receptive and active is in my relationship with my daughter. While I am out of balance to the active, she is out of balance to the receptive. Because I am too active, my behaviors and attitudes will unintentionally communicate all kinds of out-of-balance beliefs to her. Of course, the same is true for her toward me. This automatically sets up, at least in part, an adversarial relationship in which I unintentionally invalidate her by being who I am, and she unintentionally invalidates me for the same reason. Having an understanding of the receptive and active helps me to keep things in perspective.

I can observe that my daughter is too open, too sensitive, and too receptive. As a result, she can feel deeply hurt or pained over relatively small things, which causes her to become, at times, hyper-reactive—too fiery, too angry, too teary. She is a rational and deep thinker when calm, but when faced with disapproval (based on her own perceptions), her ability to think rationally vanishes and is replaced by huge waves of emotion and hot reactivity. At these times, she comes way out of herself to yell and strike out. This, of course, is the opposite of my own reactivity. I bend in the other direction; I go way in to avoid confrontation. I become quiet and communicate less. I go into my shell like a turtle and peer out from within. Safe and armored, I detach and quietly observe this seemingly absurd person who is now attacking or yelling at me.

Without awareness of the receptive and active, it would be easy for me to believe my daughter was being overtly disrespectful and invalidating, especially when I collide with her behaviors, which are the opposite of my own. In fact, that's how I experienced her early on as she grew up, but this is neither fair nor true. Her out-of-balance behaviors and attitudes, like my own, are just masking behaviors; they are expressions of her emotional woundedness and her deeper desires. So, practically speaking, I need to understand my daughter and myself at this deeper level if I want to maintain an emotionally connected and healthy relationship with her.

In more concrete terms, here is a sampling of what this means. My daughter is too receptive, so she has a tendency to be messy, emotionally reactive, and dependent upon me for things she can do for herself. She also procrastinates and loses awareness of everyday responsibilities. It would be easy for someone to hear me describe her and say that she sounds like a normal American teenager, but I don't buy that. I believe instead that all people have a unique identity formed in large part by specific emotional wounds, which originate or become visible in childhood. People come together unaware of their interior personal tilt, their particular imbalance, and then fail to see the inner cause for their outer reaction when someone makes them feel invalidated. Viewing it from this perspective is a useful, practical skill. If we know our own imbalance, we can see why our children and others set us off as they do, and we can understand when they unintentionally invalidate who we believe we should be. Then, we can begin to understand what hurts us and why, and our own reactions suddenly make sense.

I have to be careful not to take my daughter's messy room (natural vs. disciplined and orderly) or her propensity toward procrastination (waiting until the last minute versus doing) as personal invalidation because of my overdeveloped active traits. I have to try to understand that a majority of her behaviors (including her unwillingness to do things she is clearly able to do herself)—at least in part—are a reflection of what is out of balance in me, which I cannot blame her for.

Because of our opposite orientations, a part of me naturally desires to reject part of her and, of course, a part of her desires to reject part of me. It's to be expected; I am too active, she is too receptive. This fundamental difference causes both of us pain as we invariably collide with one another over common issues, but she is not trying to invalidate me, although she does, and I am not trying to invalidate her, although I do. While this dynamic generates difficulty for both of us, it allows us to dialogue about our natural tendencies and inherent weaknesses, knowing the potential impact these may have. When I lose my way and blame her for not being sufficiently active (or for being too receptive), I try to remember that I am not being fair or true. Our closest relationships are powerful living symbols that reflect our own beliefs back to us. In our ever evolving and complex relationship, my daughter continues to test my willingness to uphold the beliefs I espouse. In doing so, she unknowingly forces me to walk my talk and remains my greatest teacher. The strength of our relationship would not be possible if it were based solely on our substantial love for each other. We have something deeper, which continues to evolve as we work to understand and accept each other's wounds and imbalances. This also allows us to see one another and ourselves with greater clarity.

Final thoughts

It is very important *not* to use living symbols to intrude on another's privacy or to judge them because you can suddenly see their imbalances and fears. Please remember we are all emotionally wounded and out of balance—from the smartest scientist to the most famous celebrity, from your local clergyman to the politicians and business executives who run the world, from the psychologist whom you're seeking help from to the sweetest kindergartner—no one is excluded. We are all emotionally wounded; we are all out of balance and fear of disapproval runs our lives beyond our awareness. Use living symbols to see yourself and understand your own internal imbalance. This is their correct use.

I want to make one more very important point. Identity theory is not about you becoming a perfectly balanced human being. This is an unrealistic and unhealthy goal. Our focus will always remain on becoming ever more conscious, ever more balanced as this represents a lifestyle of awakening into health and well-being. By developing our craft, we are moving in a direction; we are not on a schedule to arrive at an unrealistic destination. The object of this work is to dismantle our fear of disapproval, not increase it with false expectations. By intentionally developing your underdeveloped, subordinate side, you begin the work of restoring balance to your entire identity. Realistically, this is all we can do. This practice offers an express route, a wormhole, if you will, from the mundane, exterior characteristics of our lives into the depths of our soul. This is what it means to see and use life as living symbols.

Exercise 9: Am I more receptive or active?

Review the lists in this chapter that identify receptive and active characteristics. Make sure everyone in your group has a comfortable understanding of these concepts. Now go around the room. Everyone should tell the group, *based on observations of living symbols*, which is more dominant within them—receptive or active—and which is subordinate for them. Reconfirm by naming those things, traits, attitudes, and activities in your life that stand out as being more or less than what might be considered standard. Then talk about what you perceive about yourself that substantiates your assessment. Group members can agree or disagree and explain why. This should create rich and interesting dialogue for everyone. If you are working alone, talk to yourself. Take the time to actually explain to yourself your perceptions of your dominant and subordinate receptive and active characteristics. Take the time to see yourself as clearly as you can. Naming things is an important, valuable act.

Questions For Discussion

1. How do I appear? If someone filmed you living your life for one week, what would you see when you reviewed the film? Would you appear to be more receptive (open, feeling, emotional, intuitive, vulnerable) or active (thinking, analytical, planning, controlling, working, doing)? Review the list of twenty receptive and active characteristics. Which way do you lean? Which living symbols (actions, job, relationship characteristics, physical attributes) corroborate this finding? Whichever way you tilt is your dominant side. The opposite is your subordinate side, which you will need to develop. Talk about how you might make this happen. Refer again to the list of receptive and active characteristics.
2. Ask yourself, where in life do I most struggle? Where do I experience repeated patterns of feeling unfulfilled or

blocked? We all struggle because we are weak in some areas; these are our receptive or active characteristics.

A. If I struggle to earn money or with employment; if I struggle to be punctual or organized; if I struggle to plan, focus, analyze, or control; if I struggle to protect others or myself—these are all living symbols of an underdeveloped and wounded active side that needs strengthening.

B. If I struggle to be open and vulnerable or to nurture others or myself; if I struggle to listen or hear; if I am emotionally reactive, have difficulty letting go and forgiving others—these are all living symbols of an underdeveloped and wounded receptive side that needs strengthening.

3. How can I work to restore balance? Explore how you might work on this in a practical way. How might you turn this activity into a craft? As an example, if my father were doing this work, he could commit to landing a real job (he never did); he could make earning a living a priority; he could devote himself to caring for and protecting his family. He could think more and react less; he could try to discipline himself and be less spontaneous and natural. These are simple, general ways of how he might begin to develop his underdeveloped side, while challenging his overdeveloped dominant side.

CHAPTER 12

Summary: Our Fall and our Wounding

. . . the loss of innocence is not a singular event in history but rather an axiom of human experience, repeated in every generation and in the consciousness of every individual. The miraculous paradox is that this universal pattern repeats itself in circumstances that are always unique.

-A.O. Scott

AT ONE TIME OUR identity was whole, and then we experienced "the fall from innocence." This is a mythological theme that appears throughout world literature, most prominently in the story of Adam and Eve, but it also happens literally in the developmental cycle of every human being. It is that crucial moment in childhood when we come to believe that we must hide parts of who we are to avoid our parent's disapproval.

We all began innocent, meaning we were born without fear of disapproval. We were not afraid to be seen naked. We were not afraid to put anything in our mouths. And we had no fear of parental disapproval. This is the universal starting point for all human beings.

As we grow from infancy into adolescence, parent-child collisions repeatedly occur that change our identity. A parent believes one thing; a child believes another. Collision. In the beginning, these collisions are merely corrective to keep the child safe: "Don't put that in your mouth!" "Go to sleep now." "Don't touch that." But as time passes and the child grows older, simple correctives become statements of direct disapproval: "Stop crying or I'm taking you home." "Don't you dare talk to me like that!" "You're doing it whether you like it or not!"

Parental disapproval occurs whenever a parent sees their child display an attitude, behavior, or belief they don't like. (Interestingly, this response is typically rooted in their own parent-child collisions). Parent-child collisions occur thousands of times throughout our formative years. After that, the results are mostly set. "Clean your room or you are not going anywhere." "Stop crying and act like a man!" "I told you your mother is right." "Stop being afraid and just do it!" There are tens of thousands of variations on these common communications from parents coping with or teaching their children.

Some parent-child collisions are direct, such as those mentioned above, but most are not. These are unspoken and indirect—the result of children simply watching their parent's behaviors and attitudes. Indirect parent-child collisions are far more subtle, yet significantly more powerful and formative. Based on our observations of our parents, we learn to anticipate their disapproval should we voice certain feelings or ask for certain emotional longings: "I see that my mom is often depressed, so I won't ask her for the emotional caring that I want so badly. If I do, it will hurt or anger her and she will disapprove of and reject me." "I see that my dad is always tense and angry, so I'll hide my desire for his love and support and just avoid him, or he will disapprove of and reject me." "I see my mom is always on the go, always working or doing, which makes her emotionally unavailable, so I'll hide my longing to be nurtured and loved by her, or she will disapprove of me." These are the types of beliefs all children form.

Whether direct or indirect, the result of parent-child collisions is the same: Fearing disapproval and rejection, we acquiesce to our parent's authority and we hide our genuine feelings and our emotional longings—along with a portion of our personal strength. This is a natural response to parent-child collisions; it is an organic part of the human enculturation process, and it happens to us all. In this occurrence, we perceive ourselves as weaker than our parents, and we lose the freedom to voice our most pressing fear, our truest pain. As a result, we lose our emotional security, and we develop a secret longing for all that we have surrendered. From children we grow into adults, and we live the rest of our lives fearing disapproval and longing for what we never received from our parents. As time passes, our secret emotional longings recede into the dark of our hidden self and become unconscious. They now lie outside of our perception, and because we cannot see them, we cannot form beliefs about them—this is the true definition of unconsciousness. We are now unaware of our deepest emotional longings.

From this point forward, our seen self will work ceaselessly to avoid our authentic feelings and emotional longings. To aid this effort, we adopt masking behaviors. These are specific behaviors we use to avoid, deny, and disconnect from our genuine feelings and emotional longings, which send us into our blind spot. When we are in our personal blind spot, we cannot see our own emotional reactivity; we cannot see that we are avoiding our authentic feelings. We cannot see that we have become defensive and closed, which means we are temporarily unconscious. Confrontation occurs. We fear disapproval, so we hide our genuine feelings and emotional longings, and we enact our masking behaviors. Now we are in our blind spot and unconscious. We are also out of balance.

Whenever we hide some part of ourselves, we create imbalance throughout our identity. Balance is represented by our receptive and active, which we use first to form beliefs (open to receive; think about perceptions received) and then as a platform from which to take action (beliefs are the basis of action). When we hide specific parts of ourselves, we are tacitly saying we prefer to appear one way versus another. Our appearance will be more active or receptive. Our preference becomes our dominant way of doing things. This means, in our decision making, we prefer to rely more on either feelings (receptive) or on thinking (active). It will be one or the other, which sends us out of balance, because the receptive and active are bound together—like the two sides of a balance scale—in a self-regulating relationship. What goes up must come down.

We grow up and leave our parent's home, but our emotional wounds remain intact, as do our methods for resolving confrontation. The outer details of our lives are living symbols that represent our inner beliefs. Our emotional wounds are a part of our belief system, so they, too, must manifest in our lives. These particular beliefs always appear as things that are not working. Why? Because they are based on fear of disapproval and fueled by our unfulfilled emotional longings, and, so, they represent inner conflict. They manifest as problems in our marriage, issues with our children, conflict at work, chronic illness, and so on. We are all emotionally wounded. We are all out of balance, and the beliefs that keep our wounds alive are visible around us as living symbols of things that are broken and not working because they represent what we desperately want but are afraid to ask for.

These painful living symbols appear as expressions of conflict between our seen and hidden selves. The two are fighting. Our hidden self yearns for integration and wholeness. Our seen self strives to keep certain feelings and longings hidden to avoid disapproval and rejection. The need to hide in order to avoid disapproval versus the desire to be seen and integrated as a whole is the raging battle within every human being. The appearance of things not working, including illness and suffering, are symbolic expressions of this inner battle between these two core parts of self. This fight is not about good and evil, as is so often depicted in literature, but about the restoration of wholeness, the integration of the two divided halves of identity.

Masking behaviors are living symbols that represent our fear of disapproval. We use them to mask our genuine feelings and hide our emotional longings. They are concrete proof that we are still emotionally wounded and have emotional longings to hide. No living symbol is more important to understanding ourselves than our masking behaviors. We still believe we need them to avoid disapproval and to survive emotionally. Our belief in the power of disapproval was the beginning of our fall, the origin of our wounding. Our understanding of belief formation, identity theory, emotional longings, and masking behaviors begins our healing.

Part Three

Healing—The Getting of Consciousness

CHAPTER 13

Confrontation: An Opportunity to Choose Again

Each man is afraid of his neighbor's disapproval—a thing which, to the general run of the human race, is more dreaded than wolves and death.

—Mark Twain

We began our journey by learning about the mechanics of identity theory. Our perceptions become our beliefs, our beliefs shape our identity, and our identity makes or chooses living symbols, which are our beliefs in visible form. When we have a new perception that appears truer than our original one, our beliefs change and, in turn, so does our identity and the living symbols that represent them. This is the immutable law of identity in action, and it is a natural process of ongoing personal change and evolution. Next, we focused on parent-child collisions, which produced our childhood beliefs about disapproval, our emotional wounds, and our masking behaviors. Together, these elements, when activated, create our personal blind spot. We explored how our emotional wounds became patterns of belief and then patterns of behavior, and why these patterns persist in our lives to this day. We have learned many concepts and how they function in precise concert as an integrated, organic system. So far, we have focused on wounding in order to understand healing. Let us proceed now with healing and the restoration of consciousness.

Confrontation as opportunity

Most of us avoid confrontation, yet we still experience it many times a day. Confrontation presents us with a juncture and a choice, because we find ourselves standing at the crossroads of our seen and hidden selves. Our seen self fears disapproval, our hidden self does not. The question is, what do *you* believe? Someone is angrily telling you you're late again, or you didn't do something right, or you shouldn't be this or that. The conflict causes you pain and upset. Feeling admonished, self-disapproval wells up from within. Now you must choose: Do you own your genuine thoughts and feelings and speak your truth? Or do you give in to your fears and hold your tongue? Do you give voice —not just to the anger that you feel on the surface—but also to your deeper emotional longings? Do you ask for what you want? Or do you acquiesce and let your fear become a show of masking behaviors?

The outer meaning of any confrontation is far less consequential than you might believe. In terms of inner work, who is right or wrong outwardly is not the point—it is your response to emotional upset that matters most. Do you accept and fear disapproval, as your seen self does? Or do you reject disapproval as a false belief, as your hidden self does? Every confrontation asks you to decide what you believe about disapproval, what you believe about your own self-worth. It is this embedded function that elevates confrontation to its highest purpose.

Because confrontations occur so often, they offer us abundant opportunities to identify and work with our childhood beliefs about disapproval and our masking behaviors. We know these beliefs and behaviors will appear during confrontation, so we can prepare ourselves in advance for a constructive, planned response instead of an emotional, knee-jerk reaction. This preparation is one of the main purposes of this book. If we come to see our present confrontations as expressions of past parent-child collisions, we can begin to perceive them differently. If we come to recognize and respect our deepest emotional longings within our confrontations, we can begin to embrace them. This is the essence of personal transformation, which relies on our ability to perceive our reaction to confrontation in the moment. The question is can you see yourself enacting a masking behavior?

We choose our masking behaviors carefully; they are meant to help us avoid our emotional truth; they are designed to minimize or make confrontation go away. Over time they become safe, comfortable, known behaviors, like well-worn jeans, so they always feel natural and familiar to us. This deception is particularly unfortunate, because this feeling of a natural fit obstructs us from seeing our masking behaviors *as* masking behaviors. The truth is we are attached to our masking behaviors; they bring us emotional comfort and escape. When we display them, we feel more like who we are than at any other time. This is an illusion. Masking behaviors represent unconscious behavior that effectively undermines the emotional quality of our lives by blocking us from identifying or acting on our emotional longings, thus perpetuating our crippling emotional wounds. What keeps our masking behaviors ongoing is our blind spot. We don't recognize our own masking behaviors because we have performed them over the course of a lifetime. Now they are a habit, as close to an automatic response as can be.

When I was a young boy, I would accompany my Aunt Ruthie to Gristede's market in Manhattan. As we arrived at the checkout, I would invariably wave many, many people ahead of us. I would continue until Aunt Ruthie, chuckling, would say, "Enough." On one of these trips to Gristede's, when I was about seven, as my aunt shopped, I disappeared. I left the store and did not tell her. I was aware my aunt would worry, but I had asked an elderly lady if she needed help with her groceries—which she did. And then this elderly lady asked me to walk her home. I was torn as to what to do. I had a knot in my stomach, but I felt compelled to help this woman. If I said no, she would disapprove of me—she actually wouldn't but that was my perception. I felt trapped by my own beliefs. So, I walked her home—a seven year old, alone in Manhattan, going off with a stranger. Perfect. When I returned an hour later, my aunt was not chuckling anymore; she was out of her mind with worry. She had never been so furious with me. I remember her screaming at me in front of all the people in the store. It was devastating and humiliating. Here's the point: Being a good person and helping others is one of my masking behaviors. Most people would not see it as such, but that's what it is. I grew up without anyone touching me, holding me, or making me feel loved or valued, and my father made me feel like I was an endless burden in his life. From these experiences, I came to believe I was unlovable, that I had no value, and that I was just not worth it. Being a good person elicited the same response every time: "You're so helpful. You're such a good person. I'm so grateful to you." Through this small, innocuous adaptation, I was able to create self-worth. I discovered I did have value. Perhaps I could be loved. By being good and serving others, I avoided my genuine feelings. Nor did I have to ask directly for my emotional longings. I could go along happily unconscious by being helpful—that is, until I had to face my angry aunt. Here, my identity created a perfect confrontation. Do I own my genuine feelings, stand firm, and tell my now scolding aunt that all I want is for her to hold me and love me. Hell no. Her vocal disapproval scared the daylights out of me, so I withdrew inside myself (another masking behavior) and answered all of her questions with, "I don't know."

The question becomes, should I continue to be a good person and help others? After all, society loves people who behave this way. The answer is yes, but only when it's authentic. When it's a cover for deeper, unconscious feelings and desires, then it's a masking behavior. If you look closely at this event, you will see how confrontation is embedded in our psychological and emotional struggles. Confrontation is a great chalice that holds our entire story.

Another story: I was born with asthma during a time when the treatment for allergy-induced asthma was minimal at best. As a child, my allergies sometimes became severe, and I would have an asthma attack. If you've never had one, and I hope you haven't, the sensation is that your lungs are filled with cotton instead of air. A deep inhalation only produces a long, shallow gasp; the feeling of suffocation attends every labored breath. It's frightening. During these events, time moves so slowly that minutes become hours. I would spend days sitting upright in a chair, mostly by myself. Lying down was not possible. Every now and then, someone might call in, "How are you doing?" And in a great and difficult wheeze, I would always answer, "Fhhhhhhhine." I was a little boy and I was terrified, but I would rather have died in that chair than bother anyone with my emotional needs—that is how strong my fear of disapproval was. Never asking for the emotional comfort that I so deeply craved, I disassociated from my emotional longings. Appearing as though I didn't need anything, I displayed my masking behavior.

The importance of learning to see our masking behaviors in real time stresses again the necessity of meeting life as a craft, of seeing mundane interactions as living symbols with deep inner meaning. In the end, if we can perceive ourselves enacting our masking behaviors during conflicts, we can bring consciousness to what has long been unconscious, and we will have in our hands a practical tool to unravel the mystery of our own conditioned behavior. Only then can we receive our emotional longings, which live quietly in our heart of hearts.

Confrontation and its three-part composition

Confrontation is composed of three structural elements that are always present just beneath the surface. Few look, so these core elements often go unnoticed. But if you do look for them, you will find them every time; see them and they will change your entire perspective of yourself and your life.

The three underlying components in confrontation are: 1) **childhood beliefs about disapproval**, which we learned from parent-child collisions; 2) **masking behaviors**, which we use to avoid disapproval; and 3) **emotional longings**, which are what we hide behind masking behaviors to avoid disapproval. In other words, when faced with confrontation, we hide our emotional longings behind our masking behaviors to avoid our childhood beliefs about disapproval, or not. These specific elements form the three-part composition of all conflicts and confrontations.

Confrontation is both frightening and upsetting because it puts our emotional longings *and* our childhood beliefs about disapproval into play *at the same time*. Whatever the nature of the confrontation may be, it will always contain these two diametrically opposed beliefs. Both become triggered and come into play at exactly the same moment with exactly the same intensity. Because they represent opposing beliefs, opposing forces, they naturally create a feeling of inner conflict. This is a universal human experience, and though we may not realize it, we must choose which one to affirm. This is the very definition of conflict. Do we accept our seen self's fear of disapproval and its pressure to keep our emotional longings hidden, or do we align with our hidden self and its belief in the value of owning and acting on our emotional longings? In other words, do we ask for what we want? Our choice determines our life's direction, which will be toward consciousness or unconsciousness, toward repetitive patterns of pain and dissatisfaction or new patterns of healing and transformation. As always, our living symbols will faithfully and accurately reflect our choice back to us.

If we do not look beyond the surface of a confrontation, if we allow ourselves to get pulled into emotional reactivity and give in to fear and worry, then we have no way to see the three critical elements that can bring us clarity. We will be too upset, and we will react instead of respond. Whenever we react, we fall temporarily into our blind spot. When we respond intentionally, we do not. Spend some time studying the following charts. They should make all of this clear.

THE UNIVERSAL STRUCTURE OF CONFRONTATION

There are three underlying components in every confrontation: **1) childhood beliefs about disapproval**, which we learned from our parent-child collisions; **2) masking behaviors**, which are behaviors we use to avoid disapproval; and **3) emotional longings**, which are what we hide behind our masking behaviors to avoid disapproval. In other words, when faced with confrontation, we hide our **emotional longings** behind our masking behaviors to avoid our **childhood beliefs about disapproval**—or not.

When we feel fear or emotional upset in our bodies, it means we're having a confrontation in the moment, amplified by **parent-child collisions** from the past. This tells us that **BOTH** our **childhood beliefs about disapproval AND** our **emotional longings** have become triggered and our **seen** and **hidden selves** are in conflict. Our **seen self** pressures us to accept our fear of disapproval and enact our **masking behaviors**, while our **hidden self** simultaneously reminds us to own and act on our **emotional longings**, meaning what we truly want. These represent opposite beliefs, opposite agendas. Now, we must choose to affirm one option or the other, and our choice will determine our life's direction, which will be toward consciousness or unconsciousness, toward old patterns of self-defeating choices or new patterns of self-healing and awakening. As always, our living symbols will reflect our identity back to us, so that we may see both the result and the meaning of what we have chosen.

Chart 4
THE THREE PARTS OF EVERY CONFRONTATION

CONFRONTATION OCCURS - I REACT UNCONSCIOUSLY

I feel fear and upset in my body. Both my **emotional longings** and **childhood beliefs about disapproval** have been triggered, and my **seen** and my **hidden selves** are in conflict; feelings of fear and disapproval rise up within me.

Start

My seen self reminds me that if I express my genuine feelings or ask for what I want, I will be disapproved of or rejected. This frightening perception appears true, so I **believe** it.

I feel intimidated by the fear and pressure I feel, so I enact my **masking behaviors**

I hide my **genuine feelings**; I disassociate from my **emotional longings**. I do not ask for or act on what I want.

My unconscious reaction calcifies old beliefs and emotional wounds. Old patterns of fear of disapproval are retained. My **identity** does not change, so my **living symbols** stay the same. I am in my blind spot.

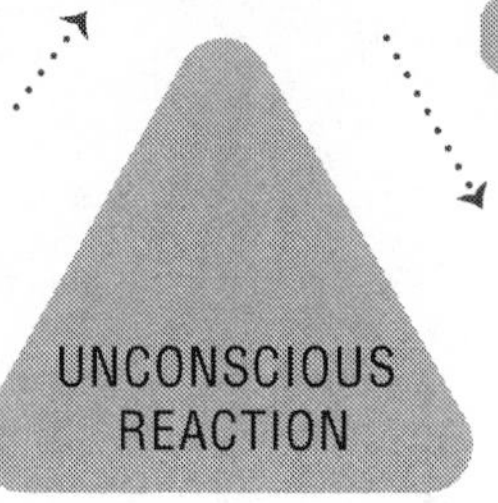

OR

CONFRONTATION OCCURS - I RESPOND CONSCIOUSLY

I feel fear and upset in my body (which will lessen over time with repeated effort). Both my **emotional longings** and my **childhood beliefs about disapproval** have been triggered, and my **seen** and **hidden selves** are in conflict; feelings of fear and disapproval rise up within me.

Start

My seen self reminds me that if I express my genuine feelings or ask for what I want, I will be disapproved of or rejected. **I reject** this harmful, false belief and step away from my reactivity.

I look for and own my **masking behaviors**.

I name my **genuine feelings**. I own and act on my **emotional longings**.

My conscious response shifts my perception. As I repeat this effort, old beliefs and emotional wounds heal, which changes old patterns of self-defeating, reactive behavior. My **identity** shifts and **new living symbols** appear that represent a healing of my fear of disapproval. I can see constructive changes in myself and in my life, as can others around me.

CONSCIOUS
RESPONSE

A full-page, color version of this chart is available for free download at TheCraftOfLife.com.

As you enter more deeply into this practice, the sheer repetition of the above sequence will surprise you, as will its utter simplicity. You may have a thousand confrontations from a thousand parent-child collisions, but your responses will be literally the same with each one. That is what makes all of this complexity manageable. Historically, you have probably focused on who is right and who is wrong, which is a masking behavior that has distracted you. We all must eventually choose between our pressing need to be right and our deeper desire to be loved, accepted, and respected. The need to be right is the last major masking behavior that everyone must surrender in order to receive their deeper emotional longings. Now you will learn to look beyond right or wrong and focus on your response to the confrontation. This skill will change your life. The precise nature of confrontations change, but your response to them does not. Knowing this is key.

Let's take another look at John, one of the twins from Chapter 7. He is the brother who, fearing his father's disapproval, consistently works hard and does a good job. His wounding parental beliefs were the following: I should not expect anyone to see or understand me. If I do, I will be disapproved of. I should not express my genuine feelings, especially anger. If I do, I will be disapproved of. John's masking behaviors were to work hard and be compliant. By working hard he keeps his genuine feelings hidden and unconscious, and he never has to deal with his deeper emotional longings for acceptance, support, and love.

John is now forty-three years old. His boss asks him to work on Saturday, but John is exhausted and doesn't want to. Further, he has promised to take his young son to the zoo. However, when John tells his boss that "he doesn't think he can," his boss becomes visibly disappointed. He tells John that he relies on him, that no one can do this work better. The manager is a proxy for John's father, although John doesn't see this in the moment, because he is more focused on the "right response" to his boss. John feels 1) emotional pain, 2) he believes that due to his refusal he has failed so, 3) he fears disapproval. These feelings come directly from the tension of this specific confrontation, which is a parent-child collision, happening in real time. On one hand, John feels a genuine need to rest, to be with his family, and to take his son to the zoo. On the other hand, he believes the facts of what his boss, his father proxy, has said: Indeed, John is the best person for this job because his work is meticulous and fast, and the job is for an important client. But John also feels the threat of his boss' disapproval, which is a proxy for his father's disapproval. With these feelings from the confrontation, John's childhood beliefs about disapproval automatically rise to the surface. He perceives that his boss disapproves of him. Feelings of self-doubt and self-disapproval begin roiling within him. But John's focus is on the confrontation and not his reaction to the confrontation, so he is unable to see much of anything. He is being swept away by a wave of emotion, and his masking behaviors are poised to take over. He is falling into his blind spot.

If John were aware of what was occurring, he would see the specter of his father standing behind his boss, arms folded, reminding him of two of his commandments: *If you do not work hard, expect my disapproval,* and *if you directly express your hurt and anger, I will overpower, disapprove of, and reject you.* John is not conscious of this dynamic, but he feels it in his body; he has feelings and sensations that he felt as a boy in his father's presence. He feels his throat swell and tighten. He feels angry that his boss is pressuring him to work on Saturday. He feels sad at the thought of not taking his boy to the zoo; he feels anxious knowing that his wife will disapprove of him, but this anger and sadness and fear get caught in his swollen throat, and John hears himself saying, "All right, I'll be here at 9:00 a.m." John has enacted his masking behaviors—to acquiesce and work hard—and he kicks himself for doing so. Now he is angry with himself for capitulating and being indecisive and weak, yet he asks himself, "What else could I have done?"

His boss thanks him, tells him he is a real asset, and that he is grateful to be able to count on him. John goes home and tells his wife he has to work on Saturday. She is angry. His son is hurt that his father has disappointed him again. The boy feels less loved, less protected. John loves his son dearly and promises to make it up to him, but the boy does not really believe this nor cares anymore, because now he is learning his father's wounding beliefs. Unbeknownst to him, though, this is the legacy of his grandfather, which is the legacy of his great-grandfather and so on. Even at forty-three, as a polished professional, as a good husband and father, John still cannot confront *his* father's wounding beliefs because he is not aware of them. Only now John is living this out with his boss and most of the other authority/father figures in his life. John must work hard to avoid disapproval, and he must never express his hurt or anger directly. As a result, his truest emotional longings remain secret and hidden. For the millionth time, John has upheld his father's wounding beliefs perfectly, and because of it, he feels trapped. He feels emotionally disconnected from his wife, his son, even himself, but he does not understand why. Perhaps he will visit his doctor and get a prescription for an antidepressant. His masking behaviors fit like comfortable, old jeans. He wears them and they feel natural; they feel like they represent who he is.

John, like so many of us, has a good life, a good marriage, a good family, but all lacking a critical piece—a certain emotional connectedness that he deeply longs for, that he lost during childhood. Emotional fulfillment comes when we take up the building of life and relationships as a serious craft. In his mind, he is doing his best, but no one in his family seems to understand. His feelings of loneliness amplify and he becomes depressed, not because he has a clinical problem, but because in the depths of his soul he is emotionally exhausted. He is like an empty lake, and he does not know what to do.

Why do we do this to ourselves? In nature, the fear of death is the strongest fear of all, but in humans, it is disapproval; disapproval is an emotional death that feels like personal annihilation. This is why our adaptations to it (our masking behaviors) are so dramatic, so powerful, so effective. Death by disapproval generates dreaded fear—it is visceral. To avoid it, we learned to hide our true feelings and conceal our deepest emotional desires.

Confrontation resolution: Is it conditioned or free?

How do we know if our resolution to confrontation is conditioned or true? This is a crucial question. The ultimate veracity of identity theory comes from measuring the output (living symbols) of the lives of those who put it into practical use. A colossal fallacy of our time is that spiritual and emotional growth cannot be measured. In fact, they can and must be measured, otherwise a given system of thought or practice has limited value at best. The movement toward consciousness must be quantifiable. If we do not know where we are in our self-development, then, by definition, we are lost, and lost is another synonym for unconscious. If we are investing the time and energy to practice a system meant to promote personal transformation, then we should expect to reliably measure the degree of our transformation. Without reliable measurement, we can practice but remain unhealed and unconscious and not know it, and then fool ourselves into believing that we have changed when, in fact, we have not. This is a serious hole to fall into but not uncommon.

Naming our masking behaviors opens a path to measuring our growth. Once they are written down and learned, we are able to witness ourselves acting unconsciously, and, as a result, we can experience our genuine feelings. This is a game changer. In the preceding example, John was thrust into a parent-child collision when his boss asked him to work on Saturday. John did not want to, but he agreed to anyway. John's acquiescence was a masking behavior designed to avoid disapproval. He resolved his confrontation in a manner consistent with his father's beliefs. He demonstrated his belief that hard work is essential to avoid disapproval and that one should censor one's true feelings and not express hurt or anger directly. John, albeit unconsciously, believed his father would have approved of his resolution. If I brought all of this to John's attention, he might claim that he believed he'd done the right thing, that he did what he himself wanted to do, that he preferred to have the day off but that life brings responsibilities that we must keep. If I asked John what he thought and felt during this incident, he would have to admit feeling angry at his boss for pressuring him to work on the weekend, sad at not being able to take his son to the zoo, hurt that his boss had so much power over him and so on. Since John did not own any of these feelings, he could not express them in an appropriate manner. His actions were inconsistent with his feelings, which he betrayed by responding to the confrontation with acquiescence. Although John avoided his boss' disapproval and feelings of failure at work, he also sacrificed his self-esteem and his emotional relationship with his wife and son. This is what most of us experience every day in real life.

Seeing confrontation resolution differently

Confrontations that threaten us with feelings of disapproval and failure and deny us our emotional longings are frightening, disturbing experiences. At least they appear so. However, there is much more to these loaded interactions. Now we must begin to challenge *our beliefs* about confrontation. We must learn to see confrontation for what it truly is: an opportunity to become conscious and to heal ourselves by reclaiming the personal power we surrendered to our parents long ago. We adopted masking behaviors to avoid our parent's disapproval. And we are still trying to avoid their disapproval, only now we are doing so unconsciously through other relationships—such as with our spouse or partner or our children, as well as with colleagues, friends, organizations, and businesses; in other words, with anyone or anything that represents our fear of disapproval.

To discover our true identity and restore our ability to fully feel, to find our personal strength, we must challenge the way our parents taught us to resolve confrontation. This old way of giving our power to them is no longer true for us; it simply does not work. I am not advocating that we reject our parents, but only their wounding beliefs, which do not serve us, and, in fact, only hurt us by causing us to make self-defeating choices. This should not challenge the love between you and your parents. In fact, this love will only increase as your unique identity becomes untangled and differentiated from their identity, and you realize how much of your fear of disapproval is a projection. Nor does it demean or diminish the many important and strengthening beliefs and values they also taught you. Since our parental relationships represent our earliest beginnings, they are the correct starting place to identify our earliest wounds. It is not my intention to blame parents for the ills of the world (I am a parent, too), but to point to an organic mechanism in the process of human development that keeps us all bound and shackled with fear. Bear in mind that all parents were also children and most children will become parents. We are all walking the same path in the same shoes.

Exercise 10: Identifying my emotional longings

When you were growing up, there were specific emotional desires that you wanted from your parents but never received. For whatever reason, they could not or would not give these to you, so these emotional desires went unfulfilled. These represent specific forms of emotional sustenance that you learned to do without, believing you could not ask your parents directly for them without incurring their painful disapproval, rejection, or abandonment. This was your perception, and the success of this important exercise depends completely on your willingness to look at your parents and simply say what you experienced. You are not being asked to judge or criticize them, to disrespect them, or to not love them; you are only being asked to look at them and your childhood experience and to own the truth of whatever you experienced, of whatever your perceptions may have been.

If you love your mother, but you experienced her at times as being mean or harsh, then that was your experience and you will need to own that. If you are devoted to your father because he is such a kind and gentle man, but he failed to provide you with sufficient emotional protection, then that was your experience and you will need to own that. In my own case, my mother died when I was two and what I wanted but never got from her was physical affection, emotional nurturing, and love. I could never ask her for these things, and they became my deepest emotional longings. My father was self-absorbed and a compulsive gambler; what I wanted from him was emotional and financial support, protection, and stability. I could never ask him for these things without him exploding, so I never did. Between my dead mother and my narcissistic father, I developed my sense of emotional longings. Now you are going to get closer to your own sense of emotional longings.

Sit quietly, as if for meditation. Breathe from your belly. Allow yourself to become calm and centered. Allow yourself to recall memories from your childhood, specifically times where you felt pain, fear, or anger and wanted your mom or dad to help you ease these disturbing feelings. They didn't, and you believed you could not ask them to. So your longing for comfort went unanswered. Now name what it was that you wanted but did not or could not get.

Your emotional longings

At the back of the book, in the Forms and Charts section (see Table of Contents) or at *www.TheCraftOfLife.com*, you will find Form 2: *Identifying My Emotional Longings*, which you will use to compile your own emotional longings. Chart 16: *A List of Emotional Longings*, is also available in downloadable, searchable format at *www.TheCraftOfLife.com*. This list will help you to identify your own emotional longings.

We'll begin with your father. On Form 2, write down a scene from your childhood in which you were in pain, fear, or anger and wanted comfort or help from your father, but he could not or would not give it to you. Write down several more that come to you naturally and easily. Now reread what you have written and ask yourself, what did I long for from my father in each of these instances?"

Now repeat the same exercise for your mother.

Use the third page of Form 2: *My Emotional Longings Are* to compile your emotional longings from the first two pages. Try to name a minimum of four and a maximum of eight. To give you a concrete example, here are my emotional longings:

1. To receive help, caring, and support both emotionally and financially.

   (Neither my father nor mother gave me any of these.)

2. The courage to express my anger and have confrontation with my father.

   (My father had an explosive temper, so I learned to fear anger and never express it directly. I learned not to confront him or others.)

3. To receive affection, emotional protection, and love.

   (My father had no ability to provide any of these and my mother was dead, so neither could she.)

4. To be seen, recognized, and accepted for who I am as I am.

(For a homework assignment in seventh grade, I wrote a poem about a boy in incredible pain. It was genuine and heartfelt—something I rarely bothered with. I was not a great student, and my teacher asked me if I had actually written it, implying that I had not. This hurt me far beyond anything he was aware of. I told him I had, and he gave me an A. Then, in an extremely rare action, I showed my poem to my dad, who read it and immediately asked if I had actually written it. I was devastated. No one could see me, recognize me, or accept me for who I was. This was my perception and my experience.)

5. For people to be who they claim to be.

   (My father was never who he claimed to be; he was a narcissist and a con man, and this caused me persistent pain and anguish. I could never ask him to change his ways because I feared his angry response.)

6. To receive rational responses during confrontation.

   (My father was an emotionally reactive, irrational man, and he was at his worst during confrontation.)

Here is a short version of Form 2 with examples filled in.

Form 2
IDENTIFYING MY EMOTIONAL LONGINGS

Age	Write a brief description of a childhood memory in which you felt deeply upset and ardently wanted comfort, support, understanding, or help from your **FATHER**, but he could not or would not give these to you.	I Felt	What did you long for from your **FATHER** in this scene? What could he have done to make you feel safe, protected, or loved? These are your **emotional longings**.
	EXAMPLES		
8	*My father comes home angry and out of control AGAIN!!!*	*Angry, hurt, scared, unprotected*	*To feel safe. To feel protected. For him to demonstrate self-awareness, consider-ation, and self-control.*
6-18	*My father did not earn enough money to allow for all of the extras that I wanted like piano lessons, a bigger apartment with privacy, family trips, etc. We had barely enough but no more.*	*Unhappy, unsafe*	*For him to be a better earner, protector, provider. For him to inhabit his strength as a man.*
4-18	*My father abandoned the family when I was a boy. His absence left a huge gap that affected me in more ways that I can even recognize.*	*Unsupported, unprotected, unseen, unloved*	*For him to be there acting like a good and strong father. Earning money, protecting the family, caring for all of us with strength and awareness. Being there for my mother who was forced to raise us alone.*

Age	Write a brief description of a childhood memory in which you felt deeply upset and ardently wanted comfort, support, understanding, or help from your **MOTHER** but he could not or would not give these to you.	I Felt	What did you long for from your **MOTHER** in this scene? What could she have done to make you feel safe, protected, or loved? These are your **emotional longings**.
	EXAMPLES		
10	*I come home from school and my mother is drinking in the kitchen, obviously under the influence.*	*Scared, Angry*	*To stop drinking. To deal responsibly and maturely with the emotional pain and dissatisfaction in her life. To communicate with me honestly—even though I was a kid.*
8	*My mother criticizes me again for not doing something exactly the way she wants it done.*	*Hurt, Angry*	*For her to see and respect me. For her to not be critical, harsh and hurtful.*

This form is available at the back of this book and as a full-page, editable version for free download at TheCraftOfLife.com

It's time now to fill in your emotional longings. Once you have your list, you will need to test them out to see if they're correct. First, in your imagination, one at a time, speak each emotional longing to the parent you associate it with. Imagine yourself not as an adult, but as a child, and speak the emotional longing—perhaps for the first time—directly to your mother or father. As you do, see if it feels true. You should feel an emotional resonance. If you do, keep the emotional longing. If you don't, look again, because you just haven't found the right words yet to describe the emotional void you felt growing up.

Once your list passes this first test, use it again to revisit old or current relationships with spouses or partners. If your list is accurate, you should have experienced or be experiencing similar patterns and feelings in your most intimate relationships. That is, a sense of unfulfilled emotional longings. If you don't have this experience, something is off, and you need to take a closer look and try again. The truth is all human beings re-experience their unfulfilled emotional longings from childhood in their present adult relationships, unless they have done some form of inner work to change, improve, or heal the wounds that these longings come from. Here is one final test: for one week, watch yourself whenever someone causes you emotional upset or pain. Ask yourself, "If this person said or did the following, would I feel emotionally satisfied?" Compare your response to your list of emotional longings; they should match.

I am asking you to triple check your emotional longings for the following two reasons:

1) They are crucially important to the inner work we will do later on. If they are not accurate, our work will not be effective.
2) We will use this list in Chapter 15 to identify our childhood beliefs about disapproval—another crucial element to the inner work we will be doing.

CHAPTER 14

Belief and Personal Transformation

To perceive the world differently, we must be willing to change our belief system, let the past slip away, expand our sense of now, and dissolve the fear in our minds.

—William James

THE LAW OF IDENTITY, also known as story creation, is the process by which our identity converts our beliefs into perceptible forms or living symbols, such as our work, marriage, finances, health, hobbies, attitudes and so on. Story creation is ongoing. It can never be stopped, so our identity perpetually manifests itself in its current state for us to see. In this way, mind becomes matter and energy takes on form.

If we want to change what we see in our lives we must start where all change begins and that is with the underlying organic force of story creation. How can we take this process, which is the custodian of change and perpetually present, and channel it for our own benefit? Fortunately, the answer is not complicated. We gather and focus this natural force by having a new perception that appears truer to us than our initial perception. This is the only way beliefs change, so it is the only way we may change ourselves, because our entire identity is based on our beliefs.

When we perceive something from a new perspective and it appears true to us, our perception shifts and the meaning it once held spontaneously transforms. This, in turn, literally forces our identity to follow suit and change as well. New perception creates new belief, which changes identity, alters our decisions and actions, then gives rise to new living symbols.

Here is an example of how a belief changes. There is a masterpiece of immense value painted by the great Dutch artist Johannes Vermeer. One day experts discovered it was actually a fake by the master forger Han van Meegeren. The painting instantly dropped in value, even though it appeared exactly the same. If we had not been told by "experts" that it was a fake, we would still believe it was a genuine masterpiece with its original value intact, and we would admire it for its greatness. The painting had not changed, but our new, truer perception of it had, which, in turn, changed our belief about its worth.

Here is another example. We dream that we are being chased by a knife-wielding maniac. In the dream, we run for our lives. The terror we feel causes our heart to pound and perspiration to bead on our forehead. These physical responses bear witness to our belief about the imminent danger of this crazed man. In the dream, we run through the night, but he gains ground. We look back and see light glinting off the point of his sharp blade. We run up the road as fast as we are able, but exhaustion sets in. Our terror becomes deep and primal. Our alarm clock goes off and we awake. Instantly, we realize we were only dreaming. There is no maniac with a knife; no one is chasing us. We've had a nightmare. This new, truer perception dissolves the terror we were experiencing only a moment ago. We suddenly feel hungry and think about breakfast. Again, a new, truer perception forms a new belief, which changes the meaning and value of our initial perception, which changes our decisions and actions. In this case, we stop running for our lives and go make pancakes, which shows how dramatic change can be once our perception shifts.

Here is a third example. I visit my ninety-year-old Aunt Ruthie who lives alone. I notice how dirty her white carpet is and offer to have it cleaned. She laughs and says I must be imagining things because she vacuums daily as she has for fifty years. I bring a light from another room and shine it down on a particularly dirty part of the carpet. I invite Aunt Ruthie to look. She is shocked by what she sees. In the brighter, more concentrated light, she perceives food stains on the dirty carpet and, instantly, this new, truer perception changes her original beliefs. She is embarrassed. I comfort her. The issue is not about her cleanliness; it is about her poor eyesight. She asks me to have someone clean the carpet as soon as possible. Aunt Ruthie's beliefs have changed because her perception of her carpet has changed, and, as a direct result, her decisions and actions have changed.

The important points are these:

1) We believe in perceptions that appear to be real or true.
2) A belief changes *only* when we gain a new, truer perception of what we initially perceived (which means our original perception was wrong).
3) Personal transformation occurs *only* when we change a previously-held belief.
4) Change (or transformation) is a mechanical process that can be studied, understood, and quantified because it is based on cause and effect. The cause is a shift in perception, which has the effect of changing belief. This transforms our identity, which redirects our decisions and actions. New beliefs then appear as new living symbols: Aunt Ruthie no longer defending her dirty carpet and instead having it cleaned. All change, personal or collective, is based on this simple but profound formula.

Controlling the formation of beliefs

Beliefs form automatically whenever we perceive something that appears to be real or true, but there is an exception to this process. It is possible to use a combination of will and intelligence to suspend beliefs. By slowing the process of perception, we may control the formation of beliefs. This concept forms the basis for a powerful new tool, but it requires an act of will or self-control. We must first grab hold of our emotionally-charged reactions, then use our intelligence to consider other possibilities. By using our will and our intelligence in tandem, we slow both our perception and the automatic nature of the belief-formation process, and, almost magically, the belief cannot form because we have temporarily suspended it.

Now we have emotional space and within it lives the possibility of acquiring a new perception. If we take the time to view things from this new vantage point, and if our new perception appears truer than our initial emotional reaction, our identity will shift. By this simple act, we have moved closer to the truth, which is an apt description of personal transformation. Psychiatrist and Holocaust survivor Victor Frankl wrote: "Between stimulus and response there is a space. In that space is our power to choose our response. In our response lies our growth and our freedom." By intentionally observing ourselves in the throes of conflict, we experience emotional space; it is from this fresh perspective that we may choose to respond with new awareness instead of reacting emotionally; in so doing, we discover a doorway to consciousness and healing.

A woman in customer service makes a mistake on a customer's order. The order ships and the customer receives the wrong product. He calls and yells angrily at the woman for making this dumb mistake. The customer claims the woman has ruined his upcoming family plans by sending the wrong product, and there is no time left to reship it. The customer demands to speak with the woman's boss to complain. Waves of disapproval wash over this woman. Her own internal sense of failure magnifies. Normally, this would send her on a downward spiral of self-disapproval, fear, and depression, but instead she checks her initial emotional response and uses her intelligence to examine the situation. Yes, she made a mistake, and it did wreck the customer's plans, but, in truth, it was a simple human error. She transposed two numbers, so the warehouse sent the wrong item. This is the kind of mistake that anyone could make. She had made it before and will likely make it again.

The woman recognizes that this customer is acting as a proxy for her father, who disapproved of her whenever she failed at anything. She feels the old parent-child collision and the old feeling of disapproval. She perceives her childhood beliefs about disapproval pressuring her to be right all the time, and she sees her masking behaviors rising up, causing her to become stoic and silent about her pain. The woman realizes she does not need to have a big, dark emotional reaction because this is an ordinary, acceptable mistake, and she perceives in this instance her childhood beliefs about disapproval are wrong and damaging, because they are amplifying her sense of self-disapproval and undermining her sense of security. They are causing her to buy into this angry customer's criticisms. She thus chooses not to disapprove of herself. She chooses not to give in to her childhood beliefs about disapproval or enact her masking behaviors. As a result, she owns her mistake and apologizes to the customer, then turns the situation over to her manager and moves on with her day without feeling heavy disapproval hanging over her. Actually, she feels good about the whole event because she gained self-control instead of losing it. She has turned a negative into a constructive experience, reclaimed a small bit of her personal power and expanded her own consciousness. She has transformed her own identity.

Whenever a confrontation generates fear of disapproval, it offers us the opportunity to manage our disapproval consciously instead of reacting unconsciously. This is an opportunity for a new perception and thus a new belief. Our worst fears may be manifesting (someone is disapproving of us because they believe we have erred or failed), but so is our opportunity for personal growth, which can only come at this precise moment.

Ironically, the moment of disapproval is our best opportunity for insight and change. But we dread disapproval, and we fear parent-child collisions with their threat of rejection and abandonment. Our seen self works continuously to avoid both. When we encounter them we are meeting our worst nightmare. It is completely understandable that our initial reaction to disapproval is fear and pain. However, if we can form a new relationship to these dreaded but almost daily encounters with disapproval we can transform ourselves, because the moment of disapproval is the one vantage point that offers us the opportunity for a fresh perspective and a new perception. Now we must train ourselves to stand in the very place that we habitually avoid, because it is from this exact point that we can see our masking behaviors, own our emotional longings, and heal ourselves by awakening.

A path to unconsciousness or awakening

Confrontation can only lead to one of two places: unconsciousness or awakening. The following two charts lay out the sequence for both.

Chart 5
CONFRONTATION LEADING TO BLIND SPOT

An event triggers conflict: I feel pain or emotional upset in my body, or I observe myself enacting a masking behavior.

(Some people struggle to feel emotional pain or fear. Consequently, these people must use masking behaviors as their recognizable trigger. See yourself enacting a masking behavior and then go to #1 below.)

I feel frightened, hurt, or angry because I feel accused or attacked.
(I don't realize it, but I am re-experiencing a parent-child collision from childhood.)

My deepest emotional longings unconsciously rise up within me, creating a dual pressure to hide them or ask for them. I become emotionally reactive (or stoic) and fall into my **blind spot**.

UNCONSCIOUSNESS OCCURS AT THIS POINT AS I REACT FROM FEAR.

Now, the same sequence of events happens in the following chain reaction:

1) I unconsciously accept my **childhood beliefs about disapproval**.
2) I surrender my emotional strength and hide my **genuine feelings**.
3) I unconsciously enact my **masking behaviors**.
4) I disassociate from my **emotional longings**.
5) I react from my **receptive** or **active**, whichever is dominant, which means my reaction is out-of-balance.
6) I am now in my **blind spot.** I am responding unconsciously to self or external disapproval, which perpetuates unsatisfying life patterns.

Chart 6
CONFRONTATION LEADING TO CLARITY

An event triggers conflict: I feel pain or emotional upset in my body, or I observe myself enacting a masking behavior.

I feel frightened, hurt, or angry because I feel accused or attacked.

(I don't realize it, but I am re-experiencing a parent-child collision from childhood.)

My deepest emotional longings unconscioulsy rise up within me, creating a dual pressure to hide them or ask for them. I become emotionally reactive (or stoic) and fall into my **blind spot**.

UNCONSCIOUSNESS IS OVERTAKING ME, BUT I AM AWARE OF IT

I remember that my pain, anger, and fear are **cues** telling me to **slow down** and **step away** from my reaction.

Instead of an unconscious, automatic reaction, I choose to reflect on my situation. Emotional space becomes available. My decision to stop and consider things sets off a new sequence of events.

CONSCIOUSNESS RETURNS AT THIS POINT

1) I recognize and reject my **childhood beliefs about disapproval** and see the **parent-child collisions** from which they came.
2) I name and own my **genuine feelings**.
3) I recognize and reject my **masking behaviors**.
4) I name and accept my **emotional longings**.
5) To the other, I own what I said or did without equivocation.
6) I act on my **emotional longings**; if appropriate, I ask for what I want.
7) I have shifted my perspective and avoided my **blind spot**. I have acted on my **emotional longings**, which promotes authenticity in my life and in my relationships. I feel a sense of hope and strength as I develop new skills and greater awareness.

In chart six, please note the three ovals on the left, which identify three steps. These represent locations on a map—a map of consciousness and unconsciousness. At any given point you will be in one of these states. The skill we are working on is identifying where we are on this map of consciousness, right now in real time, and then deciding where we want to go from there. This simple practice is extraordinarily powerful. It is a true step in self-healing and transformation, because it represents our decision to awaken when we are unconscious and in our blind spot. As we make this effort we begin to see ourselves more clearly and to realize it is we who block ourselves from having what we want by choosing to remain asleep while awake–not because we are weak or lack intelligence, but rather because we never saw this circumstance so clearly. And our fear of disapproval, especially self-disapproval, has proven too much to overcome.

Intentionally seeking a new perception for the purpose of changing a belief is a simple skill. It can be acquired only by learning specific techniques and practicing these repeatedly until the skill is mastered; it is one of the main tools used to intentionally build a quality life.To end this chapter where we began, the brilliant psychologist and philosopher William James wrote: "To perceive the world differently, we must be willing to change our belief system, let the past slip away, expand our sense of now, and dissolve the fear in our minds." Amen.

Exercise 11: Tell me how I've hurt you

This exercise is about having a new perception and changing an old belief, which means seeing something old with new eyes. The intent is to precipitate transformation. New perception creates new belief; changed belief alters identity.

Part 1: Friend

Invite a close friend over for a visit, but do not give them any specifics. Explain that you are doing inner work for self-improvement and are required to do an exercise with a close friend. Ask if they will help and participate. Meet in a private, quiet place where you will not be disturbed and will feel emotionally safe.

1) Read the following to your friend: You and I have had a long relationship. During this time, I know that I have said or done things that have hurt you. But, believe it or not, I may not be aware of these. Please, think for a moment, and then tell me, very specifically, one thing that I have said or done that has caused you real emotional pain. Don't be concerned that it makes sense, that it is rational, or that I am even at fault—the only criteria is that my words or actions have hurt you.
2) Now remain silent; listen and observe. In this exercise, you may not respond, refute, or argue.You may only *listen.* Open your heart and your mind and listen. *Be receptive.* Do not defend. Do not disagree. Just try to understand this other person's pain—*really understand it*—because for this short time you are allowing yourself to feel what the other is feeling.
3) When the person is finished speaking, respond naturally—*BUT you may not disagree, defend, refute, or say anything about what you have heard.* This is a listening and observation exercise. Your job is to stay open and receptive and to try to understand—even feel—the other person's pain.
4) When finished, thank your friend for helping you.

Part 2: Parent or child

Repeat the same exercise with one of your parents. If your parents are not alive or cannot participate, then you may substitute one of your siblings or children.

Part 3: Spouse or partner

Repeat the same exercise with your spouse, partner, or boyfriend/girlfriend.

Questions

1) In any of the three interactions, did you experience a new perception? Did you see something old in a new way? Explain.
2) Did your new perception seem truer to you than your initial perception? Explain.
3) Did your new perception change what you had believed up to that point? Explain.
4) Did you have the feeling that this change in your beliefs simultaneously transformed your personal identity as well? Explain.
5) Do you now have a better understanding of how a change in perception transforms beliefs? Explain.

Group instruction

Each member of the group should do this exercise and then gather together for a discussion to exchange insights and experiences.

CHAPTER 15

Follow Your Pain & Discover Yourself

Our very life depends on everything's recurring
til we answer from within.
—Robert Frost

OF ALL THE THINGS we need to see with new eyes, pain is the most significant. We need a new perception of pain, so it gains new meaning and purpose. Think about the many forms through which pain manifests in our lives: loneliness, fear, humiliation, sadness, shame, physical injury. Whether it comes from a broken bone or a wounded heart, a scraped knee or a bruised ego—pain is something we strive wholeheartedly to avoid. If it should happen to befall us, we try to free ourselves of it as fast as possible, because pain has an obvious, self-evident quality—*it hurts*—and being seen in pain is, for the most, a humiliating experience.

Pain is associated almost exclusively with negatives. It is linked to failure; it evinces loss, illness, and death. Emotional pain is the worst. It is embarrassing to be seen displaying it. Culturally, emotional pain is a sign of weakness that calls for disapproval, unless you are a child, in which it is slightly more acceptable. Largely, white men have established our cultural perception of pain, which is to value it most when it's endured. This reveals a profound ignorance. We tend to respect those who suffer in silence and who do not bother us with their emotional needs or suffering. Emotional invulnerability remains a long-standing, almost worshipped, character trait within our culture.

Since pain is viewed as something that attracts disapproval, our societal solution is to hide it. So we hide our pain from others and we hide it from ourselves, and once it is thoroughly hidden, peace appears to be preserved. But while our pain may be gone temporarily, our wound remains deep within as the source of our pain. We have a headache, so we take a pain reliever. Our pain goes away; however, our headache is still there, but we are now disconnected from pain. If we feel down and melancholy because we are alone and vulnerable, we might drink, take pills, watch TV, go shopping, work longer, or eat more. Our loneliness and pain still exist, but we are no longer aware of them. If we are angry at our spouse or our kids, we may leave home and go back to work, find a diversion, or visit a friend. Our anger and pain are still present even though we have lost ourselves in these other activities. We feel pain, so we distract ourselves. Time passes, we forget our conflict, our pain dissipates, and we go on to the next thing. Our ability to become unconscious of pain has become the fundamental coping mechanism (read masking behavior) within our culture. We have chosen to live distracted from our pain or unconscious of it, and by doing so we avoid disapproval for having it. This confers the appearance of a "normal" life with normal relationships, and normal is automatically considered healthy. But this is a colossal fallacy.

The real question to ask is the following: What might we gain if we embrace our pain and increase our awareness of it instead of rejecting or running from it? Here is a story that speaks to these questions.[1]

---

1. I heard someone tell this story long ago and, regrettably, I do not know its author or origin.

There was a group of cowboys on a cattle drive. They worked hard moving their herd across the range. At the end of the day, the cowboys gathered beneath a large pine tree and made a fire. They ate their dinner and then settled comfortably into their bedrolls to sleep. The next morning the cowboys awoke to discover something strange had happened during the night. While they slept their legs had become entwined in a ball, and try as they might, they could not free themselves. Their tangle was so bad that none of them could tell whose feet and legs belonged to whom. They pulled and tugged, but because they could not recognize their own legs or feet, they could not get free. At that moment a man walked by and saw the cowboys in their predicament. He went up to them and said, "Hold on. I'll get you out of this." The man bent down and picked up a sharp pine needle. He took careful aim at one of the protruding feet and jabbed it. "Ouch!" yelled one of the cowboys, "That hurts!" "Well," said the man, "This foot belongs to you." The man stuck the pine needle into another foot. "Yow! That hurts!" said another cowboy. "This foot must belong to you," said the man. He continued in this way until the cowboys, one by one, were able to recognize their feet and legs and get free.

Pain has a profound function. It is the bridge between us and the lost parts of our identity. If we avoid our pain, we have cut that bridge and have no way to locate our wounds, the source of our pain, which, ironically, ensures that our pain will continue. If we embraced our pain when we felt it instead of pushing it away, if we owned it instead of disconnecting from it, we would have a practical way to pinpoint the source of our pain and begin a permanent healing process. Without pain we have no way to connect our present adult self with the self that was wounded and rejected in childhood. In other words, the adult who suffers from a wounded heart or broken spirit has no way to locate the source of his or her pain, without which healing is not possible.

In the end, healing is all about finding our wound; pain is only a symptom, but it will lead us where we need to go.

There is an additional irony here concerning our fear of pain. When we own it and name it, we gain clarity, and then our pain subsides. It is our avoidance of entering deeper into our emotional pain that actually magnifies it. When we learn to embrace our pain and name it for what it is, we suddenly understand, at a deeper level, our emotional wound, the source of the pain, and then this wound, just like a physical wound, begins to heal because we have reintroduced rational order to our emotional reactivity. In that moment life again makes sense as we see the source of our pain and how profoundly it skews our perception. It is at this juncture we perhaps realize that our perceptions of whatever we are reacting to are misguided and, as a result, we begin to understand that our wound and the fear it generates are running our lives.

The traditional approach to pain

We are taught that if you have pain, the solution is to fix it. This is the traditional western approach. You must analyze your situation, discover the cause of the pain, and remedy it as quickly as possible. If you've got a problem, fix it. If you have a splinter in your foot, find the splinter and remove it. If you have a drug problem, stop taking drugs. If you are overweight, stop eating. These solutions are so logical and make so much sense that any other course of action appears mystifyingly wrong.

Unfortunately, these solutions fail miserably when applied to human relations, where they lead to judgment, broken communication, and further estrangement. This is because the "if you've got a problem fix it" solution focuses solely on the active half of the issue, the thinking side of the matter. However, this perspective fails to recognize the receptive/feeling side of the problem, which is where the pain resides, which is precisely why purely logical solutions are ineffective and false.

In couple's counseling it is common to hear one spouse push a practical solution on to the other to fix a problem. In one of these types of situations, a husband agreed to be home for dinner by 6:00 p.m. to join his wife and two daughters for their evening meal. This was their arrangement, but the husband rarely made it home on time. He would arrive home ten to twenty-five minutes late each night, and always with a rational justification. To the wife, there were no acceptable excuses for being late so consistently: "He should just be on time!" The kids had to eat, and it was extremely important to her that they do so as a family. The husband had agreed, thinking it was possible, but something unpredictable regularly made him late. After months of this behavior, the wife was fed up and furious. She would launch into harangues over his unfairness and inconsideration. To her the situation was black and white: her husband had a family responsibility that he was not fulfilling. The husband, feeling his wife's disapproval, defended himself with a litany of justifiable excuses: *I had to finish a report for my boss; I got caught up in a conversation with a coworker; I hit unexpected traffic; I forgot a file on my desk and had to go all the way back to get it*. He could not understand her unwillingness to be forgiving and flexible over these delays, because he always made it home on time to join the family meal while in progress. They argued back and forth without either giving ground. They had reached a standoff and were stuck—very much like those cowboys entangled in a balled-up mess—so what this couple needed was for a passing stranger to refocus their perception by poking their feet with a sharp pine needle.

Understanding that the situation was causing them both pain pointed directly to the required solution. I asked them to stop and receive their pain and talk about what they felt (receptive) as opposed to what they thought (active). I asked the husband how he felt when he came home late again to confront his angry wife. As simple as this question might sound, it is much harder to do than one might imagine. The husband struggled a long time to find words that accurately expressed his emotional state. He said, "I feel like she shouldn't attack me." But this is not a feeling. This task of identifying his feelings was new and, therefore, uncomfortable and difficult because he wasn't skilled at it. For him, naming feelings was itself a source of pain. Finally, he said that he felt angry because his wife was continually attacking him and hurt (that one was harder for him to come by) because he had no intention of being late. He was working hard to support his family and his wife's angry reprisals made him feel unappreciated, disrespected, and unloved. He also felt terrible that he was habitually late and causing his wife so much distress. He thought it was important to have family dinner together and he very much wanted to do so, but he just couldn't seem to get a handle on being on time, which was personally embarrassing. This was his truth, and his wife heard him when he spoke it, perhaps for the first time.

Everything the husband had said up to this point was honest and factually correct, but it was not entirely truthful, because he omitted his feelings of pain and embarrassment, which were a significant percent of what he was experiencing. To his wife, this had made his justifications sound false or hollow, so she did not believe him or accept what he said. This is why she never really heard him. She *sensed* that he was not being truthful, though she could not prove it to him logically, which is what was revealed in their dialogue. The husband's willingness to become emotionally expressive changed everything. *Again, any perception that appears to be true will become a belief; a perception that does not appear real or true does not become a belief.* Initially, the wife's perceptions of her husband's excuses did not appear true, so she did not believe him. Therefore, his words had little effect on her. This is the entire power of belief formation as it occurs in relationships between people.

I asked the wife to tell us what she felt after listening to her husband. She said she felt deeply sorry, because her intention had never been to hurt him or to make him feel disrespected. She loved and cared for him, and she felt gratitude for his hard work. Aside from these feelings she also felt angry that she worked so hard to keep the household and family in good order, but received little recognition or appreciation from her husband for any of it. She felt hurt and unloved that he often judged her as doing less than him. She asked him how he might feel if she came to his office and criticized his sloppy desk or the cool tone with which he spoke to his assistant. She said arriving late for dinner at precisely 6 p.m. every day had absolutely nothing at all to do with the love and respect that she felt for her husband, but his continual excuses and justifications about it certainly did.

The wife had been unaware she was treating her husband harshly, because she herself felt misunderstood. Up until now, she could not see past her husband being wrong on this matter. It was not her intention to hurt him. Although she was very appreciative of him and his hard work, she did not express it sufficiently. This couple had remained largely unaware of their feelings. By asking them to name their emotional pain and talk about it consciously, they discovered deeper, wounded parts of themselves. They momentarily became untangled from one another and, for the first time in a long while, they distinctly heard and saw each other. Of course, we did not reach a permanent resolution in one session, but we did introduce a new dimension to this issue and to their relationship. By owning and communicating their emotional pain, by being willing to listen and to hear each other, they gained greater understanding of themselves and one another, which shifted their perceptions and beliefs. We then incorporated this simple practice of communicating emotional pain into every disagreement they had from then forward until it became a learned skill for both. With communication restored, trust naturally followed.

Ironically, our avoidance of pain consigns us to an endless cycle of pain, because the unspoken hurt we are avoiding continues accumulating inside of us like water in a reservoir, so our identity keeps manifesting more and more living symbols (broken relations, illness, aloneness, all manner of problems) in an attempt to get us to finally awaken and deal with our secret pain at its depth. It is only when we decide to embrace our pain and use it constructively that we end this cycle and move in a new direction toward authentic healing through consciousness. In the end, we all must find and work with our wounds, and it is our pain that will lead us there.

Childhood beliefs about disapproval

The wounds children carry are largely the result of two things: their inability or unwillingness to ask their parents (or their proxies) for what they emotionally long for, and their parent's (or their proxies) inability or unwillingness to insist that they do. The entire structure of childhood beliefs about disapproval rests on these points, which reduce down to broken, fear-driven, communication between parents and children: children are afraid to speak, and parents are typically unaware but also afraid and unwilling to listen.

If children believe their parents will disapprove of or reject them for expressing their true feelings and emotional longings, they will hide their true feelings and enact masking behaviors instead. Until it is addressed consciously, this cycle continues unabated with proxy-parents into adulthood and old age. Conversely, children who are taught by example to express their pain, fear, and anger, to insist that their feelings be heard and validated, and to ask directly for what they want emotionally, will be strong enough to experience any childhood beliefs about disapproval without lasting ill effects.

The truth is we need people, especially our children, to tell us directly when we have hurt them with disapproval. And we need to develop the skill and maturity to hear their words and accept them instead of rejecting them. Their words—often based on misperceptions—are still living symbols of something broken, something not working. This type of imperfect communication may cause us, in the moment, pain, embarrassment, and frustration, but it is pain worth having, because it asks us to examine the rightness of our beliefs within our relationships. It asks us as emotionally mature and responsible human beings to become conscious of our behavior, to become conscious of our role, within that relationship. This willingness to hear the other at a deep level may be the greatest gift one person can offer another, that a parent can offer their children, because it is a true expression of love and respect and living proof of one's desire for healthy relations. Reflect on your experience with Exercise Eleven in the last chapter when you went to specific people and asked them to tell you how you have hurt them.

Different names for emotional pain

Emotional pain goes by many names. What follows is a partial list of common feelings that represent some form of emotional pain. When we have these feelings, we are in pain. It is not necessary to memorize the list, but rather to understand that when I mention pain, I am referring to everything on this list as well as dozens of other feelings not mentioned. Emotional pain covers a lot of territory, and it is important you understand this. Further along, when we advance to other exercises, this understanding will become crucial. All listed terms are a variation on the same theme: when you feel these, you are in emotional pain.

Chart 7
WORDS THAT MEAN EMOTIONAL PAIN

A
Abandoned
Abused
Accused
Addicted
Afraid
Aggressive
Alarmed
Alone
Angry
Annoyed
Anxious
Appalled
Ashamed

B
Belittled
Betrayed
Blamed
Bored
Bothered

C
Closed
Cold
Confused
Cowed
Criticized

D
Defeated
Denied
Depressed
Deprived
Despair
Desperation
Despised
Devastated
Diminished
Disappointed
Disapproved of
Discouraged
Disgusted
Disinterested
Disregarded
Disrespected
Dominated
Doubtful

E
Emasculated
Empty
Enraged
Excluded

F
Fatigued
Frustrated

G
Grief
Guilty

H
Hated
Hatred
Heartbroken
Helpless
Hesitant
Hopeless
Horrified
Hostile
Humiliated
Hurt

I
Impotent
Incapable
Incompetent
Indifferent
Inferior
Infuriated
Insulted
Invalidated
Irritated

J
Jealous
Judged

L
Lonely

M
Manipulated
Mean
Melancholy
Militant
Miserable
Mocked

N
Nervous

O
Offended
Oppressed
Overconfident
Overpowered
Overwhelmed

P
Panicked
Paralyzed
Paranoid
Pathetic
Pessimistic
Powerless
Pressured
Provoked

R
Regret
Rejected
Repelled
Repulsed
Resentment
Restless

S
Sad
Scared
Skeptical
Self-conscious
Self-hatred
Shame
Shut down
Shy
Stressed
Stubborn
Stuck
Suppressed
Suspicious

T
Tense
Terrified
Threatened
Timid
Tormented
Tortured

U
Unappreciated
Unattractive
Uncertain
Unfulfilled
Unhappy
Unworthy
Upset
Useless

V
Victimized
Vindictive
Vulnerable

W
Weak
Worn out
Worried
Worthless

A full-page, color version of this chart is available for free download at TheCraftOfLife.com.

Exercise 12: Identifying my childhood beliefs about disapproval

We have all experienced thousands of parent-child collisions over differing beliefs while growing up with our parents or guardians. They believed one thing, we believed another, and bam! A collision occurred. Some of these collisions were direct—our parents telling us what we should or shouldn't do, whom we should or shouldn't be. But most collisions were indirect. They were the product of us watching and listening to our parent's beliefs, behaviors, attitudes, and opinions, and then drawing our own conclusions based on what we perceived.

This process is analogous to crossing a railroad track. We look both ways, usually multiple times; we listen for the loud whistle; we feel for a distant rumble on the tracks. Only when we believe, based on numerous perceptions, there is no train coming do we proceed to cross the tracks. All of our perceptions and effort are intended to bring about a safe crossing. This is exactly what we did with our parents. We watched them closely. We listened to them carefully. We formulated our own beliefs about what they would likely disapprove of and then we adapted. We were looking for a safe crossing, so we trained ourselves to not let them see certain behaviors, to not ask them for specific emotional comfort or support in order to avoid an anticipated response of disapproval, rejection, or abandonment. This was our perception of our parents and our response to what we perceived. Whether our perceptions were factually correct had nothing to do with it. As long as our perceptions appeared true to us, they became our beliefs; they became our identity.

The question is, how does all of this live within you right now? What behaviors or parts of yourself do you still hide, fearing your parent's disapproval? What emotional longings do you still keep concealed from your spouse or partner because you fear their rejection or abandonment? In this way, we have made our partners proxies for our parents. Please take out your list of emotional longings. You will need it for this next exercise. To help you, here, again, is my list:

My emotional longings are . . .

1) To receive help, caring, and support both emotionally and financially.
2) The courage to express my anger and have confrontation with my father.
3) To receive affection, emotional protection, and love.
4) To be seen, recognized, and accepted for who I am, as I am.
5) For people to be who they claim to be.
6) To receive rational responses during confrontation.

To identify your childhood beliefs about disapproval, simply take each of your emotional longings and write them out as the literal, opposite statement. These opposite statements are your childhood beliefs about disapproval. As an example, here are my childhood beliefs about disapproval as compared to my emotional longings, which are listed above.

1) I should not ask for help, caring or support—emotionally or financially—or I will be disapproved of and rejected.
2) I should not express anger or have confrontations, or I will be disapproved of by my father.
3) I should not ask for affection, emotional protection, or love, or I will be disapproved of, rejected, and abandoned.
4) I should not want to be seen, recognized, or accepted for who I am, as I am, or I will be disapproved of.
5) I should not ask other people to be who they claim to be, or I will be disapproved of, rejected, and abandoned.
6) I should not ask to receive rational responses during confrontation, or I will be disapproved of and rejected.

As you can see, the basic format for all childhood beliefs about disapproval is: I SHOULD OR SHOULD NOT—followed by the belief, then ending in—OR I WILL BE DISAPPROVED OF. The belief is almost always about asking or not asking for something, wanting or not wanting something, doing or not doing something, being or not being something. Try to keep your responses within one of these four formats.

If you anticipate more severe degrees of disapproval, add disapproved of and rejected to your sentences. If you expected the ultimate punishment for asking for what you wanted, add disapproved of, rejected, and abandoned. This gives you three varying levels of disapproval, which indicate three ranges of fear that live inside you. As your expectation of stronger disapproval rises, your fear and reticence rise as well. In other words, while it is hard to cross the tracks when you see the train coming in the distance, it is far more difficult when the train is close, and you see it speeding toward you with incredible power and velocity.

Take a moment and consider the relationship now between the three key elements of all confrontations: *childhood beliefs about disapproval, emotional longings, and masking behaviors.* While growing up we perceived our parents and formulated beliefs about who we should not be, how we should not behave and, most important of all, what emotional comfort we should *never* ask for. These become our childhood beliefs about disapproval. As a result, we must hide specific elements of our own identity, specific behaviors, genuine feelings, but, most important of all, we must hide what we want most from them. These are our emotional longings. Now, instead of asking for this precious and crucial support, we adopt behaviors that assist us in disowning and disassociating from what we want most. These are our masking behaviors. In the end, we are all left with unfulfilled emotional longings, which create a deep, perpetual wound in our psyche, a wound originated and sustained by our personal fear of disapproval.

At *www.TheCraftOfLife.com*, you will find in downloadable, searchable format *Chart14: A List of Childhood Beliefs About Disapproval*. Please use this list to assist in identifying your own childhood beliefs about disapproval; adapt them in whatever way helps as you write down your own. You will also find in the charts and forms section at the back of the book or on the website, *Form 3: Identifying my Childhood Beliefs About Disapproval*. Use this to make your compilation.

My emotional longings are . . .

Copy your list of emotional longings on the form to prepare for creating their opposite statement, which will be . . .

My childhood beliefs about disapproval are . . .

Now use your list of emotional longings to create opposite statements. There should be one for each emotional longing.

Once you are done, you will need to test these statements out, just as we did with your emotional longings. For one week, observe yourself responding to felt disapproval, rejection, or abandonment. Watch your responses to any feelings of disapproval, rejection, or abandonment, regardless of how small or seemingly insignificant. Now check your list. Do your written beliefs represent what you believe in moments of conflict when you felt disapproved of, rejected, or abandoned? They should match perfectly. If not, adjust the language. If you adjust one of your childhood beliefs about disapproval, then you must go back and also adjust the language of its related emotional longing, because they are two sides of the same coin. Childhood beliefs about disapproval and emotional longings always mirror each other.

In the next chapter, you will compile all of your personal information onto one sheet called *My Responses to Disapproval Form*. Once this is complete, you will begin your work of consciousness building and self-healing in earnest.

Form 4
IDENTIFYING MY CHILDHOOD BELIEFS ABOUT DISAPPROVAL

	MY EMOTIONAL LONGINGS ARE *From Form 2b, copy your list of emotional longings into the spaces below.*
	Examples *a) To be seen and supported emotionally, especially by my father (or his proxies).* *b) To be met calmly and rationally (instead of with a reactive, irrational response), especially by my mother (or her proxies).*
1	
2	
3	
4	
5	
6	
7	
8	

	MY CHILDHOOD BELIEFS ABOUT DISAPPROVAL ARE *The format is: If I ask to be (**fill in your emotional longing**), I will be disapproved of and rejected.*
	Examples *a) If I ask to be seen or supported, I will be disapproved of and rejected by my father (or his proxies).* *b) If I ask to be met calmly and rationally, I will be disapproved of and rejected, especially by my mother (or her proxies).*
1	
2	
3	
4	
5	
6	
7	
8	

This form is available at the back of this book and as a full-page, editable version for free download at TheCraftOfLife.com

CHAPTER 16

My Responses to Disapproval Form

Your vision will become clear only when you can look into your own heart. Who looks outside, dreams; who looks inside, awakes.

—Carl Jung

YOU ARE NOW GOING to organize your story on to one sheet of paper. You're going to compile your fears, wounds, and deepest desires into one readable, easy-to-understand form. This is a profound activity. It gives rise to an extraordinarily powerful tool that you will have for the rest of your life. If you use this tool, you will gain clarity in all situations at all times. When you fall into your blind spot and become unconscious, you can use it to reawaken. You can use it to understand your reactions to conflicts and issues in your life. Understanding yourself at a much deeper level, you can use this simple, powerful tool to stop looking at others as the reason for your pain and finally become the loving, authentic person you are, which means healthy, satisfying relationships become possible.

To start, we first need to recognize that conflict and confrontation have a universal structure. Look beneath the surface of any confrontation and you will always find the same three elements: childhood beliefs about disapproval, masking behaviors, and emotional longings. Neither the size nor the magnitude of a confrontation makes any difference. It doesn't matter if someone cut you off on the freeway or if you've received a diagnosis of lung cancer or if you're facing a sudden financial catastrophe or if someone has eaten the last cookie you were saving for yourself. All of these seemingly different, unrelated conflicts of differing importance have the same three elements as their internal construction. Nor does it matter if the confrontation is between you and someone else or within you.

Your objective now is to train yourself to look for these three elements. Seeing past confrontation's veneer and recognizing them is a cornerstone of the Craft of Life, because it is the level at which you will find your truth. Perhaps you had a confrontation with someone at work, or you encountered someone rude at the supermarket, or you had too much to eat or drink and berate yourself for it. Typically, we process such events by talking about them with family and friends. We talk, we complain, we vent. We voice our anger and hurt. Others listen. They offer sympathy and understanding. They try to validate our position: *the other person was wrong; you were right; I'm sorry this happened*. These are the ways most of us process conflict and confrontation. This is the kind of dialogue that goes on everywhere, in every household, throughout the world.

While this venting may allow us to feel better for a short while, it only calcifies our unawareness and unintentionally sets more firmly in place the patterns we would like to change. To stop this cycle, we need to develop a new skill. We must use our will to perceive confrontation differently. We must use our will to see past the surface of the event and look deeper because the same three structural elements will always be present.

The amazing part of inner work is that we relive our childhood story daily. It never ends. In fact, it is the glue that holds our life together. We are born. We experience parent-child collisions throughout childhood and adolescence. We mature and age. Throughout our lives we continue to have confrontations and conflicts, and they all appear to be different, occurring with different people at different times and over different events. Yet, at their depth, they are always the same, and they always have the same internal structure. If you want to transform yourself, this is good news, because once you learn to identify the same three fundamental elements, you only have three things to look for and consider. Observing ourselves experience this endless repetition is what allows us to transform. As you practice this skill, it will become second nature. Learning to see past the veneer of conflict or confrontation to its three deeper components is a life-changing ability.

Assembling *My Responses To Disapproval Form*

You will need the following five items:

1. Exercise 5, Chapter 7: Form 1: Masking Behaviors' Journal
2. Exercise 10, Chapter 13: Identifying my Emotional Longings
3. Exercise 12, Chapter 15: Identifying my Childhood Beliefs about Disapproval
4. Blank Form 5 (back of book or in full size at www.TheCraftOfLife.com): *My Responses to Disapproval*
5. Chart 7, (Chapter 15 or at www.TheCraftOfLife.com): Words that Mean Emotional Pain

First, enter your name and date at the top of the *My Responses to Disapproval Form*. Next, enter the information from one through three in the appropriate sections. Now, using the chart: Different Words that Mean Emotional Pain (#7), fill in the top nine GENUINE FEELINGS that you consistently hide from others into section three. At this time, leave My Source Belief (sections six and seven) blank.

Now review again the Confrontation's Three-part Composition chart, except this time, when you see the general labels for 1) Childhood beliefs about disapproval, 2) Masking behaviors, and 3) Emotional longings, insert your personal statements for each of these. Now you are overlaying your personal story on top of the universal structure of conflict and confrontation. It is like overlaying your physical body on top of the universal human skeleton that lives beneath it. It is your story that, like your physical body, makes this universal structure you.

You now have in your hands a tool of enormous value. This will become increasingly clear as we move forward in our journey together. It is like having a fine instrument—a Martin guitar or a Steinway piano—without yet knowing how to play it. Please be patient. Music lessons will begin shortly.

Exercise 13: Observing the three parts of every confrontation

For one week, set aside time to reflect on conflicts or confrontations that occur during your day. Have your *Responses to Disapproval Form* nearby as you review the confrontations. You may be in conflict with others, with organizations, or with yourself. Here is a list of questions to help guide you in your review:

1. Were you aware that conflict/confrontation was occurring?
2. If yes, did you feel fear or emotional upset in your body? Where?
3. Did you react emotionally? What was your reaction?
4. Did you hear an internal voice threaten you with disapproval for voicing your genuine feelings or asking for what you want? The voice may sound something like this, "If I say this or do that or ask for this, so and so will disapprove of, reject, or might even leave me."
5. Did you yield to this pressure of disapproval? If yes, what masking behaviors did you enact? Check your *Responses to Disapproval Form.*

6. Did you blame someone else or hold that person at least partly responsible? Did you feel a sense of injustice that something unfair or wrong was happening to you?
7. Did you disengage from or lose sight of your emotional longings? Were you too afraid and reactive to ask or act on what you want?
8. What did you see in the moment? Did you react or did you respond?
9. Can you now see that both your emotional longings and your childhood beliefs about disapproval (now self-disapproval) were active and in play at the same time over the same issue?

As you do this exercise, you are practicing several concepts simultaneously:

- You are learning to recognize the three structural elements that underlie all conflicts and confrontations: childhood beliefs about disapproval, masking behaviors, and emotional longings.
- You are also learning to recognize the natural flow between these three elements as confrontation moves from one element to the next.
- You are learning to recognize the deeper truth of your own story in real time within real conflicts and confrontations.
- You are beginning to perceive, understand, and organize conflicts in a new way, which opens the door for a shift in perception, belief, and identity.

This exercise is beneficial to do as part of a group. There will be much to share, investigate, and learn together. In the beginning, it may feel difficult and awkward to talk about, but after practice it becomes easier. Now you are coming into clarity.

Form 5
MY RESPONSES TO DISAPPROVAL

Name: ______________________________ Date: ____________

When I feel fear or emotional upset in my body, it means I'm having a confrontation in the moment, amplified by parent-child collisions from the past. This tells me that **BOTH** my **childhood beliefs about disapproval AND** my **emotional longings** have become triggered and my **seen** and **hidden selves** are in conflict. My **seen self** pressures me to accept my fear of disapproval, while my **hidden self** simultaneously reminds me to own and act on what I truly want. These represent opposite beliefs, opposite agendas. Now, I must choose to affirm one or the other.

These are my **childhood beliefs about disapproval.** None are true anymore.	
1	
2	
3	
4	
5	
6	
7	
8	

These are the **genuine feelings** I typically hide. My seen self pressures me to conceal these.							
1		3		5		7	
2		4		6		8	

My **masking behaviors** lead me into my blind spot. My seen self pressures me to enact these.			
1		5	
2		6	
3		7	
4		8	

My **emotional longings** are what I want. My seen self pressures me not to ask for or act on these.	
1	
2	
3	
4	
5	
6	
7	
8	

Our **seen self** wants us to remain unconscious by perpetuating our emotional wounds.
When we hide our emotional longings behind our **masking behaviors** because of **childhood fears about disapproval**, then we remain unconscious and our identity cannot change.

Our **hidden self** wants us to become more conscious by healing our emotional wounds.
When we recognize that we are enacting **masking behaviors** because of **childhood beliefs about disapproval** and, instead, act on or ask for what we want, then we are breaking old beliefs and patterns, restoring personal integrity, and building consciousness. And, then, nothing can prevent our identity and our lives from transforming.

This form is available at the back of this book and as a full-page, editable version for free download at TheCraftOfLife.com

CHAPTER 17

Separating our Pain from our Wound

What's left of kisses? Wounds, however, leave scars.

—Bertolt Brecht

WE NEED TO CLARIFY further two words: pain and wound. Pain is what we feel when we're physically or emotionally hurt. The pain we feel comes from a wound, but it's not the wound itself. The wound is the source of the pain, but it's not the pain that we feel. Their relationship is very clear: the wound is the cause and the pain is the effect.

Emotional pain is a special messenger asking a particular question. It is a call for help from deep within—a cry from a neglected, forgotten part of our own identity. Pain invites us to go beyond its self-evident feeling of hurt and to look deeper for its source, which is our wound. In this way, pain was designed to initiate healing; this is pain's true purpose.

When a confrontation befalls us, we get sucked into an emotional vortex. Someone says or does something that hurts us and, in the blink of an eye, we react emotionally or defensively, enmeshed in conflict. Someone tells us, "That's not the right way to do it." Or, "Late again—what a surprise!" Or, "How could you waste money like that?" Any one of these or thousands like them pull us into the roaring rapids of emotional conflict. Words are spoken to us; feelings of fear and disapproval arise; masking behaviors come out; and our genuine feelings and emotional longings remain submerged. Flailing about for emotional survival, we are consumed by our pain. So we argue our position to prove we're right. We fight back because it feels natural and makes sense. Fighting feels justified and necessary. We fight back to hold on to our self-worth, but underneath we are trying to prevent what feels like personal annihilation. We might say, for example, "It is the right way to do it. You don't know what you're talking about!" Or, "Hey, you're late all the time. Don't give me *your* bullshit!" Or, "It's not a waste of money. I was trying to do the right thing." Or we say little or nothing and withdraw inside of ourselves. Or we discuss the situation as if we were lawyers negotiating a contract.

In all of these instances, our pain, our fear of disapproval from others or ourselves, drives us onward, and even though we may not realize it in the moment, the same fears are driving the other person's reactions as well. Pain fuels both of our reactions. But our immediate pain is not the real issue, so it's the wrong place for us to focus. In these moments, our wound is the cause of what we're feeling; our pain is only the effect. The skill that we all need to learn and eventually master is separating our pain from our wound, because they are completely different and each one sends us off in two very different directions: one toward consciousness and one into unconsciousness.

Conflict always has embedded in it the cause of our immediate pain and the old childhood wound buried beneath that has now become triggered. We can always see the issue at hand, but we rarely see the childhood wound, the result of our many parent-child collisions. Nor do we see our emotional longings, which, unfulfilled, remain the beating heart of our wound. We feel pain, we get angry and hurt, we feel invalidated or denied, and so we react. It is what we know to do, but our reaction is fully programmed. It is like a dog with a ball. Someone throws the ball; the dog reacts and chases it. Someone throws the ball again; the dog chases it again. Someone says or does something that hurts us, and we react to the pain as we always do: we chase the ball, believing in the moment that the ball is what it's about. But it's never about the ball. It's never *really* about the confrontation. It isn't about who left the toilet seat up, who left the dishes in the sink, or who isn't fair. Each is just a distraction, for it is the pain that keeps us from seeing our wound and claiming our emotional longings.

If we could identify our emotional wounds and learn them well, we would be in an entirely new position. Confrontation occurs. We feel pain. Yet, instead of reacting, we first stop and look for our deeper wound. Of course, we must deal with the issue at hand. But, if we are to remain conscious, we must also see our wound as distinct and separate from the pain we are feeling in that moment.

Our craft continues by perceiving our confrontations differently. Every pain-fraught confrontation is rooted in an old parent-child collision. There are no exceptions. Parent-child collisions mean the same five things every time. If you memorize the following steps, you will strengthen your ability to see and transform your pattern of reactivity in a very deep way:

1) **pain results from parent-child collisions**, so we
2) **hide our genuine feelings** and
3) **surrender our emotional longings** and **personal power.** We then
4) **hide behind our masking behaviors**, leading us to
5) fall into **our blind spot**.

Now, all we can feel is our pain, and we cannot see our wound.

Here is the story of a couple. Both the husband and wife had done identity theory work so they had the benefit of common language, concepts, and perspectives. Both knew their own stories well. The husband bought a vase for his wife. She received the gift and put it on their fireplace mantle. The husband said, "It would look better on the table." The wife disagreed. The husband stood his ground, "No, it would look better on the table." An argument ensued and tempers flared. About three minutes into this heated argument, the wife said to the husband, "We're both having parent-child collisions. We're both reacting from old childhood wounds. We aren't really fighting about the vase." Silence. A minute later the husband said, "You're absolutely right." They looked into each other's eyes and, without another word, both understood what had happened. They felt a greater trust in one another and a stronger emotional connection. They both let the argument go. This experience represented a quantum leap in their individual inner work and in their marriage. They learned to step out of their blind spots and see what they could not see before. They demonstrated the ability to separate pain in the moment from wound in the past, resulting in clarity.

Let's look at this scenario from the opposite perspective. What if they had not separated their present pain from their childhood wounds? They would have had the same experience they've had for thirty years. There would be no clarity, no understanding, no resolution—only more pain. The husband insists the vase would look better somewhere else. The wife disagrees. Neither gives ground and neither thinks to look for a deeper wound from childhood. So they fight. First about the vase, then about how the husband is always telling his wife the "right" way to do things, but she refuses to listen because her husband is wrong much of the time and his mode of communication invalidates her. She tells him he is a bully and a jerk. This hurts the husband's feelings, so he tells his wife she can't even put a vase in the "right" place. And so it goes. In the end, both bring out their masking behaviors, which hides their genuine feelings. They go away mad and emotionally disconnected and, of course, unconscious. They then spend hours ruminating about what took place. They tell themselves they've married the wrong person. They talk about it with friends, relatives, and therapists. The vase consumes enormous energy, draining time and love from their marriage. The conflict becomes exhausting.

Now let's expand on what actually occurred. The wife had practiced the skill of stepping back in confrontations and looking for her masking behaviors. Masking behaviors are the entry point for all that follows. Recognizing and owning our masking behaviors is the doorway to healing. The wife saw herself feeling pain from disapproval. She then watched herself shut down emotionally and go numb. She recognized her reaction as a masking behavior. This told her she was hiding her genuine feelings, so she named the feelings she was hiding: judged and hurt. Her husband had said: "The vase is in the wrong place." Which she understood to mean, "I can't do anything right. I'm a failure—*again*." The wife recognized these beliefs as part of her childhood beliefs about disapproval.

As a child, her mother always made her feel like she couldn't do anything right. Her husband's words led her to believe her husband was a proxy for her mother. By going through this two-minute process, the wife realized she was projecting her fear and pain onto her husband. He wasn't really repeating her mother's disapproval, he was simply stating his opinion: the vase would look better on the table. He was not judging her. But it felt that way because of her childhood wounds. So she separated her present pain from her childhood wound and gained clarity. The pain was the initial belief that she put the vase in the wrong place and had failed again. Her wound distorted and amplified the situation, fueled her inner feelings of disapproval, failure, and rejection, and caused her to fight back for her own emotional survival. The pain issue was where to put the vase; the wound issue was how to deal with self-disapproval and self-rejection, which she felt from her husband's words.

Through understanding, the wife stepped out of her blind spot and learned her perceptions were misguided. She learned more about the skill of separating pain from wound in order to gain clarity. She learned that her husband was indeed a trustworthy partner, and that he, too, was also driven by his own childhood wounds, which were the source of his reaction. In the counseling session following this argument, the wife also told me she was bowled over by how much time and energy she was saving weekly by reaching resolutions quickly or not fighting over issues that had vexed her in the past. This is just one of the practical payoffs of identity theory. The husband had a similar experience and similar realizations.

A great benefit of completing your *Responses to Disapproval Form* is having your masking behaviors compiled into a clear, short list. If you memorize them, you'll know to look for them. When you see yourself engage in masking behaviors, you'll see what you could not see before. This is extraordinarily transformative, for it means your unconscious behavior is now conscious. You are experiencing clarity. Now you have a concrete starting point for locating your deeper wound and reclaiming your hidden emotional longings. The wife's emotional longings included the following: to be heard and respected, to be validated and understood, and to not be the one at fault all the time. She felt these when her husband agreed with her that they were both having parent-child collisions, which not only ended their argument, but also reaffirmed their love and bond as a couple. It is worth mentioning that this couple—like most married couples—thought seriously about divorce as a solution to their marital differences, which they perceived as unsolvable. Their issues and the breakdown in their marriage were solvable, but, first, they both had to learn to see themselves differently before that could happen. Now they can talk about their stories and their wounds, not just their pain.

How personal transformation occurs

The story of the vase provides a clear example of how personal transformation occurs. When the wife separated her present pain from her past wound, she gained a new perspective. It was as though she shined a brighter, more concentrated, light onto the situation—as I had done for my Aunt Ruthie and her dirty carpet—so she could see what she could not see before. From this step came new perceptions and new beliefs about herself and her husband, which caused her to change her behavior (she stopped fighting and considered alternative actions). Her new beliefs resulted in better decision making and wiser actions, which changed the content and tone of her communication. Moving forward, the husband and wife will less likely engage in arguments without first considering their newfound perspectives and beliefs. As they practice and become more skilled at resolving their conflicts in this new way, they will use their masking behaviors less, they will hide their feelings less, and their unfulfilled emotional longings will diminish as they are gradually fulfilled. As this happens, their hidden selves will begin to integrate into their seen selves. They will gradually move toward balance and wholeness. All of these transformations occurred because the wife chose to see her masking behaviors and separate her present pain from her past wound.

A deeper look at confrontation

We've arrived at a point where we need to take a closer look at our responses to confrontation, which is the gateway to personal transformation. In every confrontation, the two fundamental components of our identity—our seen and hidden selves—rise up and stand for their specific beliefs. Each wants you to choose it over the other, but the beliefs each represent are diametrically opposed. You must choose one, but only one. So each presses you for your allegiance. This is the underlying reason why confrontation is so powerful, disturbing, and uncomfortable; however, it is a reason for which we often have little awareness. We think the conflict is about who was disrespectful or who scratched the car. We don't realize that the conflict has awakened the most primal components of our identity and sent them into a battle for survival. Regardless of how large or small a confrontation, each one stirs up the same response: we feel the upheaval in our guts as our seen and hidden selves fight it out like gladiators in the arena of our minds. This is not an overdramatization; the inner conflict that occurs during moments of confrontation is profoundly deep and primal.

When confrontation unfolds, we must choose which beliefs to uphold and which part of our self to stand with. Do we accept our seen self's fear of disapproval and hide our emotional longings, or do we embrace our hidden self's belief in the value of owning our genuine feelings and acting on our emotional longings? Our choice literally determines our life's direction. Do we choose unconsciousness, or do we choose consciousness that brings new patterns of healing and transformation? Or, do we continue down the tired path of repetitive patterns of pain and dissatisfaction? These are the two choices we have—it's one or the other.

Option 1: We choose our seen self (an unconscious choice)

Confrontation occurs. We experience pain, anger, and/or fear. We feel attacked and invalidated. Our childhood beliefs about disapproval and our emotional longings are now in play. It is time to choose. We unconsciously decide to uphold our seen self and its dreaded fear of disapproval. So, we enact our masking behaviors and disassociate from our emotional longings. Moving forward, we generate living symbols that reflect our oldest emotional wounds, our deepest fears of disapproval. We remain mostly unconscious. We continue to experience pain and dissatisfaction in our key relationships. Everything in our lives that isn't working remains mostly status quo.

Option 2: We choose our hidden self (a conscious choice)

Confrontation occurs. We experience pain, anger, and/or fear. We feel attacked and invalidated. Our childhood beliefs about disapproval and our emotional longings are now in play. It is time to choose. We consciously decide to uphold our hidden self and its authenticity. So we look for our masking behaviors, then resist or stop them even as we enact them, and we take possession of our emotional longings; we ask for or act upon what we want. Moving forward, our new actions generate new living symbols that reflect healing of our deepest emotional wounds, which lessens our childhood beliefs about disapproval. In other words, visible change occurs. We become more conscious as everything in our lives that wasn't working suddenly, mysteriously begins to. This process is so completely organic that it seems invisible and incomprehensible. Actually, it is as visible and comprehensible as a seed sprouting and blossoming into a flower.

When we begin to see confrontation as an important and meaningful occurrence, we repeatedly have new, truer perceptions of old beliefs, which helps heal our identity. Then everything and everyone connected to us heals as well because we are harnessing the power of belief formation and setting in motion the alchemy of life. To make this happen, we must step out of our blind spot and see our hidden self apart from our seen self, and then we must choose one or the other consciously.

What to expect as you begin this practice

I had a client named Renee who had done all the foundational work of identity theory. She was part of a group that studied each chapter, and, in addition, she saw me for individual counseling. Growing up, Renee felt loved by her parents, but she never felt supported by them, either emotionally or financially. Her mother, feeling caught in an unsatisfying life, could not relate to her children beyond her own pain and unhappiness, and, so, regularly displayed masking behaviors of defensiveness and denial, as in, "I wasn't being critical; I was just being truthful." Or, following a cutting remark, "Don't be so sensitive. I didn't mean anything by it." On the other hand, her father consistently avoided confrontation with his wife, and, so, although a kind and gentle person, was not able to offer Renee true support or protection. Further, her father did not earn much money, so the family got by but had little extra for anything else. Renee could not have the things she really wanted, such as dance or piano lessons. Not having enough money or emotional support became the basis for her childhood beliefs about disapproval. What Renee wanted was to be seen, validated, and supported, both emotionally and financially. These became her unfulfilled emotional longings.

Renee's seen self believed that if she directly asked her parents for her emotional longings, she would be misunderstood, which would upset and hurt them, and open herself up to their disapproval and rejection. Her hidden self, however, believed the opposite: that she must act on her desire to be seen, validated, and supported, or her deepest childhood wounds would never heal. These are the two conflicting beliefs from the two conflicted parts of self that rise up within her at every confrontation. With all of this identified, Renee was ready to begin this practice. Then something happened to her that most everyone undertaking this work should know about and expect to happen, because some variation of it often occurs.

Renee began working with conflict and confrontation and developing new perceptions and beliefs. She practiced watching her responses to both, and she began to see her seen and hidden selves pursuing their different agendas. She worked to build a conscious, collaborative relationship between these two disparate parts of self, and she began to make real progress, which she felt and saw in her life and relationships. One day Renee was driving on a local road, reflecting on these recent changes. She thought, "Maybe I really am supported? Maybe things *are* changing for me?" She felt a quiet, but deep, happiness in her heart.

That's when a car crashed into her. A driver had come out of nowhere, made an illegal U-turn, and crashed into the side of her car. No one was hurt, but the timing could not have been more precise.

When I saw Renee next, she appeared beaten down, discouraged, and almost broken. She had reached the chasm that all of us must eventually face. This is one of the toughest parts of any true inner journey. The seen self can be a wild beast, especially when cornered. At first it goes along with the new collaborative relationship with the hidden self—it appears to be win-win for both—but as progress is made, the seen self realizes that going further will lead to its own demise. That's when the wild beast emerges and often with remarkable power and vengeance—think of the terrifying roar of a lion. The seen self will now fight tooth and claw for its own survival. Your own identity will now begin to manifest conflict after conflict, creating the appearance that things are not only not changing, but growing progressively worse. Your seen self will begin to tell you that you should never have even started this process. But you did and now you are fully aware of your masking behaviors, so you have crossed the point from which you cannot go back even if you tried. This is the edge of the chasm and the only option now is to marshal your resolve and cross to the other side.

I have witnessed many people traverse this difficult inner terrain. The length of time it takes is proportional to how much we cling to old beliefs and behaviors, how much we resist seeing and naming our masking behaviors for what they are. Eventually, we must all come to a place where we tell ourselves, "I am sick of this. I don't want my wounds, my fears, my destructive beliefs running my life anymore; it isn't worth it. I am selling out my own soul by upholding a set of beliefs that only hurt me." Finally, we relax our grip and let our main masking behaviors go. We surrender. For many, this means moving away from the anger that we feel at the surface and dropping down deeper into our true emotional longings. When we do this, suddenly, as if by magic, we find ourselves transported and standing on the other side of the chasm. The sense of relief that we feel in this moment is enormous. We understand we can never go back; we don't want to go back, and we see in front of us a new, unexplored landscape of identity with fresh possibilities. The feeling is extraordinary.

Renee wept as she told me of her car accident. It was proof that change was not really possible or too hard. She said that being supported was a pipe dream and the universe made its point by totaling her car. The despair she felt was deep and real. We talked again about her seen self and her hidden self. We talked about where she was and what she needed to do next. She was in transition; she was so much further along than she could see at this difficult moment. As we talked, she felt my commitment to her courageous inner work. She could recognize that other friends were supporting her too. Her deepest emotional longings were starting to be fulfilled but she hadn't really noticed. Many living symbols were present in her life that proved this. She decided to keep fighting for the inner transformation she so longed for. We began to work with the following exercise, which is about separating pain from wound, seeing your past in the present, seeing your seen and hidden selves, and how each co-creates the conflicts that befall you—all so you will choose one over the other. In the end, the only thing we control is this choice, and our choice determines whether we become free or not.

Exercise 14: The Clarity Exercise/beginner level—Stop, feel, see the past

To learn the craft of identity theory and free yourself from fear and reactivity, to build a caring, authentic relationship with yourself and others, plan on using this exercise in its different forms for a long time to come. I use a version of this exercise every day in my own life; it's powerful because it's amazingly effective. The purpose of this exercise is to reduce emotional reactivity and promote consciousness so you may gain clarity about yourself, your life, and the decisions you choose to make. Its practice is the basis for living life from the inside out instead of from the outside in. If you invest time and effort in this exercise in its various forms, you will be rewarded with profound self-discovery—not just immediately, but at increasingly deeper levels for decades to come. The final version of this exercise, which appears later in this book, takes approximately 60 seconds.

Step 1: Recognize you are having a conflict or confrontation

Whenever you feel emotionally upset, overtaken by pain or fear, you are experiencing conflict or confrontation either with someone or yourself. This is where this exercise begins. Now you can start training yourself to recognize conflict and confrontation as they occur. This is similar to training yourself as a new driver to stop your car when you reach a stop sign. In the beginning, it took awareness, but eventually it becomes like second nature. Whenever you feel pain, fear, or emotional upset, *STOP* and recognize that you are having a confrontation. The details do not matter. Nor does it matter who is right or wrong, what is fair or unfair. The only thing of consequence is that you learn to stop and recognize when you are having a confrontation, because this simple act breaks the pattern of automatic, conditioned reactivity and initiates the process of awakening. Healing starts simply with the realization, "I am having a conflict."

Step 2: Name your genuine feelings

Once you realize you are having a confrontation, your next step is to name your genuine feelings. Again, do not respond to the conflict or confrontation nor engage in who is right or wrong. Just name and own your genuine feelings. This is your point of focus. It may be helpful to use the chart of feelings in the back of the book to help. Name your feelings regardless of what they might be. These feelings represent your personal and private truth. Say them to yourself: I feel ___________, and I feel ___________, and I feel ___________. By naming your feelings instead of hiding them, you are consciously breaking the oldest of childhood taboos. You are intentionally embracing what you have habitually hidden for a very long time.

Step 3: See the past in the present

Now comes the critical part. This step is the key to unlocking your story. Every conflict or confrontation is rooted in old parent-child collisions. There are *no exceptions*. You might believe there are, but I assure you there are not. You will be surprised to discover this is true as you move further along in your practice. Your effort at this step is to see how your story—your childhood beliefs about disapproval and your emotional wounds—enter into and amplify your present conflict, making you feel like what happened decades ago is happening once again. This is not actually the case, but it feels that way. Your work now is to see all of this clearly, to see your childhood story re-energized in the moment, making you feel exactly as you did growing up when you were overpowered and wounded by your parents.

Repeat this practice over one or two weeks or until you can do steps one through three quickly and easily. You need to come to a measurable level of skill with this exercise and be able to demonstrate it, or your practice will not be effective. This early incomplete version lays the foundation for the next, more complete level of this same exercise, which you will find in the following chapter. Bear in mind that our goal is deep, permanent transformation. These are not simple, self-help exercises. You are doing them to transform yourself, your life, and your relationships in a true and meaningful way. Do not expect to change wounding beliefs that you have held for decades in a week or even a month. That isn't going to happen. To give you some perspective, when

I work with a group, if a participant makes the effort, powerful transformation typically occurs over a nine-month period. If a person continues on in the coming year they may finally be able to face their source belief, which you will read about in a later chapter. Profound healing and transformation are possible in a relatively short period when compared to how long you have lived out your childhood beliefs, but expecting to change them in this moment or in a week, is looking for a magical cure that does not exist. For now recognize that you are undertaking a heroic journey that requires a new level of strength, stamina, and commitment. The potential rewards are enormous.

Summary: The Clarity Exercise/beginner level

Preliminary steps:

Take out your *Responses to Disapproval Form* and *The Three Parts of Every Confrontation* chart. Study each one for a period of time until you know and understand them well. You need to know your own story thoroughly, and you need to understand the three key elements of confrontation on a feeling level and not just as intellectual concepts. Now you are ready to begin.

Step 1: Recognize you are having a conflict or confrontation

If you feel pain and emotional upset in your body, this means you are having a conflict or a confrontation. Do not react. Recognize what is happening.

Step 2: Name your genuine feelings

Instead of reacting emotionally, use your will to step back and name your feelings. Say to yourself, "I feel __________, I feel __________, and I feel __________, etc. Now own what you feel, because these feelings represent your personal and private truth.

Step 3: See the past in the present

Know your story and understand how your childhood beliefs about disapproval are influencing and amplifying your current conflict, thus creating the illusion that you are being attacked and wounded as you were growing up. Observe how the past distorts the present, causing you to overreact and fall into in to your blind spot.

CHAPTER 18

Reclaiming Your Power

Nobody knows what you want except you. And nobody will be as sorry as you if you don't get it. Wanting some other way to live is proof enough of deserving it. Having it is hard work, but not having it is sheer hell.

—Lillian Hellman

THERE WAS A CHILD born to a family. Her mother and father loved her, and the child felt loved. The father worked long hours to support his family. He worked hard to make a better life for his children than he ever had. But he did not have enough time or energy for the child, so she grew up believing work was more important than spending time with her. This was her perception. The mother also worked hard. She kept the house, she cooked and cleaned, and attended to extended family, all while working a regular job as well. She was often tired and frustrated. She did not have enough time or energy to spend with the child, so the child grew up believing work was more important than being with her. This was her perception. The child wanted time with her father, but she was afraid to ask. She feared his reaction. She feared being scolded, disapproved of, or rejected. All of these responses would be painful, especially because she loved her father. The child wanted to spend time with her mother, but she was afraid to ask. She feared hurting her mother's feelings, and she feared being scolded, disapproved of, or rejected. All of these responses would be painful, especially because she loved her mother. So the child learned not to ask for what she longed for. She learned to hide what she wanted most. As a result, the child felt a quiet ache in her heart, a subtle pain of something unfulfilled. She felt this every day, but, as years passed, as she grew older, this feeling became normal, and she lost awareness of her unfulfilled desires.

The child became an adult. She left home and began her own life. She spoke to her mother and father frequently. She loved them and they loved her. She found herself in many relationships. In each of them, she experienced an emotional void, as if something were missing. She worked too hard; her partners worked too hard. She often felt abandoned and alone, but she could not bring herself to broach this subject directly with anyone. The words got caught in her throat; the feelings stuck in her chest. At times she cried, and at other times she became angry. She often drank too much. But her pain did not lessen. She went to therapy. She talked about her feelings when her partners did not pay enough attention to her, when she felt abandoned. But her pain did not go away. She had many relationships over many years, and they all seemed to end in a similar place. She believed she was trapped in a pattern she could not break free of, but she could not see it plainly; she could not understand it clearly. So her solution was to work harder to find the right relationship. But life is not about finding the right relationship; it is about building one.

We all must reclaim the power we surrendered to our parents in childhood when we bowed in fear to their perceived greater strength and stature. It is this power that we now need in order to conquer our fear of disapproval and be strong enough to build healthy relationships. Lacking this critical strength, we are unable to stand our ground calmly and simply ask for what we want. So our emotional longings remain unfulfilled, and these are what keep our deepest emotional wounds alive. Unfulfilled emotional longings create and sustain emotional wounds that never heal, cannot heal, until they are fulfilled or no longer desired. Both of which can only happen when we begin to ask directly for what it is we truly want. By not asking, we avoided our parent's disapproval and survived our childhoods, but, now, by still not asking, we unintentionally maintain a belief system with which we create intimate relationships that remain quietly, privately unsatisfying.

You and I are the child in the story above. Our stories are different, but the framework is the same. There were things that we learned not to ask for from our parents or caregivers—emotional nourishment we desperately craved. These unasked for yearnings became our secret emotional longings and, to this day, we would rather pull out our tongues than ask directly for any of them—our fear of disapproval, rejection, and abandonment is that strong. This leaves us in a precarious position. If we do not ask for what we want, we can never have it. It will not magically fall from the sky or be presented to us on a golden platter by our "soul mate." Magically receiving what we long for would undermine the purpose of life, which is the evolution of all people to become more conscious—more balanced and whole by reclaiming our personal power. We must have our power in order to challenge our fear of disapproval so that we finally have nothing to hide. Hiding is the foundation of all our emotional wounds and not-hiding is the only action that will heal them. Not-hiding requires strength and courage—more strength and courage than it takes to run a marathon or be an eighty-hour-per-week CEO or fight in a war with people dying all around us.

Our seen self understood that our longings, if asked for, would lead to disapproval and rejection, so it banished them into the dark unconscious part of our identity. Locked in our hidden self, our emotional longings disappeared. Unable to perceive these precious parts, we lost the ability to form beliefs about them. So, over time, they seemed to disappear. We have all hidden our deepest emotional longings for years. Now we must practice the skills of tracking our hidden self so we may find our emotional longings again. It is time to ask for what we want, for only then can we heal our deepest wounds. To do this, we must regain the power we surrendered to our parents so long ago, the power we gave up in our earliest parent-child collisions.

My story

My mother was diagnosed with terminal breast cancer just after I was born and died when I was two. I have no memory of her, and I imagine we had very little physical contact during the brief period she survived. My father was a petty criminal and a compulsive gambler who never held a regular job. When I was twelve, and again at fourteen, he did two stints in prison related to Mafia-run gambling operations, or, as we came to say when asked, "My dad's away on a business trip." My father also had a violent temper; he could spin out of control at any time over any frustration. And pretty much everything frustrated him.

From the earliest age, I understood that what my father wanted from me was for me to want nothing from him. Any request, no matter how small or insignificant, was a burden to him, which he met with disapproval, irritation, or anger. As I grew up, I saw my father lose his temper hundreds of times. Anger and frustration were his way of dealing with the world, and the stress I felt around him was close to unbearable. I never knew when the next explosion would come; I only knew it wasn't far off. To survive, I withdrew into my shell like a hermit crab, encasing myself behind thick, invisible, protective walls that no one, especially my father, could penetrate. Though I am acutely aware of it, withdrawing from others and into myself remains my number one masking behavior. It is how I deal with pain, fear, or volatility.

What I longed for most was for my father to awaken from his unconsciousness and see me; I wanted him to recognize my deep emotional need to feel loved, protected, and supported by him. I wanted my father to stop being emotionally reactive, to stop exploding so quickly. I wanted him to control himself and comport himself with consciousness and sensitivity. But, of course, none of this was possible. Regardless, these were my deepest longings.

After one last great blowup, I left home at seventeen. Before leaving, I'd gone head to head with my father many times. Once he slapped me in the face, so I punched him in the mouth and knocked him on his ass. I will never forget him crawling out of my room on all fours, overpowered and defeated. Contrary to what you might imagine, this did not restore my power or heal my emotional wounds; in fact, it deepened them by reinforcing my unfulfilled emotional longings. In that moment, I experienced myself as being alone in the world with only myself for protection—the opposite of what I longed for

I learned early on to fear my father's anger and reactivity. Confronting him directly, especially as a small child, was out of the question. So I learned to hide my genuine feelings, subordinate my own power, and enact masking behaviors whenever he blew up. I often withdrew into myself or hid in my room or went off alone. I believed I could not let anyone know my real feelings of pain and fear without risking disapproval, so, unintentionally, I did not give myself permission to actually feel them. As a result, I became an expert at explaining my feelings as if they were concepts. I could not express anger, but I could explain why I was angry. This became another masking behavior.

All of my masking behaviors represent fearful hiding to avoid disapproval, an abdication of power as a way to get by. By never owning my anger, by not asking for what I longed for, I never had to confront my father directly, which allowed me to avoid his disapproval and rejection and, of course, his temper. Avoidance of disapproval by staying apart and remaining quiet and within myself formed the core of my emotional life. So when I left my father's home to start a new life, I believed I was leaving the worst of it behind. I remember feeling afraid and unsure at setting out on my own, but I also felt deeply relieved. I felt the exciting possibility of living my own life, on my own terms for the first time. What I had no understanding of was how my emotional wounds from childhood, my beliefs about disapproval and my fear of my father, all came with me like parasites feeding on my soul.

As I lived my new life, I invariably encountered angry, reactive people or other authority figures, and I unconsciously perceived them as proxies for my father. Everyone, from the angry waitress at the coffee shop, to an overreactive coworker, to a judgmental professor, became my dad, or at least made me feel that way. Of course, I reacted accordingly every time: I felt fear of disapproval, so I hid my power. I enacted my masking behaviors and I disassociated from my emotional longings. Whenever confronted by anger or authority, I enacted what I call my "hiding" behavior: I would silently disappear right in front of the other person's eyes.

All of this came to the fore when I met the woman who would become my wife. We have now been together thirty-eight years. Apart from the many wonderful bonds we share, my wife has a temper: she reacts with anger to things that make her angry. She is openly confrontational in matters where she believes confrontation is called for. This sounds normal and reasonable, but because of my childhood wounds, I quickly came to fear her losing her temper or going out of control. This created all kinds of problems for me, for her, for us. At first, I was unable to see or understand what was going on, because I found myself living again with my father. I am an eminently reasonable person, so I could not come to terms with continued outbursts of irrational anger, which struck me as mostly unreasonable and unnecessary.

During this phase, I blamed my wife for her anger and unreasonable stance. I dealt with her anger by enacting my masking behaviors: I withdrew and became stoic while surrendering my emotional longings (to be seen, loved, and supported), and I thought a lot about leaving (my main method for coping). I spent many years repeating this pattern, which felt natural to me. Over time, we talked, examined, argued, and read about this issue, and we saw therapists. Not much changed though. In truth, I could not see the problem clearly, so I could not resolve it effectively. I understood the connection to my father and my childhood, but I could not verbalize my emotional longings nor see how my masking behaviors were hiding my genuine feelings and emotional longings. I always thought these coping behaviors were just me being me. I could not have been more wrong.

I watched and worked on this issue for many years–decades, actually—and then one day I had a quiet epiphany. After years of repetition, after years of experiencing my wife's anger as the same as my father's, I saw her anger not as anger but as an expression of her own pain; in other words, anger was her masking behavior. I suddenly realized my wife's anger was not about me; it was not about what I did or didn't do; it was not about whether I was inadequate or incompetent; it was not about whether I left dishes in the sink or was late for the thousandth time. It was simply my wife's way of expressing her pain, which was part of her wound that traveled back to her childhood and her parent-child collisions. This realization changed everything.

For years I feared her blow ups and losing control because I believed they were about me, so I avoided them at all costs. This was a complete surrendering of my power. Instead of confronting her, I avoided her. My decision unintentionally made me a weaker, more fearful person. By fearing and avoiding her angry outbursts, I was tacitly declaring her and all proxies for my father as stronger, more powerful, than myself. In other words, I was allowing my wife to control my behavior. I was a prisoner of her reactivity. But now I saw my wife not as angry and out of control, but in pain that she communicated in the form of anger. So my heart opened to her. She had been, to some degree, my adversary; now, she was my partner in a truer sense, a person to whom I owed my allegiance and understanding. From this point forward, whenever she became angry, I tried to see past her anger, and, when I did, I clearly saw that she was in emotional pain—all rooted in her childhood. My mind was blown. It is like having a dog for ten years and suddenly realizing it was actually a cat all along. Anger had meant one thing, and then suddenly it had a completely different meaning.

This is the extraordinary power of belief formation in action. After many years, my perception shifted, so my beliefs changed, which transformed my identity, which in turn changed my decisions and behaviors, particularly the way I related to her. What does this mean in practical terms? I clearly saw my wife's anger as her pain, not as an attack on me, and I believed this new perception. So I changed. My wife would get angry and the new me would see her pain beneath her anger. Instead of enacting my masking behaviors by becoming silent and pulling away, I chose to stay emotionally connected in the moment, because that was what she needed, that was what I needed, and it was the appropriate response. As a result, my wife felt more connected to and supported by me, not because I said anything to her about this, not because I told her how I felt, but simply because I was meeting her in a new and different way. This was what she wanted from me all along. She wanted me to allow her to express her pain as anger and then for me to see it for what it was and to support her. I was unintentionally giving my wife some of her emotional longings, and, as a result, she became more loving and understanding of me.

In this crazy, counterintuitive fashion, we both ended up getting some of our emotional longings met, which further healed our deepest wounds. Before, I had acted out of a sense of justice or intellectual fairness: "Your anger is wrong and unreasonable, so I'll withdraw from you to ease my pain and express my disapproval." This action never got me what I wanted, but the opposite response did. Now I am stronger. I'm more emotionally available and connected, more vulnerable and more balanced, which are all new living symbols that I and others in my life can see and feel. I did not count or plan on any of this. It is the organic nature of identity work. Perception shifts; change occurs; life transforms. Suddenly we are different.

Why we must ask for what we want

Most, if not all people, feel unworthy and unentitled to have our deepest emotional longings met, and we lack the requisite strength to broach this monumental subject because we gave our power away to our parents long ago.

Our parents unintentionally sowed the belief in us that we should not ask them for something we truly wanted. We should not ask for their love or respect or validation or caring or whatever it is we believed they could not or would not give us. The creation of this specific belief was a traumatic event. We all experienced it; we all believed it, and now we are unable to ask for what we so badly want, fearing disapproval and rejection should we do so. Here is a critical point. The entire reason for asking for what you want is not to get it, but only to ask for it—to bring the words to your lips—so that you yourself can hear and own them. The problem is not that we don't have what we want; **the problem is that we don't ask for it**.

By not asking, we lose sight of our deepest personal truth. No one can hide their inner beliefs from the force of identity. If you don't ask for what you want, then you are tacitly reinforcing the belief that you don't want it. It is this belief that your identity is then forced to manifest. The reason why you don't ask is far less important than the act of not asking. In other words, not asking because of your childhood beliefs about disapproval explains why you don't ask, but it does not change the fact that by not asking you will not get what you desire and the patterns of your life and relationships will remain the same. Directly and repeatedly asking for what you want, especially with awareness of your story, stimulates healing at the deepest levels of identity and in the most practical way imaginable. When we ask for what we want, even when we believe we cannot get it, we are making our emotional longings known to ourselves. This is a necessary moment of awakening.

Regardless of what you may believe, the decision to ask or not is up to you; it has nothing to do with anyone else. It does not matter whether the other person will give you what you want, or even understand your request. You are asking so you yourself may embrace the truth that what you are asking for is vitally important and valuable to you. Further, asking for what you want right now in real time allows you to discover whether, in fact, you actually want it. The act of asking is what finally confers clarity. Asking brings us into allignment with our most deeply held emotional desires, and it is this simple act that restores our personal integrity.

In the beginning, what we all want is to reinforce our fear of disapproval by hiding our emotional longings and our personal power. This is how we survive emotionally. This is how we avoid our worst pain and fear. As we make our initial discovery by completing the *Responses to Disapproval Form* we clearly identify our story: our parent-child collisions, our childhood fears of disapproval, our masking behaviors, and our emotional longings. We study and practice to see clearly all of this in our lives. In this way we develop the craft of life. Only then are we ready to ask for what we want. This is truly terrifying, so we engage in this activity gingerly and in a long, careful progression. We test the waters. We gently risk disapproval and challenge it and grow within ourselves. Our perceptions begin to shift, our beliefs change. So our identity changes, and we see the results in our lives as new living symbols, new partners, new attitudes, new reactions, new results from new actions taken. Then we explore what we believe we want, and what we discover is that it probably isn't what we really wanted after all; it was only a place holder for something deeper.

Early in our relationship, I wanted my wife to care for me as a mother might—to compensate for the mother I never had. But what I received from her was irritation and anger. After all, she was not my mother. She denied me my emotional longings, but I could not confront her on this because I feared her angry disapproval and rejection. So I pulled away, and then she felt rejected and cast aside. As time passed, I wanted not to fear her anger but to receive her love and care instead—the same things I wanted from my father. None of this was possible until I found a way to break the cycle of unconscious behavior that has been part of my family lineage for generations. Then I saw past my wife's anger and began to perceive her deeper emotional pain. My heart opened to her; my fear of her and her reactions relaxed and dissipated. Now, I work to approach her directly. My wife is still herself, as am I. She still gets angry, but I have little fear of her anger now. I still withdraw, but I see this behavior for what it is. I still react with my masking behaviors, but far less so, and I recognize this when I do. Our relationship is not perfect, but it is moving in the right direction and in the right way.

Pulling back the curtain

There is a remarkably fitting image from the film *The Wizard of Oz*. Throughout the movie, everyone has given the great and powerful Oz their power. Everyone bows to him; everyone fears him; everyone looks to him for solutions to their problems; and no one is willing to risk his disapproval. Then Toto, Dorothy's small dog, pulls back the curtain from behind which the great Oz is standing, manipulating the fire-breathing machinery that makes him appear so powerful and terrible. In that moment, everyone sees the wizard for what he is—a man who's been pretending. He is not great and powerful after all; he is just an ordinary person. All it takes is pulling back the curtain to break the spell, to see through the illusion, to change instantly and forever the perception and belief about the great and powerful Oz. In that instant, we reclaim our power. This is what we all must do in our own lives to the people whom we have appointed as our personal Oz. We must pull back the curtain, break the illusion, and see them for who they are: ordinary men or women acting from their own pain and fear. That is all we are going to find, all we are going to see. We all fear someone acting from his or her own emotional pain and fear. Our realization in this moment of pulling back the curtain is that we are no longer a small child, and there is nothing for us to fear in this person. Almost magically, our long surrendered power returns to us. Now we are strong enough to face our fears, to act upon our emotional longings by expressing our genuine feelings.

The reclamation of our personal power is the fundamental purpose of life. Unempowered, we spend our lives encumbered by our fear of disapproval and entangled in our secret wounds. But those who reclaim their power and learn to own and express their emotional pain, those who look you straight in the eye and ask calmly and directly for their emotional longings, will see and understand themselves with profound clarity. They will find succor and relief. They will find peace and joy as their fears dissolve. Choosing not to hide is the greatest living symbol of a healed human being. It is greater than any human achievement because it requires strength and courage beyond all else.

It is time now for all of us to stop hiding. Future generations are depending on us.

Exercise 15: The Clarity Exercise/intermediate level—Seeing yourself enact your masking behaviors

It is highly recommended that you not proceed further with this next exercise until you have mastered the beginner version in the previous chapter. Short cuts will not serve you in the long run. If you honor the idea of craftsmanship, then accept the work we all must do as apprentices as payment for the remarkable strength and skills we are developing. I can assure you, from many years of experience, there is no way to cut this training short and achieve any great level of success. "Wax on, wax off," as the Karate Kid learned. There's no other way. Once you have a solid handle on steps 1-3 in the beginner version, it's time to move on to the intermediate version with steps 4, 5, and 6.

When you can clearly see your childhood story amplifying your present confrontation, you are ready to see the present situation distinct from the past. Look again at your current situation. Perhaps your partner is scolding you for leaving the toilet seat up again or complaining that you bought the wrong ice cream or that you are insufficient in some way, implying you are defective or broken. Your partner's tone sounds accusatory and feels filled with blame. But, instead of reacting, you have already successfully done the following:

Step 1:

Recognized that you are having a confrontation;

Step 2:

Named your genuine feelings; and

Step 3:

Recognized you are feeling the influence of your childhood story, the impact of many parent-child collisions, which are amplifying and distorting what you are experiencing in the present moment.

Step 4: See the present as distinct from the past

This step requires that you separate the present from the past. Try to see that your partner is only saying you left the toilet seat up or you bought the wrong ice cream as straightforward issues happening in real time. They have absolutely nothing to do with the past; there is no actual connection, only what you perceive, project, and believe. When we amplify these simple, straightforward issues, we are doing it to ourselves. We are misperceiving what is going on in the present by mistaking it for what actually occurred in our painful past. We are mixing the two together. Understanding this will allow you to separate the present from the past and see one distinct from the other.

Step 5: Stay open and receptive

When you feel the energy of confrontation and disapproval, every emotional force in your mind and body will press you to constrict and close, to defend yourself, to find a way to stop the feeling of disapproval and failure. Fight this urge with everything you have, fight it with all of your might, and, instead, use your will to choose to stay open and receptive. Stay open to other possibilities, to other ways of effectively meeting this painful situation. This activity is what permits the next step, which is by far the most important.

Step 6: See and reject your masking behaviors

Here is the critical piece, the lynch pin that holds everything together. Undo this and your healing and freedom are all but assured. Now you must see your masking behaviors in the moment as you are about to enact them, recognize them for what they are, and choose NOT to enact them because they are false and self-destructive. They are completely ineffective. They will never get you what you long for most.

I wish I could tell you this is easy, but it is the place where almost everyone gets stuck: we fail to see our emotional reactivity as a masking behavior. We simply choose to overlook this fact and then try to go on, which never works, because now we are in our blind spot. *Please take this step very seriously*. Reread your *Responses to Disapproval Form*. Learn your masking behaviors inside and out and do not permit yourself the latitude of using them without recognizing them for what they are—masks covering your genuine feelings and emotional longings.

Some of the trickiest masking behaviors are those so ingrained in us, so much a part of our identity, that we mistake them for our true identity. Some examples are depression, hopelessness, anger, rage, or chronic defensiveness—all of these and any like them are usually nothing but masking behaviors. If you accept your depression as a condition of your true self, then you will never be able to truly heal because you will believe you have an illness that is out of your control like a physical disability and all you can do is learn to live with it. The same is true for anxiety.This unfortunate belief will block you from getting at your genuine feelings or discovering your emotional longings, because you will not believe that change is possible. I have worked with many clients who have suffered for decades from depression or anxiety, and I have watched them free themselves from these debilitating conditions by using the methods described in this book. It is not always the case, for each of us chooses the depth and length of our inner journey, but much of our healing remains in our own hands.

Summary: Clarity Exercise/intermediate level

Preliminary steps:

Complete your training with the clarity exercise, beginner level. When you can do this exercise and all of its steps with a measure of skill, then you may proceed with steps four, five, and six.

Step 1: Recognize you are having a conflict or confrontation

Step 2: Name your genuine feelings

Step 3: See the past in the present

Step 4: See the present distinct from the past

You have successfully recognized the past infiltrating the present, making you feel accused and disapproved of. Now, go one step further and separate the present from the past. See the issue at hand as a stand-alone matter happening right now in real time. Stripped of its connection to the past, isolated to the present moment, the emotional energy you felt begins to subside. The present situation comes back into focus and you can see it for what it is: a toilet seat left up, dishes left in the sink, a failure to be on time, a rebellious teenager, someone else voicing their pain and frustration, perhaps inappropriately. That's all that's actually happening.

Step 5: Stay open and receptive

If you allow yourself to become reactive, you will experience yourself shutting down. You are then in a defensive mode and in your blind spot. If you believe what you have done in steps one through four, it should be possible to reject the notion of shutting down and remain open and receptive in heart and mind.

Step 6: See and reject your masking behaviors

Now comes the most important step of all: seeing your emotional reactivity—whatever it may be—as one of your masking behaviors covering your genuine feelings and emotional longings. See/identify your specific masking behavior; name it, then reject it as false and harmful. Tell yourself, "I see my masking behavior for what it is and I reject it, because it is self-injurious and blocks me from ever attaining my deep emotional longings. It stops me from becoming a conscious, free human being."

CHAPTER 19

Summary: The Healing Process

Watch your thoughts; they become words. Watch your words; they become actions. Watch your actions; they become habits. Watch your habits; they become character. Watch your character; it becomes your destiny.

—Lao-Tze

THE TRUE POWER OF belief and what it can manifest is difficult to describe and impossible to depict in a linear fashion. Beliefs are created in chain reaction at such high speed that they are not wholly perceptible. Imagine two mirrors facing one another; when we look into the first, we see our reflection in both reproduced infinitely in ever smaller iterations. One belief when formed will replicate itself at high speed, over and over, beyond what we can see or even comprehend. Old beliefs from generations past travel across time to appear in our lives as beliefs we hold today. Some distant, unknown relative threatened a great, great-grandparent with disapproval or rejection, and the effect of that lives within us now, generations later, as one of our own childhood beliefs about disapproval. We are all products of our past, influenced by the beliefs of our ancestors, and our lives are impacted now as a result of their fear of disapproval and masking behaviors, just as those not yet born will live their lives as a result of ours. Beliefs form a continuum; they began with the first person and end in a future not yet known. Beliefs are what bind our species together, making us one true interdependent family.

On a personal level, this means that when we change a false belief about ourselves, when we heal our fear of disapproval, we are liberating people whom we will never know. It is analogous to us changing something about our physical appearance—such as dying our hair blue—and then peering into those two facing mirrors. Immediately, the change to our hair appears in each succeeding reflection, vanishing into infinity. The law of identity upholds any change in belief, and so the entire network of people to whom we are now or will be connected with are transformed in some way. In the end, the strands that bind us together are beliefs. Change one significant belief and you change yourself, your life, and your relationships, in the present and the future, all at the same time, all in one stroke.

The healing process

In Chapter 2, I wrote: "Everything I am, everything I do, is a direct expression of what I believe, and I cannot change anything without first changing the perception and belief from which it came. All transformation, large and small, comes from a shift in perception and belief." So changing our perceptions and beliefs is our goal because it is the only true catalyst for healing.

Yet, when it comes to beliefs, we all have an obstacle to overcome. We have looked out and perceived the world. Some of our perceptions appeared real or true, so these became our beliefs. How do we stop upholding old beliefs that are self-defeating or self-destructive when they still appear to be real or true? We cannot just stop believing something. We cannot pretend that what we see is not real or true, when we believe it is. What, then, can we do?

The answer to this question is straightforward: we must have a new perception that appears truer to us than our initial perception. When this happens, the new, truer perception replaces the old one and changes the beliefs attached to it. Remember my Aunt Ruthie and her dirty white carpet? In one moment, she believed her carpet was clean, then, in the next, with the help of a brighter light, she believed it was dirty. Or think again of *The Wizard of Oz*. In one moment, the wizard is great and all-powerful, but in the next, he is an ordinary man. Revised perception is the only way beliefs change, and because our lives are rooted to our beliefs, it is the only way we change.

But revising our perception requires an intentional act of will. What does this mean? When we feel pain or fear, or when we see ourselves enacting a masking behavior, we must grab hold of our emotionally-charged reaction and consider alternate possibilities, which simply means to look for a new perception. This act of investigation suspends belief formation, creating the potential for choice. Essentially, by doing this, we have stepped out of our blind spot and into fresh emotional space. Intentionally looking for a new perception—a revision of our old perception—is the basis for a powerful new skill set and an essential part of the healing process.

A waiter makes a mistake on a customer's order and brings food prepared incorrectly. The customer looks at her meal and becomes angry. She tells the waiter he's incompetent, unprofessional, and shouldn't even be working at the restaurant. This is a parent-child collision—the past showing up in the present. She demands to speak to the owner, whom she says she knows personally. An avalanche of disapproval crashes down on top of the waiter. His own internal belief that he has failed and is somehow a defective person swallows him. But the waiter does not give in to this knee-jerk emotional reaction. He chooses instead to use his will and intelligence to look at the situation from a different perspective. This cancels out his masking behaviors, which, in turn, cancels out his blind spot, and he thereby remains conscious as he gradually awakens. Yes, he made a mistake, but that is all he did. A mistake does not mean he is incompetent or unprofessional. He reflects on his childhood beliefs about disapproval and sees his parent-child collisions as the source of his reaction (he separates pain from wound, past from present).

The waiter sees that through this customer his mother is once again telling him he can't do anything right and should be denied respect and understanding. Now, however, instead of feeling embarrassed and humiliated, he simply feels annoyed by this woman's over-reactive and disrespectful behavior. He says to her, "I'm sorry for not getting your order right. I made a mistake. I'll take your food back and have the kitchen fix it, and I'll get the owner. I understand you're angry and disappointed, but being disrespectful to me is not necessary or acceptable." With that, he takes her plate. The waiter walks away from this confrontation stronger, more whole than before, even if he is shaken by the whole thing. He embraced his wounds, his fear of disapproval and he owned his emotional longings—all as his customer disapproved of him and knowing that perhaps his manager would, too. This practice helped the waiter to instill new perceptions and beliefs about himself, which naturally fostered personal transformation.

Whenever a painful confrontation arises that generates fear of disapproval, it offers us the opportunity to use our will to look for a new perception and to heal. On one hand, our worst fears manifest (our parent's proxy disapproves of us because we have erred or failed again), but, simultaneously, so is the opportunity for healing, which, ironically, comes at this precise moment. Here, we have the opportunity to see our situation differently and to take new action.

The moment of disapproval is the optimum time for fresh insight. The iron is hot, so we should strike. If we can form a new relationship to these dreaded but almost daily encounters with frightening, painful disapproval (parent-child collisions), we can transform ourselves. Now we must train ourselves to stand firm in the very place we have habitually run from, because it is from this precise location that we can see the truth and thus heal ourselves with our new perception. This allows us to form new beliefs, which enables us to reclaim our previously surrendered personal power.

In order to do this, we must develop a new relationship with our pain. Pain has a profound, constructive function. It is the bridge between us and the lost, rejected parts of ourselves. If we avoid our pain, then we have cut that bridge and have no way to locate our root wounds or our lost emotional longings, which ensures our pain and confusion will continue, just as in the story of the tangled cowboys. However, if we embrace our pain when we feel it and make ourselves receptive, we will have a way to pinpoint the source of our wounds and begin to heal and transform. Without pain, we have no practical way to connect our wounded adult self with our youthful identity, which was wounded in childhood. We need to see our pain as a valuable, practical tool and a wholly constructive part of our lives—*not* as something to be feared, avoided, or reviled.

When we recognize pain has befallen us, it is time to practice the skill of differentiating our pain in the moment from our wound in the past. Pain comes from a wound, but it is not the wound itself. The wound is the source of the pain, but it is not the pain itself. Their relationship is very clear: wound is the cause; pain is the effect. The common error we make is combining these two separate issues into one muddled clump. When pain and wound are mixed together, it is virtually impossible to meet the confrontation at hand and come out with a good, clear resolution. Again, please note that this is skill-based. Separating your immediate pain from your childhood wounds is a simple concept, yet one that requires practice. Intentionally differentiating pain from wound is part of the craft of life.

"Our son stayed out late again last night, and I think he was stoned when he came home. What are *you* going to do about it?" says the frustrated and worried mother to her husband. The husband becomes angry and snaps at his wife: "Why is this my responsibility? Why don't you talk to him!" To which the wife replies, "Thanks a lot. I can always count on you for strong support." Most of us would address this as a single issue, when, actually, it involves at least three. But the couple experience this as one muddled conflict swirling about like clothes in a dryer. They cannot clearly see their problem or resolve it. They are both reacting, putting on masking behaviors, so they face one another, standing in their individual blind spots. The first issue is about their son's behavior; the second is about the spiky, emotional energy accompanying the wife's words to her husband; the third is the husband's emotional reaction to his wife's words. The husband and wife both feel pain and fear in the moment, but, while they may not realize it, their deeper wounds have already connected the past to the present, charging it with powerful emotional reactivity. The first issue of how best to deal with their son only becomes clear if the husband and wife differentiate their own childhood wounds from the current pain and fear caused by their son smoking pot. The wife feels that she has somehow failed as a mother; the husband feels attacked for being incompetent as a husband and father. From this charged emotional space, neither can see their son or help him or even meet him in a constructive way. The parents have made this issue about themselves and not their son.

"I can't believe you backed into the mailbox again. What is your problem?" asked the angry husband to his wife. The wife responds by cowing to her husband. Again, most of us would experience this as a single issue. In fact, the majority of what either person feels comes from their childhood wounds sustained in their individual parent-child collisions. The situation in the moment always activates fear and pain from our past, blowing the present out of proportion. We need to expand our field of perception to see both the past and the present simultaneously but separate from one another. In this example, the first issue for both the wife and husband are their wounding parental beliefs, fears of disapproval and masking behaviors – all seeping up from the past. Completely separate are the issues in the present moment of the wife's driving skill and the husband's habitual angry reactivity. By combining the past with the present, these mixed issues lose all clarity. As a result, no true insight is possible. Both people fall into their blind spots, then pain and misunderstanding prevail.

When we can recognize our childhood wounds invading our confrontation, we should also be able to see our deepest emotional longings. At this moment, they are present and visible. More to the point, they can be felt. We know what we want. All we need to do is name this need, admit it to ourselves, embrace it as our truth (receive it), and then, if possible, speak it aloud. Men, in particular, struggle with this because it may feel weak and humiliating to admit that what we deeply long for is to be loved and cared for. But if love and caring is what you truly desire, then you cannot have it without first admitting it to yourself, and you can never be free of it either through avoidance or denial. Owning one's emotional longings is a necessary preliminary act to receiving them. We must make these hidden abstract needs tangible, so we may perceive them and form new beliefs about them. We must bring our emotional longings into our conscious identity, so that we may ask for them.

Now, there is one step left. It is time to reclaim the power we surrendered to our parents so long ago. We do this by recognizing all of the above and then courageously overriding our fear of disapproval and rejection and asking for or acting on what we want. Often this requires allowing ourselves to feel angry. Asking for our deepest emotional longings requires the strength we surrendered during our parent-child collisions. To do this we must first release our ancient fear of disapproval so we can ask for what we want in the present. Asking for what we want in real time heals our deepest wounds from childhood, which heals our identity because we no longer have to hide our emotional longings. Asking for what we want is not a meek action; it calls for us to stop hiding, which requires incredible fortitude. It is an act of true courage. Not hiding is the greatest living symbol of a human being who is engaged in true self-healing.

Once, as children, we walked unaware through a great, green forest. As we passed a tall pine tree, we accidentally dropped the key to our home. It landed gently in the leaves, so we did not hear or feel it drop, so we walked on unaware. We walked all the way through the woods, across a great meadow to the edge of town, through several neighborhoods and, finally, standing at our front door, we realize we lost our key. We realize we are locked out of our home and cannot get in. The key is a simple metaphor for our personal power. Though we don't realize it, we lost it in childhood, but our power is still exactly where we left it. No one has taken our power; it hasn't moved an inch. Now we must retrace our steps. We must make the effort to go back, all the way through the great, green forest, to the pine tree. And there at the base of its trunk we will find the power that we lost so long ago as children in our parent's home.

With our power in our hands, we may begin to see our masking behaviors and own and ask for our emotional longings. Our unfulfilled emotional longings compose the core of our deepest wounds, so as we begin to act upon and ask for them, our wounds begin to heal at their deepest level. As they do, we begin to experience a new sense of inner balance. In the end, we realize emotional invulnerability only by becoming completely vulnerable. This is the ultimate paradox of life.

Final comments

The craft of self-healing is preparation for emotional battle. To see it as less is to underestimate the sheer terror that drives your seen self in its avoidance of disapproval and the relentless push of your hidden self for reconciliation. These two disparate parts of identity will fight each other your entire life until you begin a program of intentional integration, which is to say a program of consciousness building. Identity theory offers a thorough and proper preparation for going into emotional battle. It is similar to boot camp where men and women train to gain the greatest level of preparedness, so that when they are in the heat of the fight and consumed by their fear and pain, they remain conscious and still perform. They get the job done. When properly prepared, you will see your childhood beliefs about disapproval and parent-child collisions as the source of your pain. You will see your own masking behaviors and emotional longings. And you will not refrain from working to integrate your seen self with your hidden self or restoring balance by asking for what you want, even if faced with disapproval. In the heat of the battle, you will get the job done.

It is necessary that your daily life becomes the platform for change, because it is in the moment of conflict and confrontation that the core of this work is experienced. In my years as a counselor, I have shared highly emotional moments with clients, but I have learned that true transformation comes not through insight and dramatic, emotional outburst in my office, but through practice, practice, and more practice, done in real time, with the real people in your life.

Exercise 16: The Clarity Exercise/advanced level, the craft of life

Here are the final two steps of the Clarity Exercise:

Step 7: Identify what you want

When you can clearly see your masking behaviors and how they lead you directly into your blind spot, when you are able to recognize your masking behaviors for what they are and not accept them or excuse them in any way, then you are ready to identify what you want. Look at this current conflict or confrontation and see it as something distinct from your past story. Consider again your genuine feelings occurring right now in this moment, and ask yourself, "What do I want?" Do you want your wife to stop blaming you and to ask for what she wants from you with openness and in a respectful tone? Do you want your husband to stop criticizing you and to speak to you with understanding and kindness? Do you want your teenager to know what he just said hurt you, and that you want him to at least try to be more considerate? What do you want, right now in the moment? What are your feelings asking for? What would make your pain or anger or frustration go away? How do you want to be seen, heard, and met? These are what you want. Stop and identify what it is in this current confrontation that you most want. It should not be overly difficult; it should not be abstract; it should be self-evident. All you have to do is see it plainly and name it.

Step 8: Ask or act on what you want

Here is the final step in this exercise. You just identified what you want; now ask for it *or* act upon it in some way. Sometimes it is right to ask directly for what you want in the moment; sometimes it's better to wait for a more opportune moment. Sometimes asking isn't appropriate at all, but some other form of action is. Sometimes direct confrontation is best; other times indirect is best; sometimes no confrontation is what's called for. You must decide for yourself the right course of action. If you are authentic about making progress based on your choices, the living symbols in your life will change, because when we ask for and act upon what we want, when we identify and own what we want, we have embraced our deepest truth and our identity cannot help but reflect this change.

Living symbols never lie. The most telling living symbols express our need to hide: we know what we want but rarely or never ask for it, especially from our partner. If you see yourself holding back, wanting love, affection, kindness, sex, or whatever it might be from your partner but are unable to ask for it, then this should be your point of focus; this is the living symbol that you should concentrate on, because it represents you temporarily frozen by fear of disapproval and unable to act on your own behalf. If you get caught here, which is not at all uncommon, please seek out help from a professional, a friend, or your group, and try to find the courage to tell them what you see. This openness and awareness shared with another is a pathway to healing and getting clear of this particular hurdle. Don't hide it, but bring it out into the open. You will surely get the support and care you need to resolve it. Always remember, hiding is far worse than not hiding. Looking honestly at one of your problems—even if you are unable to change it—is far better than pretending it doesn't exist.

Summary: Clarity Exercise (advanced level)

Steps 7 and 8 complete the Clarity Exercise.

Step 7: Identify what you want

Consider what you're feeling in this conflict or confrontation and ask yourself, "What do I want?" Don't edit, censor, or inhibit yourself, but simply answer the question. Your answer, whatever it may be, *is* what you want, so own it.

Step 8: Act on what you want

Now ask for or act on what you want.

Add these steps to your practice and continue until you are able to do the complete exercise with skill and authority. Performed in its entirety, the Clarity Exercise becomes the chief expression of your ability as craftsmen and women.

CHAPTER 20

Identity Theory in a Nutshell: The Diagrammed Views

There is an orderliness in the universe; there is an unalterable law governing everything and every being that exists or lives. It is no blind law; for no blind law can govern the conduct of living beings.

—Mahatma Gandhi

I LOVE SYSTEMS. I'VE been fascinated by them since I was a small boy. Growing up, I spent countless hours constructing Rube Goldberg-type contraptions, taking apart any number of devices or just building things. I am driven to build, and everything I build is based on a system. When I look at the world, all I see is a network of interrelationships or one enormous system. So, if you want a short answer about something, I am not the person to ask, because to me everything is related to everything else. And that makes for a long story.

Identity theory endeavors to explain the purpose and meaning of seemingly unrelated connections. It starts with the idea that all life is rooted to one central energy source, which gives and sustains life. We then percieve and think and in doing so form beliefs. Through our beliefs we direct the form this energy will take. Identity is the key; it is the lens that focuses the energy of life; it is the container of our beliefs and as such determines the manifestation of our life. When beliefs change, identity changes and, in turn, so does the manifestation of life. New living symbols appear whenever identity changes, reflecting the new beliefs that identity now holds.

To do the work of identity theory, it is necessary to understand and practice the concepts that compose it. In the study and practice of these concepts, you will discover their truth and power, and far less so from the words on these pages. With this model, results will always be found in the doing. Each concept has been covered in detail in earlier chapters. What follows are these same twenty-two concepts presented in multiple diagrammed views. The diagram below shows how each concept is connected and how all of the concepts operate in unison as one whole system. These are the main concepts that compose identity theory:

1	Perception	7	Childhood Beliefs About Disapproval	13	Conflict on Confrontaion	19	Pain vs. Wound
2	Belief	8	Seen Self	14	Fear of Disapproval	20	Revised Perception or Transformation
3	Identity	9	Hidden Self	15	Masking Behavior	21	Reclaiming One's Power
4	Living Symbols	10	Receptive	16	Blind Spot	22	Law of Identity
5	Belief Formation	11	Active	17	Emotional Longing		
6	Parent-Child Collision	12	Balance	18	Pain		

As presented earlier, confrontation brings our lives into clear focus, because it forces us, in the moment, to make a decision and take action based upon what we believe. Our response to confrontation will be conscious and relatively free or unconscious and fear-based—these are the only two possibilities—and each literally will take us in a different direction.

What follows are six main diagrams showing what happens once we choose our response: three represent a conscious response, and three represent an unconscious, reactive response. The first diagram in each of these two sets is the most succinct. The second is more general but contains additional information. The third is detailed, showing examples of someone's childhood beliefs about disapproval, masking behaviors, and emotional longings. Six perspectives of the same event are presented as three conscious and three unconscious responses to confrontation.

It isn't necessary to spend time on these charts. They are merely a condensed summary of all you have read. At first glance, they may appear overly complicated and intimidating, even leading you to believe they require too much effort. If you prefer, please move on to the next chapter. However, if you hold your initial reservations at bay, I will explain the purpose of these charts and how straightforward they actually are. On a deeper level, they represent the essential concept that forms the foundation of our work together, which is to relax, let go of our initial emotional reaction, and to perceive clearly before we decide to act–the benefit of which Poppy first taught us in earlier chapters about the leaky auditorium. However, if you choose to move on to the next chapter, please still do the two exercises at the end of this one. Both are particularly important and helpful.

Identity theory represents a complex system that seeks to name and define the exact organic process by which human beings change and evolve. Change is initiated by conflict from which there is a universal flow of events that occurs within all human beings, leading to one of two states of mind: consciousness and non-reactivity or unconsciousness and reactivity. This flow is not linear, but it is sequential. Here is our first chart:

Conflict/Confrontation Occurs
We Perceive the Event
We Decide to Act (based on our perception)
Our Action Leads to
Consciousness or Unconsciousness

This simple chart gives you a simplified overview of a complex process. This is like standing a long distance from a great mountain and watching the small figure of a climber scale toward the top. From this far off vantage point, you clearly see the shape of the mountain, the texture of its trees and rocky faces, the snow covered fields near its summit, and the tiny figure climbing. What makes this so interesting is that you have just climbed the same mountain yourself, only you did so from the interior and saw up close its forests, meadows, and boulder fields. This is the long view versus the close view, and both perspectives have their unique value. You have read many chapters that contained examples of conflict resolution up close. These six charts allow you to see the same things, but from a distance.

The initial sequence for each chart is identical. The same steps lead to the same juncture. Conflict occurs and we arrive at the same crossroads, where we find two doors. Now we must choose which to go through. Door #1 leads to emotional reactivity and unconsciousness; Door #2 leads to a controlled reaction and greater consciousness. Once you choose to enter a door, you will find the next sequence.

The first of the three charts is general, the second more detailed, and the third even more so. The more detailed charts at the end take the general form of a human outline; they look like a head, albeit a funny one, atop a body. Inside the head is our mind or identity. Our identity is divided into two sections: seen self and hidden self. Once conflict occurs, I show how our inner response flows from seen self to hidden self, moving back and forth between the two again and again. I am trying to make clear the roles that these two fundamental parts of self play in everyday, mundane events. If you do decide to spend some time with these charts, start by seeing the bigger picture that I'm trying to convey. First see the head atop the body, see the mind divided into seen and hidden selves, then see the overlay of information on each succeeding chart progressing the same events but in greater detail.

Now that you have a better understanding of what to expect and a clearer vantage point from which to view these, I invite you to spend a few minutes and see if these might offer a helpful, visual summary of the entire process. If they do, please dive in deeper. If not, the next chapter awaits.

Chart 8a
REACTION TO CONFLICT
(Reactivity and unconsciousness, 1 of 3)

An event triggers conflict: I feel pain or emotional upset in my body, or I observe myself enacting a masking behavior.

(Some people struggle to feel emotional pain or fear. Consequently, these people must use masking behaviors as their recognizable trigger. See yourself enacting a masking behavior, then go to #1 below.)

I feel frightened, hurt, or angry because I feel accused or attacked.
(I don't realize it, but I am re-experiencing a parent-child collision from childhood.)

My deepest **emotional longings** unconsciously rise up within me, creating a dual pressure to hide them or ask for them.

Faced with disapproval from this proxy for my parents and my own seen self, I become emotionally reactive (or stoic) and fall into my **blind spot**.

UNCONSCIOUSNESS OCCURS AT THIS POINT AS I REACT FROM FEAR.

Now, the same sequence of events happens in the following chain reaction

1) I unconsciously accept my **childhood beliefs about disapproval**.
2) I surrender my emotional strength and hide my **genuine feelings**.
3) I unconsciously enact my **masking behaviors**.
4) I disassociate from my **emotional longings**.
5) I react from my **receptive** or **active**, whichever is dominant, which means my reaction is out-of-balance.
6) I am now in my **blind spot**. I am responding unconsciously to self or external disapproval, which perpetuates unsatisfying life patterns.

Chart 8b
REACTION TO CONFLICT
(Reactivity and unconsciousness, 2 of 3)

Produces lack of awareness and unsatisfying life patterns

This thought process happens in a matter of seconds.

This entire sequence of events is governed by the law of identity and the belief formation process

This is my Seen Self

AN EVENT TRIGGERS CONFLICT

I feel pain or emotional upset in my body.

I feel frightened, hurt, or angry because I feel accused or attacked. (I don't realize it, but I am re-experiencing a **parent-child collision** from childhood.)

This is my Hidden Self

My deepest **emotional longings** unconsciously rise up within me, creating a dual pressure to hide them or ask for them.

Faced with disapproval from this proxy for my parents and my own seen self, I become emotionally reactive (or stoic) and fall into my **blind spot**.

Unconsciousness occurs at this point as I react from fear.

I unconsciously accept my **childhood beliefs about disapproval**.

I **hide** my **genuine feelings** and a portion of my emotional strength. I believe that if I express my feelings I will receive worse disapproval, perhaps rejection or abandonment.

I unconsciously enact my **masking behaviors**. I don't see them, but they are visible to others.

I disassociate from my **emotional longings** to avoid disapproval for asking for what I want. By doing so, I deny my own truth.

I react from my **receptive** or **active**, whichever is dominant, which means my reaction is out of balance. I am reacting unconsciously to self or external disapproval, which perpetuates self-defeating life patterns.

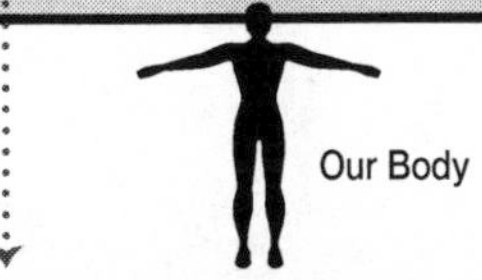

Similar conflicts and confrontations appear regularly in my life. Each one represents both my seen self's fear of disapproval and my hidden self's desire for healing and integration. These ongoing conflicts are **living symbols**. They represent the two parts of my identity, presenting me with fresh opportunities to hide or ask for my unfulfilled **emotional longings**. The choice is mine. These conflicts will occur within me and with others. They may include illnesses, accidents, twists of fate, etc. All chronic illnesses should be viewed as **living symbols** that represent persistently unfulfilled **emotional longings**.

This is our Personal Identity

A full-page, color version of this chart is available for free download at TheCraftOfLife.com.

Chart 8c
CALVIN'S REACTION TO CONFLICT
(Reactivity and unconsciousness, 3 of 3)

Produces lack of awareness and unsatisfying life patterns

This entire thought process happens in a matter of seconds.

Start here
This area represents the mind

This sequence of events is governed by the law of identity and the belief formation process

This is the Seen Self	*This is the Hidden Self*
AN EVENT TRIGGERS CONFLICT	
Calvin's girlfriend tells him she is leaving him. He feels pain and becomes emotionally upset. His chest tightens.	
Calvin feels frightened, hurt, and angry because he believes his girlfriend is accusing and attacking him, which makes him feel inadequate. He doesn't realize it, but he is re-experiencing a **parent-child collision** from childhood.	Calvin's deepest **emotional longings** unconsciously rise up within him. He feels an internal pressure to hide them or ask for them.
Faced with disapproval from his girlfriend and his **seen self**, Calvin reacts from fear. He withdraws into himself. He falls into his **blind spot** and becomes unconscious.	
Calvin has believed since childhood that he must avoid confrontation with his mother (or her proxies) and not express anger. So, in conditioned response, Calvin surrenders his power to his girlfriend, becomes subordinate, and accepts his **childhood beliefs about disapproval.**	Calvin hides his **genuine feelings** and his **emotional strength** from his girlfriend to avoid further disapproval and rejection.
Calvin enacts his **masking behaviors**: he apologizes (**masking behavior #1**), gives in and complies (**masking behavior #2**). His girlfriend sees his behavior as weak and needy. She leaves him. Calvin pouts (**masking behavior #3**). All of these behaviors are invisible to Calvin, but visible to his girlfriend.	Calvin disassociates from his **emotional longings** to be loved, understood and cared for. He wants to express his anger, but he is not able to, fearing his girlfriend's disapproval. He denies his own truth to survive the conflict.
Calvin has reacted from his dominant **receptive**; he was too open emotionally and he did not think enough about what he was feeling. His reaction is out of balance, so his emotional wounds deepen slightly with this repetition of unconscious reactivity.	

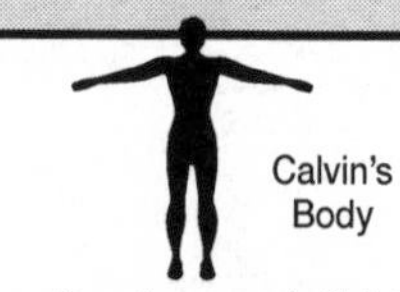

Similar conflicts and confrontations continue to appear in Calvin's life. Each one represents both his **seen self's** fear of disapproval and his **hidden self's** desire for healing and integration. These ongoing conflicts are **living symbols**. They represent the two parts of his identity, presenting him with fresh opportunities to hide or ask for his unfulfilled **emotional longings**. The choice is his. These conflicts will occur within him and with others. They may include illnesses, accidents, twists of fate, etc. All of Calvin's chronic illnesses should be viewed as **living symbols** that represent his persistently unfulfilled **emotional longings**.

This is Calvin's Personal Identity

A full-page, color version of this chart is available for free download at TheCraftOfLife.com.

Calvin's personal identity

This version includes concrete examples from Calvin's biography in Chapter 8 and represents the opposite response.

Chart 9a
REACTION TO CONFLICT
(Controlled response and awakening, 1 of 3)

An event triggers conflict: I feel pain or emotional upset in my body, or I observe myself enacting a masking behavior.

I feel frightened, hurt, or angry because I feel accused or attacked.

*(I don't realize it, but I am re-experiencing a **parent-child collision** from childhood.)*

My **emotional longings** unconscioulsy rise up, creating a dual pressure to hide them or ask for them. I become emotionally reactive (or stoic) and begin to fall into my **blind spot**.

UNCONSCIOUSNESS IS OVERTAKING ME, BUT I AM AWARE OF IT

I remember that my pain, anger, and fear are **cues** telling me to **slow down** and **step away**.

Instead of an unconscious, automatic reaction, I choose to reflect. Emotional space becomes available. My decision to consider things sets off a new sequence of events.

CONSCIOUSNESS RETURNS AT THIS POINT

1) I recognize and reject my **childhood beliefs about disapproval** and see the **parent-child collisions** from which they came.
2) I name and own my **genuine feelings**.
3) I recognize and reject my **masking behaviors**.
4) I name and accept my **emotional longings**.
5) I own what I said or did without equivocation.
6) I act on my **emotional longings**; if appropriate, I ask for what I want.
7) I have shifted my perspective, avoiding my **blind spot**. I have acted on my emotional longings, which promotes authenticity in my life and relationships. I feel hope and strength as I develop new self-awareness.

Chart 9b
REACTION TO CONFLICT
(Controlled response and awakening, 2 of 3)

Produces new awareness and healthier life patterns
This thought process happens in a matter of seconds.

Start here
This area represents the mind

This sequence of events is governed by the law of identity and the belief formation process

This is my Seen Self

AN EVENT TRIGGERS CONFLICT

I feel pain or emotional upset in my body.

I feel frightened, hurt, or angry because I feel accused or attacked. (I don't realize it, but I am re-experienceing a parent-child collision from childhood.)

Faced with disapproval from both this proxy for my parents and my own seen self, I become emotionally reactive (or stoic) and begin to fall into my **blind spot**.

Unconsciousness is trying to overtake me, but I remember that my pain, emotional upset, and fear are **cues** telling me to **slow down** and **step away** from my emotional reaction. Instead of falling into unconsciousness, I reflect on my situation. My decision to stop and consider things initiates a new sequence of events.

Consciousness returns at this point. I recognize and reject my **childhood beliefs about disapproval** and see the **parent-child collisions** from which they came.

I recognize and reject my **masking behaviors**.

To the other, I own what I said or did without equivocation. If appropriate, I express or act on my emotional longings from my receptive or active, whichever is subordinate, i.e. I ask for or act on what I want from the less developed part of my identity.

As a result, consciousness and balance increase. My emotional wounds heal slightly. My **seen** and **hidden selves** engage in a new, collaborative relationship.

This is my Hidden Self

My deepest **emotional longings** unconsciously rise up within me, creating a dual pressure to hide them or ask for them.

I name and own my **genuine feelings**.

I name and accept my **emotional longings**.

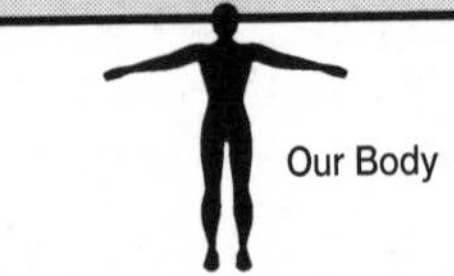

Our Body

Conflicts and confrontations continue to appear, representing both my **seen self's** fear of disapproval and my **hidden self's** desire for healing and integration, but these conflicts look and feel different than before. I have begun to demonstrate new awareness and more conscious control in my response to disapproval. The way I meet most conflict shows a shift in perception and belief; this represents true change. I am now fulfilling some of my emotional longings. I can feel them and see them manifest in the **living symbols** around me, including visible improvement in chronic illnesses, finances, and in the quality of my relationships.

This is our Personal Identity

A full-page, color version of this chart is available for free download at TheCraftOfLife.com.

Chart 9c
CALVIN'S REACTION TO CONFLICT
(Controlled response and awakening, 3 of 3)

Produces new awareness and healthier life patterns

This thought process happens in a matter of seconds.

Start here

This area represents the mind

This sequence of events is governed by the law of identity and the belief formation process

This is the Seen Self

AN EVENT TRIGGERS CONFLICT

Calvin's girlfriend tells him she is leaving him for numerous reasons. He becomes pained and emotionally upset. He feels constriction in his chest.

Calvin feels frightened, hurt, and angry because he believes his girlfriend is attacking him. He doesn't realize it, but he is re-experiencing a **parent-child collision** with his mother and his father, and it is emotionally overwhelming.

Faced with disapproval and rejection from his girlfriend, Calvin feels inadequate. He disapproves of himself for failing again. Calvin begins to shrink and withdraw but sees himself falling into his **blind spot**.

Calvin is prepared. He recognizes that his feelings are **cues** to **slow down** and **step away** from his reactivity. His decision to assess his feelings initiates a new sequence of events. He awakens and takes control of his situation instead of being controlled by it.

Calvin has long believed he must avoid confrontation with his mother (or her proxies) and not express anger--two of his **childhood beliefs about disapproval**. He decides to engage head-on in this confrontation. Calvin feels hurt, angry, and scared. He tells his girlfriend how he feels and asks calmly for a true explanation. He has awakened.

Calvin stands strong and listens. It is painful to hear, but he tries to discern the truth instead of defending himself or reacting with his **masking behaviors**. His girlfriend tells him she is leaving, because too often he acts more like a boy than a man. She explains how this makes her feel. Calvin is afraid, angry, and sad, but he rejects his **masking behaviors** and does not 1) apologize reflexively or 2) give in and comply. Instead, he remains emotionally connected as his girlfriend speaks. This requires a new degree of emotional strength and courage.

Calvin wants to be accepted, understood, and nurtured, but sees it is not appropriate to ask for any of his **emotional longings** in this situation. His girlfriend is right: he has undermined their relationship with his **masking behaviors**. With much sadness, he lets his girlfriend go. He clearly sees what he did, what he didn't do, and how he can improve in the future. For the first time, Calvin feels authentically hopeful--even though he is profoundly sad. He sees and understands the changes he needs to make. Through this process, Calvin is reclaiming his power and courage, and he can see a clear path to a better life.

This is the Hidden Self

Calvin's **deepest emotional longings** rise up within him. He feels a dual pressure to hide them or ask for them.

Calvin owns his **genuine feelings** and his **emotional strength**.

Calvin thinks about his **emotional longings**.

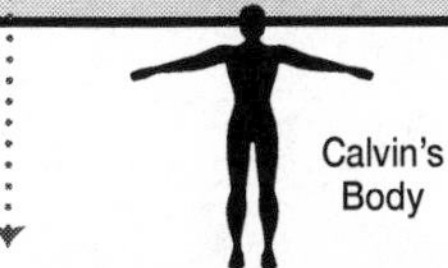

Conflicts and confrontations continue to appear, representing both Calvin's **seen self's** fear of disapproval and his **hidden self's** desire for healing and integration, but these conflicts look and feel different than before. Calvin is demonstrating new awareness and control in response to disapproval. The way Calvin now meets conflict shows a shift in perception and belief; this represents true change. Some of his **emotional longings** are being fulfilled, which are manifesting as **living symbols** around him: less chronic back pain, an improved relationship with his boss, and a richer emotional quality in his close relationships.

This is Calvin's Personal Identity

A full-page, color version of this chart is available for free download at TheCraftOfLife.com.

Exercise 17: The Clarity Exercise/mastery level

When your skills are really solid with the advanced version, you can move on to this final version, which is done very quickly and in the moment. A confrontation occurs. You recognize it simply by the feeling in your body. You immediately 1) see the confrontation; 2) name your genuine feelings; and 3) recognize the past influencing the present. This takes about 15 or 20 seconds. Next, 4) you see the present distinct from the past; 5) you consciously choose to stay open and receptive; and 6) you look for and see your masking behaviors start to arise, but you choose not to engage them. This takes another 15 or 20 seconds. 7) You realize what you want and 8) decide to act upon it. This takes another 20 seconds to initiate. Total time: approximately one minute. Result: you avoid emotional reactivity; you feel clear and centered; and you get what you want or you at least ask for it, which promotes personal intergrity and autheticity

This exercise strengthens the will as it calls directly for you to refocus your energy and attention in the moment. This self-direction will make you a stronger, more stable person across the spectrum of your entire life because self-direction, which relies on will power, is the basis for the development of any skill. And both relationship-building and the development of consciousness are most defintely skills. On a personal note, this exercise regularly brings me feelings of clarity and satisfaction, because doing it allows me to remian emotionally connected with myself and others, while pointing me down a partcular road that I need to travel next in my life.

Exercise 18: Conscious conflict resolution

Here is a similar practice in a slightly different form. It's included here because it can be used throughout your life whenever you find yourself in emotional pain. This simple practice will allow you to suspend your emotional reactivity and penetrate quickly past the veneer of whatever conflict you are having. Using it will give you clear understanding of your response, and then you will know what you need to do next to bring about a constructive result.

Form 6
CONSCIOUS CONFLICT RESOLUTION

Name who the conflict is with (another person, an organization, or yourself?).

Briefly describe the conflict.

Name 3 FEELINGS that this conflict is stirring within you.					
1		2		3	

Briefly explain why you are feeling this way.	
1	
2	
3	

Compare the explanation of your feelings to the parent-child collisions you had growing up.					
1	They are the same	2	They are similar	3	I don't see a connection (If this happens, please look again as there is always a connection between conflict in the moment and our story from the past)

If they appear to be the same or similar, can you recognize your past experience(s) amplifying and affecting your feelings in the present? Can you see how your past experience distorts your present perception?				
1	Yes	2	No	

It is not possible to effectively resolve things in the present when they are comingled with feelings and beliefs from the past. With this understanding, use your will to separate the past from the present. Once you are free of old feelings and old beliefs, describe the present conflict that remains.

Free from past feelings and old beliefs, what do you want from the other in this situation?

Now, ask for or act on what you want, but without concern as to whether you will get it or not. It is the asking, not the getting, that heals our identity; it is the asking that restores our personal integrity. Expect to feel tremendous fear of disapproval inhibiting your asking. Prepare yourself for this emotional challenge.

This form is available at the back of this book and as a full-page, editable version for free download at TheCraftOfLife.com

CHAPTER 21

Nine Points Worthy of Reflection

Only love can make it rain. The way the beach is kissed by the sea.
Only love can make it rain ... Love, reign o'er me.
—Pete Townsend from "Love Rein O'er Me"

The opposite of love is fear, but what is all-encompassing can have no opposite.
—A Course in Miracles

AS WE APPROACH THE end of our journey, I would like to emphasize a handful of points. Some we have covered before, while others are new and based on material you have now read and digested. Together, they constitute nine important details worthy of reflection and conversation.

1. It's a waste of time to argue someone out of their beliefs

Here, again, is the foundation of identity theory, which is belief formation. Once we step into the daily ebb and flow of our lives and engage in confrontation, we lose sight of the truth of this fundamental concept. A perception that appears to be real or true to us becomes one of our beliefs that we will use to make decisions and take actions. Whether our perceptions are factually correct is irrelevant. They only have to appear true to us; after which, they become one of our beliefs. Beliefs are never reliant on factual reality; beliefs are based on personal perception. If you accept and remember this concept, it will improve your life. Here is why.

Consider this universal situation that most every human being has experienced: We have a strong opinion about something meaningful to us, but another person disagrees and takes a contrary point of view. "I think red is best." "No," says another, "blue is best." This disagreement causes us pain, so we passionately argue why red is best; our underlying intent is to change the other person's opinion or show them they are wrong so we are validated as being right. But the other person does not accept our words. He resists and pushes back. This issue is also meaningful to him, and he feels hurt and irritated by our opinion and, like us, he is motivated to win the argument, to show us we are wrong in order to validate himself as right. In this instance, neither person understands that, due to belief formation, arguing is a waste of time and energy. The belief formation process trumps whatever either person says because each one's beliefs are based on their perceptions, which appear real or true to them.

What does this actually mean? First, unless you can create a new perception that appears truer to the other person than their initial perception, it is literally *impossible* for you to change their belief with your words. This is so important it warrants repeating: unless you can create a new perception that appears truer to the other person than their initial perception, it is literally *impossible* to change their belief with your words. It does not matter how factually correct or logical you are, the other person has a different perception that appeared true to him, and your opinions have little effect because they do not appear truer to him than his own perceptions. This is the direct meaning of the belief formation process and very rarely are words sufficient forms of persuasion to change anyone's mind once it is set, because perception and belief formation have already occurred within that person. Try talking a teenager into changing and see how that goes. Or a habitually late husband failing to understand why his wife doesn't believe him when he promises to be on time. Or convincing an african american who has been treated unequally for years to believe that racism is almost over because it says so in some magazine.

People do what they do because of what they believe, and rarely can we change what anyone else believes with our words. It is they, apart from us, who must have a new, truer perception of the situation for this to happen and our words are insufficient. So yell, scream, nag, explain, whine, plead, complain, overpower, and disapprove all you like, but none of these reactions will change another person's beliefs, so none of these assault-based behaviors are effective. It may change their behavior temporarily (*if you do that again, I'm leaving you*), but it will not change their beliefs. And unless beliefs change, nothing changes. So what exactly have we accomplished by arguing we are right? The answer is we have successfully polarized someone while championing our personal beliefs. In our pursuit to be right, in our need to feel validated in our position, we have created disconnection, disharmony, and driven others away from us. Now, not only do they not agree with us, but they are emotionally disconnected from us, and our relationship is broken.

Here's my point: Before you attempt to change another person's beliefs, first try to understand whatever it is they have said or done, especially if it causes you pain, by asking yourself: "What might this person *believe* which led him/her to say/do what I just heard or saw?" This is a wise and worthwhile use of time and energy. It validates awareness of and respect for the belief formation process. And whenever you want to understand your own reaction to someone else, begin by asking yourself: "What might I *believe* that is causing me to react emotionally?" This would be the right time to take out your *Responses to Disapproval Form* and search for insight.

2. If you expose someone's seen self, expect to be attacked

If you pull off someone's personal mask and expose their seen self to the very disapproval they are working to avoid, expect to be attacked and reviled. In fact, any time someone attacks or reviles you, it is because you have intentionally or unintentionally exposed their seen self to disapproval, and their attack on you is rooted in their own pain and fear.

The purpose of our seen self is to maintain an identity that avoids disapproval, especially self-disapproval. If someone believes they should always look well dressed and tastefully presented and you innocently say, "That dress is not a good color on you," expect to be attacked and reviled. If someone believes they should not make mistakes and you point out a mistake they've made, expect to be attacked and reviled. If someone believes sex should be private, even hidden, and you openly flaunt your sexuality, you are unintentionally invalidating this other person's beliefs, so expect to be attacked and reviled. The list is endless. The concept always holds true. Tear away someone's mask—intentionally or unintentionally—and you will be attacked and reviled. It doesn't matter if you are right, if you make sense, if your position is just and filled with truth. What matters is you have exposed a belief the other person is using to hide behind for their own protection and emotional survival, and by doing so you have opened them to the very disapproval they are trying to avoid. When we are on the receiving end of disapproval, it is a painful experience; when we are on the opposite end, we tend to fall into self-righteousness. The bottom line is that intentionally exposing someone's seen self is hurtful and emotionally dangerous. Most of all, it is completely ineffective. Virtually all hatred and attack come from someone whose seen self is exposed to the very disapproval they are trying to avoid, and the object of their hatred and attack will be the person or group who has exposed them. Never expect thanks for pointing out someone's failings. Do not expect them to recognize your amazing rightness above theirs. Do not expect them to give you their love, affection, and respect. In fact, you should expect the opposite.

3. Plan on meeting wounding parental figures again and again

If life requires us to face our fears of disapproval, then who better to stir up our lives than our parents and their proxies? This is another example of how the manifestation of our lives can be largely predicted. The law of identity—in its continuous push for consciousness and wholeness—will send a steady parade of wounding parental figures at us for the rest of our lives. Expect them. They will come predictably—a wounding father and a wounding mother come to threaten you with disapproval for asking for what you want. They come to reinforce your childhood beliefs about disapproval, but they will also bring you the opportunity to reclaim your personal power by facing them and their disapproval with new understanding and new skills.

There is no way to become strong except by reclaiming the strength that we surrendered when our parents first disapproved of us. To do so, we must challenge our fear of disapproval in real time. We must face our parents and their proxies (which is often us), look them straight in the eye, and *calmly* reclaim what is ours. The game board is set. Our power is on the other side, and our task is to walk across the board and reclaim it. But standing in our way is our wounding father or mother—fierce and towering, armed with swords of painful disapproval, rejection, and abandonment. We must walk past our wounding parental figure and claim our lost strength, then calmly walk back with it safely in our possession.

This game goes on daily, but now it is with our parent's proxies: our boss, our spouse, our boyfriend or girlfriend, a corporation, a friend, a store clerk, and, of course, ourselves. New permutations of our wounding parental figures are endless. They change faces and locations, but the message they carry is always the same: it is the feeling of being overpowered coupled with the threat of disapproval and rejection for asking for what we want. And, in the end, our greatest disapprover is ourselves.

4. Consider how your disapproval affects others

Take a moment and think about how you feel when someone disapproves of you. Perhaps your boss claims you are not doing a good job and you need to improve. Or your spouse complains again about your behavior. Or a friend mentions you look like you've put on some weight. Or you experience financial pressures, so you disapprove of yourself. In all of these instances and countless others like them, ask yourself the following questions: How did disapproval make me feel? How did it make me feel, even in small ways, toward the person who disapproved of me? Take a moment, think about it, and name some specific feelings. Create a list of the disapproval you received and your feelings in response. Now read your list. This is exactly how others feel when you disapprove of them: the pain of disapproval is the pain you are inflicting on others when you disapprove of them. Consider this the next time you disapprove of someone.

I don't want to imply we should create a world in which we never disapprove of others, which is unrealistic and perhaps impossible. But when we ask for what we want, a lot of disapproval becomes unnecessary. All of us have a choice: we can dish disapproval or we can ask for what we want. It is we who must decide. Further, disapproval does not have to be a wounding experience. If we were willing to speak or listen to one another and not fear disapproval and rejection, then we would remain emotionally connected and all things could be openly discussed and even argued. If this were to happen, dreaded confrontations would transform from experiences of fear and pain into moments of authenticity, strength, and connection. What a better world it would be if this became the norm.

5. Making external decisions for internal reasons

If you've compiled your *Responses to Disapproval Form,* and you know your childhood beliefs about disapproval, masking behaviors, and emotional longings, then you are in the unique position to make life decisions in a new and better way. For the first time, you can begin to understand external situations from an internal point of view and use your understanding of your own story to help you make decisions.

This skill represents a milestone because you now have the ability to make decisions based on your knowledge and understanding of your personal responses to disapproval. In other words, you can view a new job opportunity and ask yourself whether the person or company that you're about to work for is yet another iteration of your wounding parental figure. If the answer is yes, you can choose to say no and immediately consider a healthier alternative, or you can choose to take the job and work through the issues. This is very different from showing up and expecting your job to be just a job; you are now expecting your job to be an extension of your inner life and identity, which gives it new value and meaning.

You can look at a potential new love relationship and ask yourself: am I able to ask this person for what I emotionally long for? Will they hear it? Will they allow me to speak it? Will they help me to get it? Are they even capable of giving it to me? How much of this person looks, sounds, and feels like another iteration of my wounding parental figure? Based on factual answers to these and similar questions, you can choose to say no to a potential love relationship and immediately consider and seek out a healthier alternative that will not suck you back down into your childhood wounds. Or, you can choose to enter the relationship—not just as your latest love—but as your latest opportunity to do your inner work and, thereby, heal your deeper wounds and clarify old misperceptions in order to claim the love you long for.

This concept of looking closely at a new situation or relationship and considering its potential effects based on knowledge of your childhood beliefs about disapproval, masking behaviors, and emotional longings means that you are now bringing your inner life into your outer life, your inner work into your outer work, your unconscious self into your conscious self, and for the first time these two disparate worlds become intentionally integrated. You are now harnessing a power beyond all description. And you are not using it to get rich quick or find your "soul mate," but rather you are courageously living a conscious life from the inside out. By doing so you are healing yourself and your relations at the same time in the deepest manner possible.

6. In the end it's all about balance

Every human being is to some degree emotionally wounded and out of balance. We are either too receptive or too active. We are this way due to the myriad parent-child collisions we suffered growing up. During these painful confrontations we hid one side of ourselves (receptive or active) while inflating the other. This allowed us to avoid further disapproval from our parents and survive emotionally, but it left us wounded and out of balance: "I don't care how you feel!" communicated your parents (so we became too active). Or, "You can't do anything right!" (so we became too receptive).

To make this right, we need to strengthen whichever side is underdeveloped. If our receptive side is underdeveloped, then our life work must be to strengthen it by intentionally becoming more open to ideas and feelings, to input and criticisms from others, to consulting our feelings, sensations, and intuitions before we act, and to owning and expressing our deeper feelings with others. If our active side is underdeveloped, then we must strengthen it by intentionally becoming a more thinking, analytical person. We must be willing to plan before we act, to think through and ask questions before we move in a direction; we must show discipline by organizing our thoughts and our activities; and we must develop our ability to protect, plan, and support ourselves and others.

Intentionally strengthening the less developed side of our identity is the general work we all need to do, though it is effort we typically avoid because it feels unnatural and uncomfortable. We can choose to address our imbalance head on, which gives us the highest probability of changing what we already believe is not working in our lives, or we can accept our imbalance and do little or nothing. We can tell ourselves: "This is who I am naturally. I can't change, and I'm not sure I even want to." In which case life will carry us forward in its own time, as we slowly evolve emotionally, but in complete obedience to the law of identity. Living consciously or unconsciously is our choice, but the entire organic movement of life is toward balance and wholeness, and nothing can stop this predetermined progression.

It's important to emphasize again that balance is not our destination or our goal; it is our direction. This work is about taking conscious action on your own behalf and trying your best to move forward. It is not about setting false, unattainable goals and then disapproving of yourself for failing to reach them. The gradual reawakening that accompanies this process rewards the practitioner with a happier, richer emotional life, and neither enlightenment nor perfection are required.

7. Chronic illness is a living symbol of unasked for, unfulfilled emotional longings

I have three chronic illnesses: allergies and asthma, which I was born with, and diabetes, which I developed later in life. I have spent a great deal of time thinking about my illnesses, what they mean and how to treat them effectively. I have continued to address them from the perspective of belief, identity, and emotional wounding. As a result, I do not see my illnesses as disconnected conditions that befell me by happenstance. Instead, I see them as living symbols of my unfulfilled emotional longings that have traveled through my family lineage to find me in this present moment. I can clearly trace this route through three generations: myself, my parents, and my grandparents. Each of us experienced a loss or absence of love, nurturing, and protection from our parents, siblings, and/or children. These profound losses created deep, unfulfilled emotional longings so entrenched in my family's psyche that their only appropriate manifestation after so many generations was illness. In the end, it turns out that our individual pains, our particular fears, are not particularly individual.

When we view chronic illness as a stand alone condition and not as a living symbol of unfulfilled emotional longings, we are mistakenly seeing the effect, the disease, as the actual problem, which means we are confusing the symptom for the source. As a result, our treatment is ultimately ineffective. If you see a psychiatrist and display symptoms of depression, you will likely be prescribed medication to help your condition. In many cases, your symptoms will abate, and you will feel better. But this is an ineffective solution in the long term, because all of your fears and pain, all of your family's fears and pain, are still intact, only further removed from your awareness. You are taking pills now but have little clarity about your inner emotional wounds or the organic mechanics of identity that control how and why your wounds manifest. Further, your seen and hidden selves continue to generate inner conflict, which will likely increase in an attempt to break through the anesthetizing effect of your medication.

Although you have disconnected from your emotional pain, you are still in pain, because the beliefs in your life that have manifested as depression are still fully alive and active within you, even though you have less motivation and awareness to deal with any of this effectively because you now believe medicine is your solution. This isn't an attack on the judicious use of medicine when it is required. I take medication every day in support of my own illnesses. I am pointing out what happens when we mistakenly see and treat a symptom while overlooking the cause. This has serious practical ramifications. In a report published by Medco Health Solutions in 2011, one out of four women between the ages of 40 and 60 are on antidepressants. Further, an additional study published in 2013 in the journal *Psychotherapy and Psychosomatics* found that nearly two-thirds of more than 5,000 patients diagnosed that year with depression did not meet the criteria for a major depressive episode, as described in the Diagnostic and Statistical Manual of Mental Disorders (DSM), which is the clinical source used by psychologists and psychiatrists in diagnosing mental illness. These two statistics speak volumes. We are a society in serious emotional pain, and we deal with it in the most cost-effective manner by erasing the symptoms of our pain while leaving the deeper cause untreated.

This perspective of seeing and treating external symptoms without considering the unfulfilled emotional longings from which they actually come is an oversight that permeates our medical world. We don't need to disparage doctors, nurses, and technicians. They play a crucial role, and I respect and deeply appreciate the knowledge and skill these practitioners possess. However, my point remains: physicians are expected to treat symptoms, and they are armed with medicines and procedures for this purpose. Medical professionals then unintentionally pass the belief on to their patients that treating the symptom is all that is required, but this is not the case–it only produces temporary results. Medicine does not operate on the premise that the mind and the beliefs composing it are the root source of chronic illness. Few see identity as the origin of physical manifestation, so few medical practitioners see identity as the cause and disease as the effect.

What does this mean for you? Like me, if you have a chronic illness, try viewing it as a living symbol—a physical manifestation of your unfulfilled emotional longings. When you do this, you will see that your beliefs about disapproval are grounded in not asking for your emotional longings, fearing disapproval should you do so. Chronic illness is a living symbol of emotional longings chronically unasked for and unfulfilled. That is what illness is. We hide our genuine feelings; we disassociate from our deepest emotional longings, so we develop chronic illness, which is always an amalgamation of our personal unfulfilled emotional longings and our family's. This is the genetics of consciousness and the organic flow of beliefs across time.

8. Nurture yourself with small acts of nourishment

The practice of identity theory as a craft requires us to engage our will in order to refocus our perception.The exercises throughout this book train us to look past life's surface for the root cause of our pain. In doing so, we discover the inner truth of our emotional reactivity. Some will experience this model as an intellectual endeavor—in other words, thinking our way to healing. I would argue that this is not the case. This is a practice of will that frees the mind through right perception, followed by right action. It is primarily experiential, not intellectual.

As we face our fears and take the fight to our seen self, we will at times find ourselves in the painful embrace of the dark night of the soul, and, then, we will need emotional sustenance. If we become anxious and afraid, we will need emotional release, succor, and comfort. It is wise to identify and assemble in advance a list of actions that will give us comfort, so that when we need them, they are ready for our use.

Below is a list of suggested small acts of nourishment that have worked for me and others. Add anything to your list as long as it is not a masking behavior. Get in the habit of doing these practices to support your inner work with conscious kindness. Think of these small efforts like watering a rose bush. Water it regularly and it will thrive; stop and it will certainly wither. The idea is to nourish your inner self regularly with care.

- Walk or hike in nature
- Have meaningful conversations
- Dance
- Sit in a park or beautiful spot
- Swim
- Clean and organize a small area
- Work in your garden
- Sing
- Listen to music
- Sit under the night sky; look at stars
- Hug your child
- Meditate
- Sit in the sun and feel its warmth
- Play with your pet
- Take a bath
- Sit and breath consciously
- Care for someone who needs it
- Walk outside
- Create art
- Watch moving water—the ocean or a stream

Do anything that connects you to something bigger than yourself, something that fills you with a sense of greater order and meaning.

9. Vulnerability is our ultimate strength

I never cease to be amazed at how many deeper truths are paradoxical. For me, the following is one of the most important examples. It has to do with our cultural definition of strength. We perceive strength as power, might, action, and stamina. Strength appears as a model of leadership: an authority commanding others with great vigor and endurance. Most of all, our cultural model of strength is someone who, by sheer force of will, overcomes pain and limitation to achieve his or her goals. It is what we respect and value. But this definition of strength represents only the first half of human evolutionary development. It's opposite—vulnerability—is a different form of strength, which is necessary to bring about the next generation of human development.

In order to heal ourselves we must marshal our inner forces and face our deepest fears of disapproval by asking for what we want. If we do this repeatedly, we reclaim the personal power we surrendered to our parents in childhood. When we are well into this healing process, something changes; we reach a point where we must face our fear of disapproval in a new way. We must begin to see external disapproval from others as them reacting to their own wounds from old parent-child collisions. For a while, we must allow ourselves to be bombarded with anger, attacked, and misunderstood, while remaining wholly open and receptive during the entire experience. The power we must harness to accomplish this is, paradoxically, vulnerability. In the end, the only true control we have is to remain open and vulnerable at all times. This is the way we conclusively demonstrate that our fears have no power over us, and, by doing so, we reclaim our lost power. When we are able to remain one hundred percent vulnerable, it is because we have no fear of life, no fear of disapproval, no fear of any other human being. We are fearless and so we are open and completely receptive, which is the truest kind of strength—the ultimate strength—and it has nothing to do with big muscles, expressions of toughness, or displays of power.

Only when we are vulnerable are we truly capable of giving love to others and, by so doing, to ourselves. In the absence of fear, in the presence of openness, giving love becomes possible, and with it the doorway to the spiritual cosmos becomes available once again. In the end, quite literally, all that remains is love, and vulnerability is the only road that will take us there. But vulnerability does not just happen. We must work at it doggedly and develop it as a skill. If we want to gain physical strength, we lift weights and work out, which are skills that confer strength. If we seek to become more vulnerable, we must own our wounds and imbalance, face our fears, and learn to ask for what we deeply long for. We must do this again and again and again until we are fully open and vulnerable and strong, so that we may finally give love to others and experience it for ourselves. Vulnerability bestows the greatest of gifts, which are balance, wholeness, and love

Exercise 19: Becoming vulnerable—tell me what you want from me

Here is a simple but powerful exercise for developing and experiencing vulnerability. I don't recommend you attempt it unless you feel absolutely ready. If now is not the time, just save it for the future. The whole purpose of this exercise is to experience vulnerability by allowing yourself to remain open and receptive to another person's emotional longings. When done successfully, you will be able to feel the other person's pain of unfulfilled emotional longings. Once you experience their longings, you will see deeply into another human being's soul, which is something to be honored. You are not being asked to fix anything. You are not being asked to change anything. You are not being asked to fulfill the other person's longing. You are only being asked to experience vulnerability. Think of this exercise like going to see a great natural sight you may visit once in your life—the bottom of the Grand Canyon, the top of Mount Whitney, or the Fijian reefs. The experience leaves an indelible impression that lives within you for the rest of your life.

Suggested participants in this exercise are spouses, partners, and either teenage or adult children.

Without any advanced notice, tell this person that you are doing an exercise connected to this work and that you need their help. No preparation is necessary. Set a day and time to meet in a private, quiet, and secure place. Sit across from each other so you may look into one another's eyes. Read the following to your participant:

I realize this may feel a bit awkward or strange, but I am going to ask you a deeply personal question. After that, I will only listen. I will not refute or comment; I will try to understand, even if it feels like what you are saying is an attack on me. Whatever you believe from the past leading up to this moment, I am granting you the freedom and the permission to answer truthfully now, even if you believe your answer will hurt, anger, or embarrass me. My feelings should be of no concern to you during this exercise. It is only your feelings that are important.

It is perfectly common to want something from a close, important relation but to never actually ask for it directly, fearing some kind of negative response, whether it is defensiveness, disapproval, outrage, hurt, anger, or pain. In other words, I believe that certain things I do or say may have caused you ongoing pain, but you do not bring this to me because you believe I cannot or will not hear what you have to say. I'm sure there is truth in that. I understand this but I am actively working on breaking through this barrier and learning to be vulnerable, open, and accepting. Please help me by answering the following questions:

1) Name one attitude or behavior that you don't often get from me but would satisfy you emotionally if you did. Take some time to reflect before you answer.

2) When you don't get this from me, how does it make you feel? (Give your participant a copy of Words that Mean Pain *from the back of the book.)*

3) Describe what it is that you want from me but aren't getting. Tell me how it would make you feel if you did.

I am not saying I can or will give this to you; it may be something I have to work on; it may be something I believe I can't give you, but I am saying I'm willing to make myself open and vulnerable to listen and understand your feelings of pain and unfulfilled longings to better understand you and our relationship. I am trying to become more conscious by understanding how you believe I cause you ongoing pain and unfulfillment in our relationship, and I promise to try to work with it as best I can. I am going to close my eyes and sit calmly and quietly. Please take whatever time you need, and, when you're ready, let me know. Do you understand? Do you accept? If the answers are yes, then let's begin.

Close your eyes. Relax. Breathe slowly and deeply from your belly. In your mind, open your heart to this other person, open yourself to the words they are about to speak, and try to fill this person with love. Remind yourself that you are pursuing the truth and their words will help take you closer—even if these words initially cause you pain or embarrassment by pointing out some deficiency. Try to receive their words without fear or emotional reaction. Look for the truth that they contain. No matter what you may believe, truth is buried in their words, so consider them carefully. Do not invalidate this person's position. The point of this exercise is not to give your subject what they want but only to remain open, receptive, and vulnerable throughout, and then to consider, with great respect, whatever it is they have to say. Another human being is voicing their pain; receive this pain with the honor it deserves.

Once the person has spoken, repeat back to them what they have told you to ensure that you understand. Ask, "Did I hear you correctly? Did I understand?" If the answer is yes, thank this person and tell them you will think deeply about what they have said and will get back to them sometime in the future. If the answer is no, have the person tell you again until they confirm that you understand.

Go off by yourself to a quiet place and contemplate your experience. Do not try to fix anything; do not try to reason things out; do not try to figure who is right and who is wrong—*resist all of these impulses*. Simply let the other person's pain of unfulfilled emotional longings expand in your heart until you can feel what they feel. Do not stop until you feel their pain in your own body. If it doesn't happen in that first attempt try again later or the next day and keep trying until this happens. Only when you can feel their pain will you know for sure that you have reached a place of openness and vulnerability.

Now communicate back to your subject what you learned, what you might do—whatever it is that you believe you need to say. This concludes the exercise.

CHAPTER 22

Our Tragic Belief in the Impossibility of Emotional Fulfillment

Listen to the MUSTN'TS, child, Listen to the DON'TS, Listen to the SHOULDN'TS, the IMPOSSIBLES, the WONT'S, Listen to the NEVER HAVES, then listen close to me—Anything can happen, child. ANYTHING can be.

—Shel Silverstein

YOU ARE ABOUT TO read the most important chapter in this book. It's about the greatest block to consciousness and self-healing that anyone will ever face. I have known and worked with many people who have devoted themselves to inner work for years, even decades, and all eventually reach a point where they cannot seem to change any further. In this moment, we have the sense that we are permanently stuck.

We believe we know our emotional wounds and what we shouldn't do in our lives, yet the old patterns we've worked so hard to change still continue. We feel the same fear and pain we've always felt when threatened with disapproval or loss. Try as we might, we are not able to fully free ourselves from reacting with upset, anger, and fear. When we arrive at this point of self realization, it is puzzling and disconcerting, frustrating and upsetting. Our core issue is like old-fashioned fly paper—so ridiculously sticky that try as we might we can't shake free of the damn thing. In this chapter we will identify how this happens, why it happens, where it comes from, and exactly what you will need to do to breakthrough the final barrier to greater consciousness and true healing. Be forewarned, there is great subtlety at this point. It is easy to miss, but, going back to where we began with Poppy and the auditorium leak, we find that perceiving clearly is precisely what is required.

To grasp what we are about to explore, you need to have a strong, working understanding of all the concepts up to this point in the book. You need to have a solid understanding of identity theory and the mechanics of transformation through perception and belief. You must know your own story well: your childhood beliefs about disapproval, your masking behaviors, and your emotional longings. You will also need a true understanding and respect for the ongoing battle between your seen and hidden selves and how they jointly manifest the two sides of every conflict to support their individual agendas. In other words, you need to be at the level of a journeyman/journeywoman in this craft in order to really understand this last bit of material. It will be a deeper, more studied look at what you already know. As I said, this last step is incredibly subtle. It lives right in front of your nose, but to most it remains invisible. Further, you must have actually done the required inner work preceding this juncture, because only then will you be able to see what we are about to examine.

After much practice and effort, after thousands of pieces played and performed, a pianist who has consistently focused on continuous improvement will *spontaneously* acquire a new, unexpected level of skill and experience that allows her to play with extraordinary force, expressing music more purely, more deeply. This playing could not have come before because it rests not on pure technical ability, but on a long history of effort and experience. Once acquired, an unnamable quotient appears, permitting the musician to enter so deeply into the music that a subtle yet powerful alchemy happens. Although she has played the same piece for years, she sees or hears something slightly different and now plays the piece with a new feeling that touches listeners in a deep and profound way.

This is analogous to reaching a high level of skill and perception with any discipline. Perhaps someone is a naturalist. After years and years of preparing specialized cameras, of hiding in the shadows to observe rarely seen animal behavior, of tracking creatures through forrest and brush, the naturalist spontaneously realizes a new level of awareness. He can now follow nearly-invisible tracks as if they were billboards on the highway. He sees what others don't, and it fills him with a new, deeper level of nourishment from a new, deeper communion with nature. Again, this comes from years of practice and repetition, coupled with the desire to continuously improve, which is the intentional movement toward greater consciousness.

Anyone who invests deeply and consistently in any particular discipline, regardless of the activity, will with right practice and long effort experience a profound yet subtle shift in perception that produces a whole new level of skill and consciousness. Typically, this is territory traveled alone. If these individuals chose to explain their process, then, theoretically, others could learn and follow at a faster pace, which is what I am endeavoring to do here. There is no magic involved, only focused, disciplined effort done in a clear, practical, and identifiable way, which, in the end, produces the quantum leap in growth that I am attempting to describe.

Sucking the marrow from the bone

A fundamental question in life is, who is responsible? We feel pain and fear, so who is responsible? We began by revisiting our youth and examining the thousands of parent-child collisions we had growing up. From the most important people in our lives, we learned to hide certain feelings or not ask for specific kinds of emotional support as a way of avoiding their disapproval and rejection. Our unasked for, unfulfilled emotional desires created an emotional wound that gave rise to our hidden, secret emotional longings and our fears of disapproval. Perhaps we blamed our parents or the situation, so we accepted it and let it go. Whatever we took to be the truth became our story, which is now the foundation of our out-of-balance emotional lives. We live from this foundation right now and the beliefs that gave rise to it influence our every decision and action. We are not trapped, rather we are all rooted like trees in the earth, and the ground in which we reside is our story from childhood. Do not underestimate the nearly limitless hold, the gargantuan effect, this has on us every day. It is our root system from which we grew and continue to grow from.

In the first phase of our inner work, we learned our story and how it influenced us. We also learned to see our parents as equals rather than as superior or dominant to us. In other words, we worked to drop the vertical relationship of them above us, wielding the power of disapproval, and changed it to a horizontal relationship of us and them on the same level of equal power. This transformation occured as we came to understand and accept that our parents were wounded by their parents and are rooted to their story in the same way we are to ours. They are wounded and out of balance; we are wounded and out of balance. They were denied specific emotional care and validation from their parents, which, to this day, they still yearn for. We were denied certain emotional care and validation from our parents, which, to this day, we still yearn for. So we learned in the truest sense that parents are not to blame; they are the origin of our wound and bear responsibility in its creation, but they are not to blame, for they are only unconscious adults struggling with their own childhood wounds. With this understanding, we see blame, anger, and hurt are no longer appropriate, and we recognize them as ineffective responses that fail to move us toward healing and deeper consciousness. Instead of moving us closer to what we want, they move us further away, which is painful.

This is equally true of premature forgiveness. The cliché "My parents did the best they could. I don't blame them for anything," bypasses the deeper work of feeling our childhood pain of unfulfilled emotional longings and using that pain to find and take ownership of the lost parts of ourselves, including our personal power. We are only fooling ourselves with old clichés like the one above. Distracting us from becoming conscious or working effectively to heal is a continuous strategy of our seen self, but we can never fool our identity, which will always manifest the emotional quality of our lives based on our true beliefs. Living symbols never lie; they are mirrors of our self in which we can see all of our emotional pain, both conscious and unconscious. We cannot hide because our truth always shows up in the form of a skin rash, a car accident, a chronic illness, lack of money or protection, or ongoing dissatisfaction in our lives and relationships. All of us must one day allow ourselves to feel and own our pain, or we will progress no further because we never actually hold our personal truth in our own hands.

As we reconcile our relationship with our parents, the question of who is responsible remains. We feel pain and fear, so someone must be responsible. Where does our attention go next? We outgrow our parents and our issues with them, and then we focus on our spouse or partner because they are our new source of pain and dissatisfaction. Sometimes we leave our partners to find new ones, only to experience the same pain and dissatisfaction again. In reality, it is we who choose our partners, and it is we who choose to stay with them, yet we blame them for our unhappiness. We tell ourselves, "If only they would change, if only they would awaken and become reasonable or different in some way, then I could be happy." But what we learned about our parents we also learn about our partner, who is acting from his or her own story. Our partner is wounded and out of balance just as we are wounded and out of balance. Our partner believes he or she cannot express genuine feelings to us or ask for emotional longings just as we cannot ask these things of them.

As we live with this profound realization, we come to see our partner's attacks on us as their own masking behaviors, covering their own fear and pain, which they see us as responsible for. How ironic! We begin to understand and accept that they, too, are acting from their own unfulfilled emotional longings, just as we are. Again, we come to a place where blame is neither appropriate nor effective. We realize once again that blame, which is always based on the false belief that we are right, moves us further away from what we really want, not closer to it. Blame keeps us clinging to a punctured life raft; eventually we come to realize that holding our partner responsible for our dissatisfactions is a waste of time, which causes us to finally abandon that deflating boat.

When you see your parents as wounded and out of balance, you are really seeing them as individuals. You can then see their emotional wounds without judgment or excuse. If you come to understand and accept their emotional deficiencies and failings as ordinary espressions of humanity, and if you come to see the same thing in your spouse or partner, and you withdraw the last remnants of blame and projection from all, then you are left with the only person who actually controls your emotional life. And that is you. Finally, after so much work and effort, the focus is on the right place and the right person. There are no further distractions. You fully understand and truly believe that all of the work now is with yourself. The living symbol to watch for, which will let you know you've arrived at this place, is you will no longer speak of others as the source of your pain. You will not complain about coworkers; you will not vent to friends and family about your partner or spouse; you will not see yourself as a victim of anyone or anything because none of these people causes you significant pain any longer. You are now ready to confront yourself at a deep level of identity. Be prepared, for you are about to confront the most powerful, clever, and motivated adversary you will ever face: Your seen self, which ". . . will not go gently into that good night."

Our seen self: The final barrier

Quite frankly, we do not understand or appreciate how desperately our seen self will fight to survive or to what degree it will go to keep control of you and your identity. Let me express this in the starkest terms: your seen self is a sociopath and it will do virtually anything to protect its existence and keep your fear of disapproval firmly entrenched. It is through fear of disapproval—particularly for voicing your genuine feelings or asking for your emotional longings—that your seen self controls you. And it will not stop its efforts. In our seen self, we are combating our greatest nemesis, and so we must ready ourselves for heightened battle. To prepare for anything less is to be unprepared, for given the slightest opportunity, the smallest of openings, your seen self will vanquish you; it will successfully block you from speaking your genuine feelings and attaining your emotional longings and ever getting free of the roots that hold fast to a story that keeps you from what you truly want. The seen self does not want you to be happy, free, or conscious; it wants you to remain afraid, anxious, and reactive. That is its agenda, that is its purpose. Because when you are afraid, anxious, and reactive, it wins, it survives, it remains in control of you, your beliefs, and your identity.

Our seen self is clever and devious beyond description. It's always planning, it's always prepared in order to create multiple layers of defense. The ingeniousness behind its efforts is amazing and must be witnessed firsthand in one's own life, because the deeper we go the more stunning are its efforts in a laser-focused quest for survival and control.

The seen self begins with simple disapproval. It sets up the belief that if we express our genuine feelings or ask for our emotional longings we will be disapproved of by our parents and later by their proxies. Once we recognize this game and begin to move through it, the seen self reveals a deeper, more sinister layer of disapproval, which comes from our spouse or partner. The seen self's resistance first appears as a simple blockade with the danger of disapproval; next comes a barbed wire barrier of rejection; after that, a mine field of abandonment; after that, an armed battalion of "I'm leaving you"; and after that, a five-ton bomb with the message, "You are a defective failure." In other words, each new blockade carries greater, deeper fear and threat of personal annihilation. The farther you get in your own healing, the fiercer will be your seen self's fight for its survival, which is threatened by your increasing clarity and understanding. As you progress in your inner work, your seen self's fear-based territory is shrinking. The ground it stands on literally is getting smaller, which is clear evidence that it is in danger of annihilation. So it lays down blocks and obstacles, illnesses, accidents, and twists of fate—all designed to convince you that you can never have your emotional longings fulfilled. If you get past most of these obstacles, the seen self is ready with its most potent defense. **The seen self will make your most fundamental masking behavior look, feel, and appear to be your genuine self**. This is where inner work turns subtle, because discerning what is true becomes difficult to see.

If you let down your guard and accept your most fundamental masking behavior—your most basic form of emotional reactivity as an expression of your genuine identity or your truth—then seen self has successfully positioned you so that you can neither see nor change that particular masking behavior. "It's me being me," you say to yourself. "What is there to look at or change? I am who I am; I want to be who I am. I'm comfortable being me. This is my truth!" But you are mistaken, because the behaviors that are most fundamental to your sense of self are only masking behaviors, blocking you from both your emotional longings and true authenticity. These deep, organic masking behaviors are rooted to a source belief that is our personal ground floor, for this source belief is the one belief on which all our other beliefs rest. We accept our source belief as our most fundamental personal truth, when, in fact, it is our most fundamental personal lie. It is the false belief that serves as our very foundation, which gives rise to our masking behaviors and hides our deepest emotional longings. Please understand exactly what this means. Your source belief will insinuate itself into every other belief you have and, by doing so, color your perception about who you are. It will touch every detail, every aspect, every relationship of your life. Your source belief is your roots and all the beliefs that grow from it become the trunk and branches of your tree, which represents your life.

To dig down to this source belief, we must return to where we started and see it with new eyes—with a new vision based on all of the inner work we have done thus far. We must have one more new perception—one that has the power to change absolutely everything. This is the *originating* belief in disapproval that started it all; the mother of all our pain; the origin of our fear and dissatisfaction.

Let's say we perceived that our father was a good man, but too weak and complacent to actually protect or care for us, and our mother was a rageaholic. Our father never protected us from our mother because he feared her anger, and he never confronted our mother about her ongoing unhappiness because it was easier to avoid it. Our mother never confronted our father about his weakness and complacency, for it, too, was easier to avoid. So we watched our parents in a largely loving, collaborative relationship live out these other dynamics over many years and, as a result, we formed the belief that being seen and supported by our parents was just not possible. Our father would not protect us from our mother's anger and unhappiness; our mother would not protect us from our father's weakness and complacency. And to express our genuine feelings to either would only cause them pain and elicit further disapproval and rejection. When we reach this understanding, which happens in some form to all of us, we have birthed our tragic belief in the impossibility of emotional fulfillment. We have reached a tragic conclusion about some emotional fulfillment we believe we can never have, should never ask for, should never even want. We have now formed the roots of our tree.

Perhaps we believe that finding the right partner and being loved and supported are hopeless pursuits. We then populate our life with situations and people who support our belief in this specific hopelessness: a friend who never finds the "right" partner and complains about it, a family that continuously demonstrates the absence of love and support, a job lacking real support, which equates to feeling unseen and unloved. Unfortunately, all of these living symbols reflect back to us our deeper source belief, which helps us keep it alive by reinforcing our perception that it is true. In other words, since we continually perceive the fulfillment of our source belief, we accept it as true. In this way, seeing is not believing, rather, believing is what produces seeing. It is what converts our perceptions into beliefs—and it is an extraordinary subtlty.

In the end, we create a life based on our source belief, but we don't realize it because a) this source belief is rooted too deeply to see clearly, b) we mistakenly perceive the living symbols generated by our source belief as true, and c) we may be simultaneously working externally to break the same pattern that we are working internally to uphold. Hence, we are living at cross-purposes, but don't realize it. This is part of the subtlety mentioned earlier. We may be breaking down our negative beliefs and patterns, yet deep down we are also building them back up and sustaining them. In the end, we must come to realize that we are the problem.

This issue is most visible in our relationship with our spouse or partner. We all have seemingly endless mundane interactions that contain our full story with all of its pain and fear. Here is the kind of dynamic that I hear endless variations on: a wife's masking behavior is to respond quickly with anger and irritation; her husband's wound is from being overpowered by an angry, irritated parent. Whenever the husband perceives his wife becoming angry or irritated, he is immediately cowed; he shuts down and goes into defensive mode with his masking behaviors on full display. This is a typical dynamic that seems minor and insignificant, yet just beneath the surface are deep patterns and beliefs. Standing in the kitchen, following dinner and dessert, a husband asks his wife: "I feel like some more ice cream. Is that okay?" The wife bristles visibly, though the husband does not know why. The husband recoils internally and believes his wife is again judging and disapproving of him, hurling invisible darts at him. He feels attacked by her body language, in which he perceives anger and irritation. His source belief is *I can never do it right; therefore, I am not worthy of respect*. Here is what the husband does not see: he does not realize he is asking his wife's permission for ice cream, which means he is willingly handing his power over to her, instantly transforming her from an equal into a wounding parental figure with the full power of disapproval a proxy carries. Then when she does disapprove of him, the husband blames the wife for doing so. In actuality, the wife felt her husband's weakness and disingenuousness in his request, which is why she bristled. Such powerful emotions are regularly stirred over something as innocuous as ice cream.

If we pull back to gain perspective, the husband's seen self comes into view. Now we can see how it set him up to be trapped by his own story. The seen self began as it always does with a tragic belief in the impossibility of emotional fulfillment: "Go ahead and ask, but she's only going to be angry and irritated with you." The seen self then nudges the husband just enough so he asks for ice cream in a way that attracts disapproval, which keeps his story and fear of disapproval intact. Then, after the confrontation occurs, his seen self quietly reminds him of his deep-seated hopelessness: "She's never going to change; she's never going to be loving, understanding, and supportive. Why did you ever marry her?" And he believes it. In the moment, it appears to be true. To break apart this pack of false perceptions, the husband would have had to ask for what he wanted, which would mean being truthful and clear with himself on a deeper level by instead stating: "I am going to have more ice cream." Or, he could have said nothing, because he feared nothing, and then have simpy taken the ice cream he wanted. But this action would have undermined his seen self by robbing it of an opportunity. Perhaps seen self still would have whispered to the husband as he walked toward the freezer, "She's going to be angry if you take that ice cream." But if he swatted this inner voice away and reminded himself that it is only my seen self lying again, trying to control me through fear of disapproval, he would be challenging his source belief about the impossibility of emotional fulfillment. He could remind himself that, "My wife may or may not disapprove of me, but I believe she loves and supports me, and if she does disapprove of me, all I need do is own and express my hurt and anger and ask her for what I want."

When inner work is taken to this level, transformation is strong and fast, because we are undoing our source belief about the impossibility of emotional fulfillment and replacing it with the new belief that emotional fulfillment is not only possible, but necessary.

Here's another example. This one from my own life. As mentioned earlier, my mother died when I was two. My father, a compulsive gambler, focused exclusively on his own needs and desires. As a result, we never had money, and my mother could not confront my father on his self-centered behavior; after all, she was dead. My father did not recognize the emotional hole left by my mother's death, so I was left to protect, care, and fend for myself. As a result, I formed the belief that no one will ever see me or take care of me; it isn't possible because I'm not worth it. To express my genuine feelings about any part of this dynamic would only anger my father and invite his attack and disapproval. My deepest emotional longing is to be taken care of, and after decades of inner work in countless disciplines, I ended up confronting my source belief that to be seen and cared for is just not possible for me.

This was my seen self's foundation and its most potent defense. It blocked me from emotional satisfaction throughout my entire life because I refused to ask anyone to see me and care for me, and then I felt hurt and angry when they didn't. This belief in the impossibility of fulfilling my emotional longings insinuated itself throughout all parts of my life—in my identity, marriage, work, and health (both my asthma and diabetes speak to this belief). My seen self has successfully created an invisible barrier that blocks me on all levels while preserving its control and survival, because I continually mistake my source belief for who I believe I am when, in fact, it is my deepest, most fundamental masking behavior. This source belief keeps me in a state of perpetual woundedness by reminding me that I am defective: I cannot get what I want because I am unworthy of receiving it and should remain afraid to even ask.

Although this belief is not really me, it is so convincing that I believe and accept it as my deepest truth. I have populated my life with situations (via illnesses, losses, twists of fate, jobs) and people who unknowingly reinforce my source belief, and for most of my life I never noticed because I have spent a lifetime trying to break this pattern that I simultaneously work hard to uphold. Again, this is the degree of subtlety involved. As I dismantle this belief, even reaffirming to myself that it's true, yet on a deeper level I continue to build it back up and sustain it. I am hanging on, refusing to let go of this self-injurious belief. As a result, I have lived at cross-purposes within my own self, allowing my wound to run my life. One day I realized with absolute clarity that the problem was only me and my fucking seen self!

In this way, we all create lives in which it appears we can never have what we long for. We remain secretly unhappy and dissatisfied while living a "normal" life. We are caught but cannot loosen ourselves, because we fervently cling and refuse to let go of the source belief that is creating our unhappiness. We all must eventually see the bottom floor of our wounding belief system and recognize it for what it is. We must see how our decisions and actions continue to support and empower this belief, even though we are simultaneously working to heal it. Our perception may be the only way we can free ourselves from the fear and dread that drives our seen self's hurtful, malicious behavior.

We all choose to believe others block us from what we want. We hold this belief both consciously and unconsciously. Ironically, others are only fulfilling our personal belief in the impossibility of emotional fulfillment. It is we who keep this false belief alive by projecting it on to others around us. It is we who feed it credibility by believing it is true and behaving accordingly. When we are blocked from what we want, we react emotionally, often with anger, hurt, and outrage, as we believe we should whenever we experience the painful reappearance of our source belief—the denial of our emotional longings. However, it is we who hold our source belief, who feed it and keep it alive; it is we who have constructed a life of living symbols that bear witness to our source belief. It is we who created it all based on perceptions and beliefs learned in childhood. Our seen self works constantly to uphold our source belief, even as we try to dismantle it. With this understanding, we have finally come full circle. If you reach this juncture in your inner work, you will more than likely feel a combination of exhaustion and relief.

Once I had a very important meeting to attend. It was a rare opportunity both personally and professionally. I had not been sick for several years, but three days prior to the meeting, which could not be rescheduled, I caught the flu. By sheer will, I attended the meeting, but I was sick and uncomfortable throughout and fully spent thereafter. The normal take on this episode is that I had the misfortune to get sick at the wrong time—illness happens, after all. But for me, everything is a living symbol, so I asked myself, why would my identity produce illness to prevent me from attending this meeting? What does my hidden self want? More important, what does my seen self want? From this perspective, the answer became obvious: the potential outcome of a successful meeting was that I would be recognized for my talents and then receive the kind of support my seen self wants me to believe I can never have. By becoming sick and missing this meeting, I could lie in bed suffering with flu and victimitis, telling myself, "No one will ever see me or take care of me. The universe doesn't want me to break through this blockade. It's who I am. It's my destiny. I can't escape it." In truth, the universe had nothing to do with it. My identity created a situation that invited me to uphold my oldest, deepest belief. When I embrace my source belief, I unknowingly infuse it with life energy, allowing it to continue its invisible, toxic spread throughout my identity. Belief is the true mother of creation, and living symbols will always be the fruit of our belief system.

Blind spot redux

We rarely see our tragic belief in the impossibility of emotional fulfillment with clarity, because we fail to recognize our emotional reactivity as a masking behavior. If we excuse or accept our emotional reactivity as valid, as being anything other than camouflage, covering our true emotional longings, then we have slipped into our blind spot, and we are once again unaware. In this place of blinding darkness, neither healing nor emotional fulfillment are possible, and the only thing left for us is righteous indignation. We are right to feel hurt, right to feel angry. Someone else is to blame for not treating us in the right way, with the right words, with the right feeling. Or perhaps life just isn't fair. But this is false because all we need to do is not react and then ask directly for what we want in the moment. If the person across from you doesn't hear you, tell him you feel unheard and ask again. If the person doesn't understand you, tell him you feel misunderstood and ask again. We must develop the discipline of asking for what we want again and again until we realize conclusively that the other can't or won't give it to us. But if we make the tragic mistake—and we all do—of believing we can't get what we want from someone when we have not actually asked them for it, then by our not asking, we are clinging to the belief in the impossibility of emotional fulfillment. We are lying to ourselves and we are accepting the lie; we are holding on to our terrible source belief and then blaming someone else because we don't have what we want most. Yet, it is we who refuse to change and let go.

This is exactly what your seen self is working ceaselessly to make happen. When you do this, know that you have thrown your support to the part of your own identity that is working against your own self interest; your seen self is a traitor in your midst. By aligning with it, you unintentionally become your own worst enemy, and, as a result, you are undermining your own happiness and emotional fulfillment.

Why do we need our source belief?

Our ultimate fear is that if we open ourselves to the possibility of emotional fulfillment and asked for our emotional longings, if we open ourselves to the possibility of receiving them, we risk *not* receiving them. We risk being told "No!" And if this were to happen, our worst fears—our source belief—would be proven true. It would mean we are not worthy of receiving our emotional longings. It would mean we are not actually worthy of love, respect, or caring. Most people will not challenge this barrier—the risk is too great. Most never embrace the belief that they *are* worthy, lovable, respectable, or good enough. We have to see our masking behaviors for what they are, and we have to embrace our emotional longings, but mainly this has to do with learning to accept ourselves so that we can ultimately be ourselves.

But our seen self continuously whispers lies in our ear: "You're not worthy. Don't believe that you are. Don't expect emotional fulfillment. Don't expect love, caring, protection, or support. Don't ask directly or you will be rejected, disapproved of, and humiliated." And our seen self repeats these ugly lies to us over and over, year after year; it repeats them to us when we're awake and asleep. Its messages live so deep in our tissue that we mistake it for our own voice The obvious question is, what can we do about it?

Breaking through your source belief

The first step is to learn how to recognize your seen self's voice. Whenever you hear it speak to you, reminding you of your shortcomings and fears, whispering about the emotional longings you can never have fulfilled, call this voice the liar. It is crucial you begin to build this new belief about your seen self. It does not matter what it says, because EVERYTHING it says is a lie, designed so you avoid disapproval by never expressing your genuine feelings or asking for what you want. Everything it says is bad for you, injurious, self-destructive. That is all you need to know. Our seen self is cleverer than we are, so arguing with it about who is right is not only ineffective, it is guaranteed to set us up for failure. Your seen self will always tell you why something won't work, why you shouldn't do this or that, why you are forever doomed to unfulfillment, and its arguments will always sound logical and factually correct. "Don't ask him or her for this or that; he or she will become angry with you." True, the person may become angry with you, but it is only by asking that you may lay claim to what you want. And by not asking you are choosing to avoid what you want, which perpetuates your source belief. It does not matter whether you get what you ask for. What matters is that you ask for it, which is why the seen self's words are always a lie and a betrayal. Your seen self is your greatest enemy. It will fight to preserve your source belief in the impossibility of emotional fulfillment. It will fight you with sociopathic intent, threatening you again and again with disapproval and rejection in order to control you and your life. This is how it survives. It is a psychic parasite that lives off your entrapped soul.

Once you are absolutely certain your seen self is a liar, what it says is no longer important because you understand and accept that all of its words and well-presented facts are false. Now you are ready for the next step. This is the hardest part. Now you must allow yourself to feel fear—specifically fear of personal annihilation—but not be controlled by it. The only way to do this is to let go. Surrender. Stop holding on to your fear. Take the risk. Let go and fall free. Ask for what you want. Ask even though you are terrified to do so, even though you have no expectation of receiving it. Ask for what you want again and again and again. This is an act of faith. This letting go, this repeated asking, sows the new belief in the possibility of emotional fulfillment, in the possibility that, in fact, you are worthy to receive the love and support you crave.

Once you allow your perception to shift, the power of belief formation will take over and then nothing in the world can stop it. Not even your seen self. Now you are harnessing the underlying organic power of life itself—the same creative power that gives birth to stars and universes—and it will shift your identity. New perception creates new belief, which shapes your identity and gives new form to your life. Living symbols then appear to show you your new beliefs. Ask for what you want and life will support you. People will support you. But for this to happen you must first believe it **can** happen and that you are worthy of receiving it, that you do not have to be or do anything else. In other words, you are still worthy of love even though you have a temper or a big belly or are too old or have erectile dysfunction or don't earn enough money or are gay or whatever secret fears and insecurities you have that make you, in your own estimation, unworthy of love and caring.

To take this great leap of faith, you must risk personal annihilation. You must befriend emotional death and accept it as one possible outcome of many. At this moment, you must go all in. You must risk everything to break this seemingly unbreakable pattern. You must be willing to face rejection and aloneness or to lose all that is valuable and important to you: your marriage, your money, your job, all of it, any of it. That is the price of breaking one's source belief. It is the real world cost of bringing about the identity change that finally allows you to have your emotional longings fulfilled.

If you can do this, you are ready to release your source belief. You are ready to ask for or act on what you want instead of reacting emotionally. It is only by letting go of our paralyzing fear that we become free of its burning pain. In the end it is our choice either to block ourselves from having what we want most or risk everything by directly asking for what we want and then seeing what happens.

Let's say you're afraid of gaining weight. If you gain weight, you will be fat and unattractive. That is what your mother led you to believe. You wake up on Monday and weigh yourself. You're three pounds over your normal weight. Your seen self says, "You're fat. Everyone will see how out of control you are. Your mother would be disappointed in you. She will give you a look that lets you know you are fat and out of control." In the past this voice would have sent you spiraling into unconsciousness and masking behaviors. In fact, you can already see three of your masking behaviors popping up. But this time you tell yourself your seen self is a liar and its words are pure poison. You reject the beliefs it is trying to foist upon you. Instead you remind yourself that it doesn't matter if you are fat or not. You may or may not be out of control but you are still one hundred percent worthy of being loved and accepted. You accept that you feel afraid; you accept the possibility of emotional death, of personal annihilation. You own the fact that you have gained three pounds. Then you very intentionally tell your seen self to go to hell as you let go of your source belief (later on, with more practice, you will not need to get angry at your seen self; you will just be able to let go).

You decide to push it further, so you seek out your boyfriend and tell him, "I just weighed myself and I gained three pounds (this is like intentionally putting your head in the jaws of the lion). I would like this to be a non-issue and have your support, but I really need to know what you think." He says, "I think you should stop worrying about your crazy mother's bullshit. You're beautiful, and I think it's great that you're fighting against it." Or, perhaps you get this response: "Be careful, you don't want your weight to get away from you again." At which point your seen self jumps in to remind you of your failure. Again, you hear the voice of your seen self as a liar and reject its words. You remember what you want and you ask your boyfriend for it again: "My mother made me ashamed of my body and my weight. I want to get free of this damaging belief. I would like it if you would support me—it's really important to me." "Ok," he says, "How can I do that?" "Let's get together later and talk about it. Thank you for your support."

In addition to those around us, we block and injure ourselves with self-disapproval from within. We repeat the lies we have heard from our seen self. We tell ourselves how bad we are, how fat we are, how out of control and weak we are, how incompetent and unattractive we are. We remind ourselves, "Don't ask for what you want, or so and so will be angry or hurt and will not understand, and then we will be rejected and abandoned. We will be humiliated." We continually threaten ourselves with the anticipation of disapproval and rejection. Yet the simple act of asking for what we want is sufficient to undo our belief in the impossibility of emotional fulfillment.

The true discipline of inner work comes from the understanding that our story is the same story every day; in fact, every hour of every day, and the same story calls for the same disciplined response every time, because we realize we are the author of our own story, and if anyone is responsible, it can be only ourselves. This is why this practice is in the form of a craft. The only way I know how to change all of this is through the accumulation of skill and experience based on continuous effort in the pursuit of self-improvement. In other words, effort of will in shifting our perception to become increasingly more conscious.

There is no great mystery to the getting of consciousness. There is but learning to see our masking behaviors clearly, learning to act consciously with awareness of our story, followed by courageous practice, disciplined effort, and more courageous practice. Bear in mind, the joy of gardening is in no way diminished by the continual necessity for weeding. In the end, it is incumbent upon each of us to understand and master our fearful subservience to self-disapproval so we may again experience self-love and share with others our understanding and peace. This requires that we reject our self-destructive belief in the impossibility of emotional fulfillment; we must let it go in order to cut the very flow of life energy that sustains it. Only then will this false belief wither and die like an unwatered plant, and our seen self, suddenly bare, will have nothing left to protect. The freedom of our identity depends upon it.

Living with disapproval—An inconvenient truth

Our journey continues from where we are at this moment, and disapproval will be part of it for the rest of our lives. This should not be a shock or a surprise—external disapproval is common, but self-disapproval is constant. You will always have relationships, and in these you will experience emotional collisions, so the struggle to remain conscious simply goes on and with it our duel with disapproval—en garde!

Are you ready now to receive criticism from others or yourself? Can you let disapproval land in your heart like a ball of spikes and then use your skill, experience, and will to sort it out? Can you resist your natural inclination to react with a masking behavior? Can you resist your seen self's relentless push for an emotional overreaction? Are you ready to receive criticism, yet remain open and vulnerable and let it flow into you because, in truth, there is nothing in it to fear. Remember the old children's rhyme, "Sticks and stones will break my bones but words will never hurt me"? Are you ready to step away from your childhood belief that words can harm you more than sticks or stones? This is a practical question to be considered deeply by craftsmen and craftswomen; I do not mean it as an expression of judgement, for it is only our belief in the power of other's words and expressions to wound us that keeps our blind spot functioning. But words or expressions, and the energy behind them, are nothing more than a call for self-examination. And correct self-examination engaged in repeatedly is the activity that creates self-awareness and healing. What then are we resisting? What are we so afraid of? When you finally look within, you will only discover lost, wonderful, and valuable parts of yourself. There is no dark monster lurking in interior shadows, only our childhood wounds left unattended.

Truth is never easy. Speaking our genuine thoughts and feelings is a highly-skilled craft to be learned well and practiced often. This practice allows true relationships to form, which gives deeper meaning to life because it confers authenticity and vulnerability. While it is counterintuitive, speaking our genuine feelings—hurtful though they may be at times—makes love with others possible. It makes love and respect for ourselves attainable. Living a true life in which we speak our genuine thoughts and feelings is the ultimate expression of personal power, because it requires that we become open and vulnerable as we intentionally choose to face our most primal fears of disapproval and rejection and, ultimately, challenge our deepest wounding beliefs. Owning and expressing our genuine feelings asks us to be nothing more, nothing less, than who we are. When we do this, we become authentic human beings, and authenticity is the hallmark of truth and the foundation of vulnerability.

Within our minds, belief is the exclusive place where change occurs, and the only person you can change is yourself. This is an axiom of life. Learn your masking behaviors well so you know when you have fallen into your blind spot. Learn to recognize your emotional wounds when they become activated and try to control you. Work to understand your beliefs and reactions in order to know where they come from. Welcome insight from others into who you are, even when it hurts. From the center of your being, the energy of life flows outward, ceaseless and expansive. It shines through your personal beliefs like golden sunlight, giving rise to new life, while sustaining the old. This energy manifests our lives down to the smallest detail. Life force and our beliefs are part of the cosmic dance of creation and evolution. How much better it is to dance freely, without fear or shame, with an open heart and a conscious mind. It is all we can do. Stop hiding. Be who you are.

Ought not these oldest sufferings of ours to be yielding
More fruit by now? Is it not time that, in loving, we
freed ourselves from the loved one, and, quivering,
endured: as the arrow endures the string, to become, in the

gathering out-leap, something more than itself?

For staying is nowhere.

—R.M.Rilke

Exercise 20: Challenging your source beliefs

For this exercise, you're going to keep one last diary. It will contain your source beliefs, your personal belief in the impossibility of emotional fulfillment. The first thing you will need to do is write down your source beliefs. It isn't necessary that you hit the bullseye dead center—just come close. You can always refine and adjust as you do the exercise and learn more about what it is you believe.

Review your *Responses to Disapproval Form*. Now think of your relationship with your father while growing up. Based on your perceptions of him when you were a child, what was it you absolutely believed you could never get from him because he couldn't or wouldn't give it to you? You wanted this but were too terrified to ask him for it. You didn't want to anger him; you didn't want to hurt him. This is where your source belief originated. It is what creates our expectation that conflict or confrontation will likely lead to the worst case scenario, the fulfillment of our source belief. In our heart of hearts, we don't believe any other outcome is really possible, because we don't believe our father can or will change. And if he cannot change and if we are afraid to challenge him or his proxies, then we can never prove that our belief in the impossibility of emotional fulfillment is false. Our unwillingness to challenge our father and risk his or his proxy's disapproval means we still fear him. The result is that we settle for the emotional dissatisfaction and fear of disapproval we have always lived with. This is equally true for our mother.

Compiling my source beliefs

I believe that while growing up my **father** could not or would not give me:

____

____

I believe that while growing up my **mother** could not or would not give me:

____

____

In my own life, here is what I wrote:

I believe that while growing up my **father** could not or would not give me: *financial or emotional support and protection.*

I believe that while growing up my **mother** could not or would not give me: *love, affection, and nurturing.*

These are my source beliefs, my personal beliefs in the impossibility of emotional fulfillment. I have long believed that I am unworthy to ask directly for these things. As a result, I have spent much of my life rejecting financial and emotional support and protection, as well as love, affection, and nurturing, because in my heart I did not feel worthy to receive them—although I always told myself something else.

What follows is a diary that you will keep. Throughout any given day, you will encounter your source beliefs many, many times. Start by challenging these beliefs one time per day, then two times per day, then three times per day, then as often as you are able. Once you can demonstrate skill in this exercise, continue to do it for the rest of your life, only without a diary. This is a profoundly transformative piece of inner work; it goes hand in hand with the Clarity Exercise.

Form 6

Challenging My Source Beliefs in the Impossibility of Emotional Fulfillment. Do this one time per day, then two, then three.

Form 7
CHALLENGING MY SOURCE BELIEFS IN THE IMPOSSIBILITY OF EMOTIONAL FULFILLMENT

I believed that while growing up my father could not or would not give me:
I believed that while growing up my mother could not or would not give me:

As a result, I still believe that I cannot ask for, have, or am even worthy to receive these things.

DO THIS EXERCISE ONE TIME PER DAY, THEN TWO, THEN THREE

1	A conflict or confrontation occurs. Describe it:
2	Look for your source beliefs. See them. Recognize this proxy for your mother or father. Listen to your seen self's lying words, telling you what you can't have, telling you to be afraid.
3	Now reject your seen self and your source beliefs. They are not true; they are self-defeating lies.
4	Let go of your source belief, even though you are afraid. Stop upholding your belief in the impossibility of emotional fulfillment. Stop turning people into proxies for your wounding mother or father. Stop giving these people the power to hurt, upset, or scare you.
5	Accept the possibility that by asking for what you want you may lose someone or something important or that you might fail. It is far better to accept these potentialities than fearfully resisting their possible outcome. Surrender your fear of what might happen so that you may claim your strength and live conscious and free.
6	Now, ask for or act on what you want. This is what will break your source belief.
7	Affirm that you do not want to live controlled by your source belief any longer. Affirm that you can have what you want, instead of believing you cannot.

This form is available at the back of this book and as a full-page, editable version for free download at TheCraftOfLife.com

CHAPTER 23

Practice + Perseverance = Transformation

Courage is the most important of all the virtues,
because without courage
you can't practice any other virtue consistently.
—Maya Angelou

THIS IS THE STORY of Lauren (not her real name), a woman who was in one of my groups for eighteen months. She has graciously allowed me to share her story, which, in my mind, is the perfect ending to this book. This is a person who put everything you've read about into practice. We will hear about her successes and failures, her emotional ups and downs, but mostly we will hear about her slow, steady personal transformation, which came about due to her willingness to practice and persevere.

Lauren had heard via word of mouth that I was starting a new group for women. She contacted me, but unfortunately the group was already full. She received the news with genuine disappointment, but also with acceptance and equanimity. Her mature response impressed me. Two days later, at the start of our next group meeting, one member said she was leaving–she'd decided the material was not the right fit for her. I called Lauren the following day. We met, discussed the model, and the circumstances. Lauren enthusiastically joined the group at its next meeting. This was our beginning. I took note of this event as a living symbol, which alerted me to the possibility that Lauren might be a good participant, and that she might be particularly serious in her pursuit of personal transformation, which always enlivens me. After we met, I recognized she was seeking a path of authentic inner work, and I made a mental note to see how this observation would play out. Would Lauren's initial enthusiasm, her seemingly sincere desire for real change and the coincidence that allowed her to unexpectedly join the group, accurately predict a new student ready to work hard for personal transformation? I would watch for additional living symbols to prove or disprove the intention I first observed. This is a typical way I use living symbols as a practical tool. I glimpse something about a person that stands out and then watch for supporting patterns of behavior or circumstances to corroborate my initial observation. Significant identity traits express themselves in repeating patterns; as such, the same trait with the same meaning will appear in different forms. Once I am able to recognize a pattern and understand its meaning, I have a vantage point into a person's psyche that provides enormous practical value. I can meet that person with greater awareness. I can recognize their unconscious impulses and prepare in advance for what may come as our two chemistries blend and mix. This is like knowing the weather before going out. Having prior knowledge allows you to dress appropriately or bring along an umbrella even though the sun is shining and no storms are visibly present.

So Lauren began with real promise, and I was happy to have her. She brought a great deal of energy and feistiness to the group, plus a wonderful sense of humor and a remarkable intellect. A highly-educated business professional in her mid-forties, Lauren had separated from her husband three years prior and been divorced for eighteen months. Together, with her ex-husband, she shares custody of their eight-year-old daughter.

In the past, Lauren had sought help via traditional therapy, and when she separated from her husband she spent a week in an intensive, submersive psycho-spiritual process aimed at helping her break through to a new awareness of herself and her patterns. All of this was extremely helpful and promoted significant awareness and growth. But Lauren wanted to go further. She wanted to pierce the depths of the fears and emotional wounds that she saw controlling her behavior and attitudes; she wanted to work to heal them in order to become "the best me I possibly can." Lauren came to this work with sincerity and a genuine desire to learn and grow—two of the many wonderful traits she regularly exhibits.

At the inception of every group, I ask participants to think about what they really want and to share it with the group. While this may sound trite, what we want reveals which part of our identity we are willing to take ownership of next, which emotional wound we ourselves want to work on and heal next, and, from my perspective as group facilitator, it also reveals what a person sees (or does not see) about themselves. I write down each member's responses, so in the coming months I am able to watch their development in relation to what they originally stated. Lauren named two objectives: 1) to shift her relationship with her ex-husband (a relationship in which she was the object of his bullying, anger, judgment, and overpowering control), and 2) to meet the love of her life (instead of her pattern of providing care, stability, support, and love to a partner who gave little emotional nourishment in return). The first would be difficult, because it called for a change in perception and belief. The second would be harder still, because it demanded a true transformation of identity. I'm not certain Lauren knew what she was asking for in that to get what she wanted she would have to become—in many significant ways—a different person. This is how our journey began.

Lauren's ex-husband had long been the controlling figure in their relationship. Even though she had greater maturity, character, and inner strength, Lauren had subordinated herself to her husband in many ways. As a result, this encouraged his negative behavior toward her. He was a controlling, invalidating bully who could be cold, mean, and, at times, downright cruel in the way he treated her. Lauren had tremendous anger toward her ex-husband but it was mostly unowned and unexpressed, so she remained in part his depressed victim. As she described it, she had a long history of "putting my head in the sand." When our group began she still feared him and the impact of what he might say or do to her, and, most important, how it might affect their daughter. One of Lauren's strongest impulses is to be the best, most conscientious mom possible. During their divorce her ex-husband sued and won joint custody, and then on repeated occasions he forced Lauren back into court over minor, seemingly pointless details, which caused her great stress and cost much money. "Whatever I give, he wants more. It never ends . . . it never ends." For Lauren, her ex-husband had long been unreasonable, unsupportive, and vindictive toward her.

Near the end of her marriage, Lauren befriended a woman who was also married. They would meet for meaningful conversation and warm companionship.They soon became close friends. As time passed, Lauren felt her heart open as she again experienced feelings and vulnerability she had not felt for a very long time. Lauren began to feel an emotional love for and from this woman, unlike anything she had experienced before. Something was reawakening in her. Comparing the emotional experience to her marriage she said, "We did what you're supposed to do. We met, got engaged, got married. We had a two-week honeymoon. We came home. We bought a house. We spent months remodeling it. We got pregnant, had a child. I had a good job;

he began his own business. The appearance was awesome—it looked like a 1950s marriage. The perfect couple. The perfect family. The perfect future." But, emotionally, her marriage had become as dry as a desert.

When Lauren joined the group she had another meeting calendared several months in the future with her ex-husband and his lawyer. The threat again was if they could not come to terms—meaning his terms—then he would drag her back into court. Her anxiety over this threat was enormous. We set about working the situation with great intention. During group, I took Lauren's biography. Here is her childhood story:

Lauren's father developed commercial real estate, a boom or bust kind of business. Her mother was a homemaker. Both of her parents were alcoholics from an early age. Her father was functional and did his drinking away from home, but her mother could be under the influence at any time. Growing up, Lauren's mother might disappear for days. Lauren would ask her father, "Where's mom?" "With her friends" he might say, adding, "And I don't know when she'll be back." With her mother gone things were more peaceful, but there was also a noticeable and disturbing absence. Without her mother around, Lauren felt a palpable darkness, a sense that something in the family was seriously wrong. As a result, Lauren grew closer to her father. In fact, even as a small child, she was his supporter and confidant. He would routinely speak to her about his troubled marriage. When she wasn't under the influence, Lauren's mother displayed two distinct personalties: an angry, unhappy mother who could be mean and harsh, and a gentler, understanding mother who could at times be kind. This fluctuating identity created enormous instability for Lauren. When she came home from school, her stomach typically in a knot, she did not know what to expect: "Fresh baked cookies or a raving, drunk lunatic."

To further complicate matters, a favored expression of her mother's was, "It's better to look good than feel good." A charismatic personality when out in the world, her mother was an easy talker who had won beauty contests in her younger years. This focus on appearance became a major family theme. Her mother made sure the family looked well on the outside even though things were coming undone behind closed doors. Lauren's parents fought openly. They separated many times over the years. In some instances, Lauren found herself alone with her father, but far worse were the times she was left alone with her mother, who became unstable and emotionally abusive. Once, as a young teenager, when her mother was yelling at her again over some infinitesimally small matter, Lauren, feeling years of suppressed emotion within, raised her hand as if to strike. Her mother said, "If you move a muscle, I will put you through the wall." And Lauren knew her mother's threats were backed by a belt.

These incidents repeated again and again throughout Lauren's childhood and teen years. When she was in her early 20s, Lauren accidentally discovered her father had been having a long-term affair and had lent the woman a large sum of money, which further damaged the family. Since childhood, Lauren had taken her father's side and defended him loyally to her mother, especially regarding accusations of infidelity. Lauren had received beatings from her mother for taking such a contrary position. Now, Lauren felt profoundly betrayed by her father because it had always been true. He had lied to her and this realization was devastating.

Over the first two decades of her life Lauren had a multitude of parent-child collisions. Some were direct: "If you take your father's side you will be disapproved of." Some were indirect: "I must be obedient and do as my mother wants, or I will be disapproved of." We used her biography to create her *Responses to Disapproval Form*. Here is a portion of it.

RESPONSES TO DISAPPROVAL

When I feel fear or emotional upset in my body, it means I'm having confrontation in the moment, amplified by parent-child collisions from the past. This tells me that both my childhood beliefs about disapproval AND my emotional longings have become activated, and my seen and hidden selves are now in conflict. My seen self pressures me to accept my fear of disapproval; My hidden self wants me to own and act on what I truly want. Their positions are diametrically opposed, but I must choose to affirm one or the other.

1) These are **My Childhood Beliefs about Disapproval**:
    1) I should accept betrayal in my closest relationships but still remain loyal, or I will be disapproved of and rejected.
    2) I should not want anyone to see me or recognize my emotional needs, or I will be disapproved of and rejected.
    3) I should not want anyone to protect me emotionally or financially, or I will be disapproved of and rejected.
    4) I should accept when things feel dark or wrong and say nothing, or I will be disapproved of and rejected.
    5) I should not ask others to be honest or take responsibility for their words and actions, or I will be disapproved of.
    6) I should always appear like I have things together and that everything is fine, or I will be disapproved of.
    7) I should fear anger and not express it, or I will be disapproved of, rejected, and abandoned.
    8) I should accept irrational or hurtful behavior from others, or I will be disapproved of, rejected, and abandoned.
2) These are the **Genuine Feelings** that I typically hide:
    1) *Anger*
    2) *Pain*

3) *Fear*

4) *Sadness*

5) *Guilt*

6) *Frustration*

7) *Anxiety*

8) *Depression*

3) These are my **Masking Behaviors**, which lead me to my **Blind Spot**:

1) Not asking for emotional caring;

2) Withdrawing and living in my own world (to avoid others);

3) Thinking, analyzing, and planning (instead of feeling and expressing);

4) Talking confidentially about deeper things (but not asking for what I want);

5) Doing well, like getting good grades;

6) Not expressing anger;

7) Accepting mistreatment from others; and

8) Caretaking of others (while ignoring my needs).

4) These are my **Emotional Longings**; these are what I want:

1) To be seen and accepted for who I am.

2) To be truly loved.

3) To be believed in and valued.

4) To be protected and supported emotionally and financially by my partner.

5) To have peace and stability in my home and life.

6) To own and express my anger when it is appropriate.

7) To have a partner who is genuinely working their issues and will communicate about it honestly, openly, authentically.

Childhood beliefs about disapproval

It would be valuable to take a closer look at some of Lauren's childhood beliefs about disapproval and point out their origins.

1) I should accept betrayal in my closest relationships but still remain loyal, or I will be disapproved of and rejected.

This belief came first and foremost from her father. Lauren had protected him at great personal suffering only to discover later that he had in fact betrayed her by having affairs. She also suffered betrayal from her mother, who failed to give her the kind of love, protection, and nurturing that an archetypal mother would; instead, her mother put her own needs and her own dissatisfaction above her child's.

2) I should not want anyone to see me or recognize my emotional needs, or I will be disapproved of and rejected.

Childhood beliefs about disapproval come starkly into view if we visualize ourselves as children (but with our current adult awareness) asking our parents for our emotional longings. If we imagine them reacting with disapproval, rejection, or abandonment, we know for certain we have identified a childhood belief about disapproval. If Lauren, as a child, had asked her mother or father to see her and recognize her emotional needs and to put theirs aside, Lauren imagines they would have disapproved of, rejected, abandoned, or struck her. Always remember, it does not matter how our parents might have actually reacted. What matters is our perception of our parents and how we believe they would have reacted. Beliefs are based on perception and are not reliant upon factual reality. In this case, Lauren was probably correct in her assessment, but that is not the point. Her perception of her parents created the belief system that now lives within her.

3) I should not want anyone to protect me emotionally or financially, or I will be disapproved of and rejected.

Similar to number two above, Lauren's parent's unintentionally put her in a position of not asking or expecting much from them. They, too, were living their own lives as best they could, dealing with their own emotional pain and childhood beliefs about disapproval. Lauren, however, believed she had to accept the conditions and circumstances she was immersed in, as virtually all children do. I know in my own life, growing up in an extremely abnormal family situation, I still felt "normal." In this case, if Lauren were to ask her parents for the protection she deeply desired, she believed her parents would have responded with angry disapproval and rejection.

4) I should accept when things feel dark or wrong and say nothing, or I will be disapproved of and rejected.

By now a pattern should be clearly visible: If Lauren were to ask her parents for any form of emotional comfort or support, she believes, based on perceptions from childhood, she would be disapproved of and rejected. Therefore, when her mother or father had gone off and she felt afraid and vulnerable, she could not ask them for comfort. Doing so would call her parents own deficiencies into question, which is something most of us are terrified or too pained to do. The result is a childhood belief about disapproval, a deep emotional wound and a secret emotional longing. These four should be enough to give you a clear sense of the origin for all of Lauren's childhood beliefs about disapproval.

Hidden feelings

To insulate herself, which is something we all do, Lauren learned to hide specific feelings. If she were to express these to her parents, she believed they would disapprove of and reject her. Here is the list of those feelings on Lauren's Responses to Disapproval Form.

1) Anger

2) Pain

3) Fear

4) Sadness

5) Guilt

6) Frustration

7) Anxiety

8) Depression

As you can see, owning and expressing any of them might hurt, anger, or insult her parents, and set Lauren up for painful disapproval and rejection. This is why she, like many of us, bury certain feelings; they are too dangerous to voice, too threatening to hold on to. We may express them with some, but rarely or never will we express them to our parents or their proxies, and our intimate partners are always proxies for our parents. This means that without the discipline of inner work few of us develop the skill and courage required to express our genuine thoughts and feelings about our deepest emotional longings to our most intimate partner.

Masking behaviors

Although this is not a full accounting of Lauren's masking behaviors, it is a list of the major ones she learned in childhood, which still have an enormous impact on her life today. Learning to see ourselves enacting our masking behaviors represents a colossal step toward consciousness and healing. Our masking behaviors are literally the guardians of the doorway into the unconscious mind. This particular portal is one we rarely see and mostly avoid. There is little in mainstream culture that asks us to make this effort of will or explains the benefit of doing so. With all my heart I believe our willingness to peer into our own unconscious, our hidden self, is the fulcrum point on which future evolution turns. When we learn the critical importance of seeing ourselves enact our own masking behaviors and use this insight to penetrate our own fear and pain and talk openly about it, we can then model the process for our children. Only then can the world make a quantum leap in consciousness. We all must eventually integrate the unconscious parts of our identity with those parts that we do have awareness of. We will remain half-people until we do.

Through inner work, Lauren began to see herself enact her masking behaviors as a way to avoid disapproval, as a way to avoid confronting her fear and pain, and the result was unawareness. When conflict occurred, she watched herself withdraw instead of voicing her genuine feelings or asking for what she wanted. During confrontations, she reacted—not with feelings—but by thinking, analyzing, and planning. Over time, she observed herself employing her masking behaviors again and again.

Once we enact our masking behaviors we fall into fear; we drop into our blind spot and we lose awareness of our emotional longings. In these moments, we cannot ask for what we want because we ourselves cannot see it; we have severed the connection to whatever it may be. Unfulfilled, our emotional longings live in the depths of our unconscious self as a raw wound that haunts us. The more we fail to ask for what we truly want, the more chafed our wound becomes. We feel it, we hear an inner voice remind us of it, but rarely do we stop to see it clearly or ask for it directly. There is little in our lives that tells us to make this effort, and so we remain emotionally wounded and out of balance, which our lives reflect through our personal living symbols.

Deep emotional longings

If Lauren's emotional longings were to be fulfilled—to be seen, accepted, loved, valued, protected, and supported emotionally and financially by a partner who is working on their issues and willing to communicate honestly and authentically—then Lauren will have to develop the skill of voicing what she wants. She will have to learn to ask for her emotional longings clearly, consistently, and directly. Seeing one's masking behaviors, identifying and expressing one's genuine feelings, and, finally, asking for one's emotional longings requires us to face our most primal fears, to risk emotional annihilation, in real time. This is the inconvenient road to an identity becoming free.

At this point in our group work, we had completed Lauren's biography and assembled her *Responses to Disapproval Form*, so she had the basic tools to begin deeper inner work. From this new vantage point, she practiced seeing her story, her past infiltrating and amplifying the present. She worked on separating the past from the present. She used her will to allow herself to become open, instead of withdrawing and hiding, so that she could feel her feelings and name them, especially her fear. She gave herself permission to want what she really wanted and to name it in the moment. For whatever personal reason, Lauren took all of this on with intense focus and seriousness, so she experienced powerful results quickly. All of this bore out my original observations of Lauren's intial living symbols when she first entered the group.

One day Lauren came to our meeting and told us a wild neighborhood cat had adopted her. She took the cat in, but the cat, which she named Sheba, was not interested in being a domesticated feline. Sheba was a natural hunter, a skilled and able predator, and she began leaving decapitated or mutilated critters at Lauren's doorstep. Lauren was more than a bit freaked out. She felt anxiety in the mornings at the thought of what "gift" might be awaiting her and was repulsed by the bloody mess she expected to find. I pointed out that this was not a random occurrence but a specific living symbol generated by Lauren's own identity.

There is a danger in viewing all physical manifestation as a living symbol in that our seen self has the perpetual need to distract us from becoming conscious. Endlessly naming things as living symbols and getting lost in their interpretation is just such a way. As Freud once supposedly said, "Sometimes a cigar is just a cigar." I know people enjoy a kind of guilty pleasure by mining all things for a deeper symbolic meaning. Be careful because this kind of fortune telling quickly devolves into yet another distraction from your seen self. With that said, when something does stand out, when it has an impact, it may be viewed as a living symbol, and then it will yield important information about your hidden emotional longings and your identity. In all cases, a living symbol will simultaneously express both sides of the issue, meaning what you want *and* your impulse to keep it hidden. In other words, what your seen self and hidden self both want.

This was the case with Sheba the cat. During this period Lauren was doing her inner work with great vitality. Remember, her main focus was twofold: to shift her relationship with her ex-husband and to meet the love of her life. Lauren had long been cowed by her ex-husband, especially when he displayed wild, uncontrolled bursts of anger, which scared Lauren into submission and brought out her masking behavior of caretaking him at her own expense. Sheba represented a part of Lauren's identity: the part that was not afraid, the part comfortable using power and force as right behaviors. The part that was unafraid to kill (metaphorically) when killing was appropriate. These were latent in Lauren but not currently in her grasp. We discussed this in detail and decided it would be constructive for Lauren to ritualize this nightmarish event. Lauren would begin to receive Sheba's kills with gratitude as sacred offerings. She would open her heart and mind and release her disgust so that Sheba might teach her about predators and prey, about using power naturally and unabashedly. Lauren gradually learned to accept Sheba's bloody gifts. She cleaned them up lovingly, and she thanked Sheba for these primordial lessons. In the process, Lauren felt she was assimilating a new part of her own identity and was becoming increasingly comfortable with the notion of using her own power to protect herself. She was learning to choose between being predator or prey. Lauren learned to own her power and to deal a lethal blow in self protection, if needed. In this way, she learned not only to survive, but to thrive.

Week by week the group watched Lauren's progressive transformation. Then, a new lawyer appeared almost out of nowhere: a woman who wanted to take on Lauren's ex-husband in their upcoming negotiation and who was passionate about the case. This woman was different from previous attorneys. She was fiery and tough and wanted very much to protect Lauren. She was another iteration of Sheba, and Lauren gave her permission to fight with ferocity. This was another living symbol of Lauren's inner change in beliefs. A new pattern began to emerge.

On the day of the negotiation, the two lawyers sat across from one another with their respective clients. At one point during the meeting the two attorneys left the room. It was at this moment that Lauren drew a line in the sand. Without fear or anger she looked her ex-husband in the eyes and let him know the gig was up; the game was over. She told him, "From here on, you no longer control me." He had a tirade on the spot. It was the same behavior Lauren had seen for years, only this time she observed it with new eyes. (This story exemplifies why this model is framed as a craft. Lauren had practiced and prepared, so she was ready with a pre-planned response. She knew what to expect from her ex-husband; she knew what his reaction would likely be, so she was emotionally and mentally prepared. Further, she could not claim growth as a craftswoman without actually confronting her fears in real time.) Lauren waited quietly and dispassionately—as one might wait for a bus or a train—until his fit of anger subsided. She again looked him in the eye and said, "That's not interesting to me anymore. Any conversation you want to have that's positive and constructive and in our daughter's best interest, I am happy to have. But that's all I'm interested in." There was a long moment of frozen silence. Her ex-husband looked into her eyes and perhaps saw something he had never seen before, and he replied, "In that case, how are you?" Lauren was shocked. In one exchange, the spell was broken. She had pulled back the curtain on the great and terrible Oz, and their relationship has since permanently changed.

The reclamation of power is a universal experience with an interesting progression. It is almost always clumsy as a person works to take back their power from others in the most ham-handed of ways. This typically appears as inappropriate displays of anger as a person lets out what has been suppressed for years, followed by a marked sense of self-centeredness or entitlement as the person learns to tell just about everyone to fuck off in some way or another in pursuit of what they want. This is eventually followed by standing face to face with someone's angry disapproval and seeing it for what it is—false, non-threatening bluster. When we do arrive at this place, we are amazed to see there is nothing really there. The emperor has no clothes; it was us all along, projecting our childhood fears onto some proxy for our parents. And we finally ask ourselves, "What was it that I was afraid of?" Such is the power of perception and belief. In that moment we reclaim some of the power we'd surrendered to our parents so long ago and we become more whole, more balanced for our effort.

During this period, Lauren's self-acceptance grew. She was becoming more and more herself. This is no small feat. It is an incredible accomplishment. One day Lauren called and asked for a private session. She told me she had something really important to share. In that meeting, Lauren came out as a gay woman. It was an extraordinary moment. I spend my life observing people hide behind self-created masks, dodging imagined disapproval to avoid some internal beliefs that exist only in their mind. To have Lauren courageously step out from behind a mask she had worn for over four decades into the light of day is an event that I live for—when a fellow human being stops hiding. This is a day of great importance and celebration. This is a day of love and emotional connection. Healing and transformation are available because self-acceptance is happening. Whether we are gay or fear abandonment or are terrified to ask for the love and respect we yearn for, whatever our hidden emotional longing may be, the day we honor who we are and begin to ask for what we want is the birthday of our identity's awakening.

Privately, Lauren had already begun searching for a new partner; this was number two on her list of wants. She used an online dating site to meet a woman named Randy. They hit it off immediately. Lauren met this woman and fully enjoyed being with her. But Randy lived one hundred miles away, which, by living symbol standards, is a safe distance for someone so new to intimate relations who is also exploring a new side of her sexuality. This distance as a living symbol expressed Lauren's true desire for intimacy as well as her fear of it.

For Lauren, Randy had incredible blue eyes, and she was beautiful. Their connection was powerful and immediate: "It feels like I'm spending time with someone I've known a lifetime," said Lauren. But Randy was not ready. She felt a powerful connection to Lauren, but instead of developing their relationship, she'd pull Lauren toward her and then push her away. We talked about this in group and everyone (except Lauren, of course) could recognize this pattern from her own childhood story. We read Lauren's list of childhood beliefs about disapproval and saw that most of them were in play. It is uncanny how specifically we all recreate the same patterns in our lives that are rooted in our childhood wounds. The same was true of her masking behaviors and emotional longings. Lauren began to see the whole of her story unfolding in a new relationship right before her eyes. For the first time her patterns were visible, and, more importantly, comprehensible. Much of the mystery was gone. All that remained was her unvarnished personal truth, which is what Lauren saw clearly for the first time.

Now Lauren found herself trapped. She felt enormous attraction and desire for Randy, yet she could also begin to see that Randy—at least in the moment—would not be able to fulfill her emotional longings. In other words, Lauren and the group could see that Randy's behavior and Lauren's emotional longings were incongruent, and that Randy would not be able to give Lauren what she wanted. The relationship would then devolve into a another version of Lauren's previous relationships—a reflection of her own childhood beliefs about disapproval. Lauren was torn between her desire to be with a loving partner she found attractive and finding someone with whom she could engage in a conscious and healthy relationship.

Then Lauren received a text from Randy letting her know that she was now dating and sleeping with another friend, but that "I still believe we are meant to be together." I used to be amazed, even shocked, at the precision with which our wounds and patterns replicate themselves. Not anymore. Now I expect it. I count on it. Randy was clearly a proxy for Lauren's father. She was having an affair, ignoring Lauren's emotional needs while focusing on her own, and betraying Lauren without fully comprehending it. All of Lauren's childhood beliefs about disapproval went off like Fourth of July fireworks. Every one of them was happening simultaneously. Again, Lauren's childhood beliefs about disapproval are:

1) I should accept betrayal in my closest relationships but still remain loyal, or I will be disapproved of and rejected.
2) I should not want anyone to see me or recognize my emotional needs, or I will be disapproved of and rejected.

3) I should not want anyone to protect me emotionally or financially, or I will be disapproved of and rejected.
4) I should accept when things feel dark or wrong and say nothing, or I will be disapproved of and rejected.
5) I should not ask others to be honest or take responsibility for their words and actions, or I will be disapproved of.
6) I should always appear like I have things together and that everything is fine, or I will be disapproved of.
7) I should fear anger and not express it, or I will be disapproved of, rejected, and abandoned.
8) I should accept irrational or hurtful behavior from others, or I will be disapproved of, rejected, and abandoned.

The good news was we had accurately cataloged Lauren's story; the bad news was it was happening again. But the experience proved conclusively to Lauren that life happens as a rational, cause and effect expression. Life is not random nor haphazard. Our lives must manifest as expressions of what we already believe. Life happens first in the mind and only thereafter may it manifest as something material, such as a relationship. To change the outer expression, meaning the potential partners she would meet, Lauren would have to change her own beliefs, which were creating the partners she habitually manifested. This is a startling moment. After reading all the books and discussing all the concepts, after attending weekend workshops and doing years of therapy, it is in this moment that inner work becomes starkly real. It is like standing before a great mountain with the intent to climb to the top and realizing the amount of effort it will take to do so. The epiphany is that changing long-held beliefs ain't gonna be easy.

True inner work is a lifelong journey, a gradual progression from kindergarten through high school and then on to university. It is an actual life journey that naturally takes time and effort as we mature. The fact is re-education of the self takes years. But don't be deterred by this notion. The journey is rich and rewarding, and self-exploration is as exciting and demanding as exploring a new planet. Several times in my life I journeyed into nature to discover something I'd never seen before; that feeling is one of awe and inspiration. This will happen as you explore yourself, as you find lost, hidden parts of your own identity.

With the support of her new perceptions and understanding, and with the help of the group, Lauren ended her relationship with Randy. She carried this out with much awareness. At first there was pain and loss, but, in the doing, Lauren's emotional longings became more clearly defined. At this point another change occurred, Lauren again met with me in private to tell me she wanted to stop taking the antidepressant medication she had been on for fourteen years. We made a plan that included consulting her doctor, and in gradual progression Lauren stopped. As her identity strengthened, as her emotional self came into greater balance, she no longer needed the support of medication. This was another living symbol bearing witness to Lauren's deep, organic transformation.

A few months later Lauren met Irene. She was a kind and decent person who quickly demonstrated genuine concern for Lauren in a way we had not seen before. This was another positive living symbol that some belief in Lauren was shifting. But, like Randy, Irene lived a considerable distance away. That living symbol was still in place. In fact, Irene had plans to move even farther away in the near future. Lauren again watched herself as the relationship progressed. She saw her old beliefs and patterns rise up, and she worked at recognizing her childhood beliefs about disapproval, masking behaviors, and emotional longings. In a short time, everything became clearer, because the repetition was so exact. While Lauren considered Irene a gift because she was a warm, intelligent, and loving woman, there were too many other things that just didn't work between them. Lauren was getting better at recognizing when she would not be able to get what she wanted from another person.

By engaging in this activity, Lauren had ceased blaming anyone for anything. She was no longer anyone's victim. She was taking responsibility for her actions, reactions, and choices. On a deeper level she was taking responsibility for her beliefs. Life was no longer happening to her; she was participating as a co-creator of her own happiness. Instead of going on a date and then complaining about the person, Lauren would speak about the whole experience relative to her childhood beliefs about disapproval, masking behaviors, and emotional longings. The results were completely positive and constructive, albeit at times painful. Lauren was becoming a craftswoman and getting clearer and clearer about herself and her life. Going back to Poppy's Story (Chapter One), Lauren was seeing her life as my grandfather saw the auditorium building. She was seeing where her problematic beliefs first entered her life; she watched them wend their way through her identity, and, finally, she saw them appear in her relationships as unfulfiilled emotional longings. Now she understood what she needed to do to heal.

Somewhere along the way Lauren began having contact with her ex-husband, but now, Lauren's tone, attitude, and words had changed. She was barely afraid of her husband and no longer willing to be bullied or abused. Sheba was standing beside her.

I would like to tell you that Lauren met the love of her life and lived happily ever after, but that would be a fairy tale. Lauren continues dating, but, more importantly, she continues her inner work. Each of her relationships has shown quantifiable improvements, which is the progression in living symbols that one should look for—tangible evidence of life and well-being improving, of awareness increasing. Lauren's most recent relationship was the closest yet. The woman lived five minutes away. She is a psychologist who shared Lauren's interest in feelings, communication, and healthy relations. In the end Lauren clearly recognized the improbability of getting her most important emotional longings met, so she moved on. Instead of a relationship taking years, Lauren was going through relationships in months in her quest to find the right partner. This is the practical payoff of doing inner work so conscientiously.

To put this into proper perspective, we must look at where Lauren began just eighteen months prior and compare it to where she is today. Evidenced by the living symbols of her evolving relationships, Lauren's growth tells the story: her identity is changing, her awareness expanding, and her relationship skills improving. I so deeply respect Lauren for her unflagging efforts. She is someone who has caused me, by her own example, to become a better, more conscious person. Witnessing her efforts has caused my mind and heart to open further. We have helped one another; we have shared transformation. This is the power of conscious relationship.

Exercise 21: The love experiment

We often go through life experiencing others as adversaries: a waiter isn't taking care of us; a driver won't let us merge; a store clerk tries to sell us something we don't want or need; an Internet customer service agent isn't really helping, and on and on. Because of our general experience, we tend to meet others with our shields up. This is our natural, default setting.

Here is a bold experiment that I like to do as it creates new perspectives and thus new perceptions. For one day, go through your life and with every person you meet, whether you like them or not, look them in the eyes and inwardly say, "I love you." Make real eye contact and silently infuse them with your love. Do not speak any of this aloud. Order your coffee as you normally would, but look the barista in the eyes and silently tell him/her you love them, and then let your love proceed from your heart to theirs.

Though there is much written about love, this exercise will give you a real-life experience of it. Notice how others start to respond to you. Note how different it is, how different it feels in your body and in your heart. Watch how it affects you as you actually experience the power of love. And perhaps you will see that the only way to receive love is to give it.

Glossary of Terms

A

active. One of the four fundamental structural elements of identity; its function is to think. It initiates the second half of belief formation by thinking about perceptions received so identity can form a belief. (See also receptive).

B

balance. A condition that occurs when one values the receptive and active equally, employing them in equal measure through one's words, actions, attitudes, and values.

being and wholeness. Together, the seen and hidden selves are one's complete identity. As such, they simultaneously represent both the concept of being (who one is) and potential wholeness (our native condition when divided identity is integrated).

belief. A perception that appears to be real or true. Once a belief is formed, it becomes a fundamental component of identity and the basis for all decisions and actions.

belief formation. The process by which we convert perceptions into beliefs; the primary action that is the basis for all other actions; the organic process by which identity changes.

belief, new. A new perception that appears truer than one held previously, which replaces the earlier belief. It is the trigger for all transformation.

belief system, personal. The totality of one's beliefs yoked together as one interconnected, interdependent system.

blind spot. (1) The temporary inability to see one's emotional reactivity. (2) The loss of conscious awareness due to emotional reactivity. This occurs when one is consumed in the present by childhood beliefs about disapproval from the past and then enacts masking behaviors.

C

childhood beliefs about disapproval. (1) Beliefs originating in childhood that cause one to hide one's genuine feelings and emotional longings from one's parents (or their proxies) to avoid their disapproval and rejection. (2) The cause of traumatic, emotional wounds to one's identity, that lead to recurring patterns of dissatisfaction in one's most intimate relationships. (3) The result of repeated parent-child collisions.

clarity exercises. A series of four progressive exercises designed to permanently alter one's response to confrontation by facilitating a new perception. The overall effect is the gradual transformation of identity through the integration of one's seen and hidden selves.

collisions. See **parent/child collisions**.

conflict. A mental struggle characterized by opposing thoughts and feelings, which simultaneously activates childhood beliefs about disapproval and disowned emotional longings. Conflict has two sides: one representing the beliefs of the seen self, the other representing the beliefs of the hidden self. This opposition of differing thoughts and desires creates tension, which naturally elicits a feeling of inner conflict.

confrontation. An event that creates inner conflict when you are confronted with hostile or defiant opposition from others or yourself. It is composed of three underlying, structural elements: childhood beliefs about disapproval, masking behaviors, and emotional longings. We hide our emotional longings behind masking behaviors to avoid our childhood fears of disapproval, so we fall into our blind spot--or not.

craftsmanship. Demonstrable skill earned through intentional study and right practice. The results of craftsmanship in inner work are quantifiable through a visible change for the better in one's living symbols.

D

decisions and actions. Perceptions create beliefs; beliefs shape identity; identity uses beliefs as a basis for its decisions and actions, which result in one's life; therefore, one's visible life is a literal expression of what one already believes.

disapproval. A feeling of emotional pain and fear that arises when one is confronted with the belief that one has failed, is not good enough, and will be rejected; typically experienced as emotional death or personal annihilation; can come from external sources but, most commonly, from oneself.

disapproval, parental. (1) When a parent directly disapproves of a child for failing to uphold a parent's beliefs (external and direct). (2) Or, more commonly, when one, acting as a proxy for one's parents, disapproves of oneself for failing to uphold a perceived parental belief (internal and indirect).

disapproval, self. When one acts as a proxy for one's parents and disapproves of oneself for asking for something, being someone, or doing something that one believes one's parents would disapprove of.

doing and balance. Together, the inner relationship between one's receptive and active becomes an outer expression of how one performs all of one's actions, which will be either too receptive, too active, or in balance. As such, their relationship represents the principle of balance. Simultaneously, they also represent the concept of doing, meaning how one does what one does, which must be either in or out of balance.

E

emotion. Raw, unrefined feelings, associated with emotional reactivity. See **feelings.**

emotional invulnerability. (1) A state of being emotionally closed and unable or unwilling to receive feelings. (2) From a childhood need to arm oneself due to a deep fear of being hurt if open, receptive, and vulnerable.

emotional longings. Our deepest emotional desires, which we surrender in childhood to avoid parental disapproval and rejection; they remain part of our hidden self until we identify and own them by acting on or directly asking for them from our partner or a close relation in the present.

emotional strength. (1) The true strength to stand up to disapproval, withstand its force and ask calmly and directly for what one emotionally longs for. (2) The strength one conceals in one's hidden self due to a fear of parental disapproval.

evolution. Visible change occurring over time by which human beings move continuously, albeit slowly, toward greater self-awareness. Evidenced by new living symbols, it is brought about through new perceptions and new beliefs.

F

fear, personal. The feeling generated by our belief in impending death, either physical or emotional (disapproval); it forms the key block to personal transformation and self-awareness.

feelings. Emotions that have been refined through a thought process. See also **emotion**.

feelings, genuine. What one authentically feels within oneself without editing or censoring those feelings.

H

hidden self. One of identity's four fundamental structural elements; its counterpart is the seen self. The hidden self is the unconscious repository for our disowned emotional longings and surrendered personal power. It exists subordinate to the seen self but cannot recognize the seen self's fear-based beliefs, because they do not appear real or true. The hidden self persistently but wordlessly encourages its reintegration with our seen self by embedding our secret emotional longings within every conflict, thus creating choice.

hiding. The fundamental and universal technique for avoiding disapproval.

I

identity, collective. The group-image automatically produced by the sum of a group's collective beliefs; group perceptions create group beliefs and group beliefs shape group identity.

identity, complete. The seen and hidden selves together are our complete identity.

identity, personal. The self-image automatically produced by the sum of one's personal beliefs; perceptions create beliefs and beliefs shape identity; represents our current point of consciousness, meaning our sense of "I."

identity theory. A practical philosophy with the root principle that all change proceeds from identity. Identity's primary function is to impart form (living symbols) to life by using one's beliefs as blueprints. Identity changes whenever beliefs change, which changes the manifestation of one's life. This process drives personal and collective evolution.

identity, law of. The central controlling and organizing principle of life; it determines the manifestation of life by dictating that perceptible forms **must** reflect the beliefs that compose one's identity. Change occurs **only** through a change of identity that occurs **only** through a change of belief, which occurs **only** through a change in perception.

identity, divided. The mental structure of a human being, consisting of four fundamental elements: the seen and hidden selves and the receptive and active. Our identity, which was originally whole, divided in response to our need to conceal rejected parts of ourselves—the direct result of our collective belief in fear of disapproval and rejection.

identity, whole. A person's identity in its original state before accepting a belief in fear (of disapproval and rejection).

identity therapy. A form of counseling based on identity theory, which is structured around a person's childhood biography and the emotional wounds caused by parent-child collisions. These collisions form the basis of our childhood beliefs about disapproval, masking behaviors, and emotional longings. Awareness of each is required to do the inner work necessary for healing.

imbalance. A visible condition that occurs when one does not value the receptive and active equally, creating a dominant and subordinate relationship between the two.

imbalance, dominant. The part of identity, either receptive or active, that one chooses to express more openly because one does not fear disapproval or rejection for doing so. As a result, it has a far greater presence in one's life.

imbalance, subordinate. The receptive or active part of one's identity that one chooses to hide due to fear of disapproval or rejection. As a result, it is less dominant in one's life.

inner work. Effort performed to integrate the seen and hidden selves and balance the receptive and active parts of identity in order to promote greater self-awareness, balance, and eventual wholeness.

L

living symbols, personal. One's beliefs made manifest through visible forms that one creates, adopts, or that appear in one's life. These forms include objects, activities, relationships, occurrences, attitudes, conditions, twists of fate, illnesses, ideas, and values. In life, beliefs are the cause and living symbols are the effect.

M

masking behavior, personal. (1) A survival adaptation to cope with fear of disapproval and rejection. (2) Any behavior that we use to hide our genuine feelings and emotional longings to avoid disapproval—can appear constructive or destructive.

mind. The non-corporeal container of consciousness.

P

pain. A sensation of hurt from a physical or emotional wound. Pain bridges the wounded and the non-wounded parts of self.

parent-child collision, direct. A formative event during childhood in which a child violates a belief important to his or her parents that results in traumatic parental disapproval. This causes the child to hide an emotional longing, surrender personal strength, and adopt a masking behavior.

parent-child collision, indirect. A formative event during childhood in which a child anticipates traumatic disapproval for violating a belief important to his or her parents. This causes the child to preemptively hide specific emotional longings, surrender personal strength, and adopt a masking behavior.

parents. Living symbols of the gateway through which children enter life. Parents are the teachers of children and, therefore, the stewards of the future, because they pass on the beliefs by which a child will eventually construct his or her life, and, in turn, affect the world.

perception. Sensory input, meaning raw impressions received through the senses or generated within one's mind. Perceptions are the fundamental ingredient of belief formation, which is the foundation for all decision-making and action.

personal power. See emotional strength.

perspective. The vantage point from which we perceive someone, something, or a situation.

R

receptive, the. One of the four fundamental elements of identity; its function is to open. It initiates belief formation by opening, thus preparing identity to receive perceptions. (See also **active**).

responses to disapproval form. A written compilation of your personal responses to disapproval and rejection, including your childhood beliefs about disapproval, masking behaviors, emotional longings, and blind spot reminder.

S

seen self. The most influential of the four fundamental elements of identity. It continuously manages identity by perpetuating a self-image that avoids disapproval and rejection by not directly asking for one's emotional longings. (See also **hidden self**).

story. A condensed way of referring to one's childhood beliefs about disapproval, masking behaviors, and emotional longings.

T

thoughts, genuine. One's spontaneous and uncensored thoughts.

transformation. A natural change to identity that occurs when one adopts a new belief based on a new perception.

W

wholeness. Our native condition when divided identity is integrated. (See also being and wholeness).

wound. The root source of any physical or emotional pain.

Charts and Forms

HIERARCHY OF CONCEPTS

THE CRAFT OF LIFE AND IDENTITY THEORY

1) The Law of Identity - The central controlling and organizing principle of life; it determines the manifestation of life by dictating that perceptible forms *must* reflect the beliefs that compose one's identity.

2) Perception - Sensory input, meaning raw impressions received through the senses or generated within one's mind. Perceptions are the fundamental ingredient of belief formation.

3) Belief - A perception that appears to be real or true becomes a belief. Once a belief is formed, it becomes a component of identity.

4) Belief Formation - The process by which one converts **perceptions** into **beliefs**; it is the primary action that is the basis for all other actions. It is also the process by which identity changes.

5) Identity - The self-image automatically produced by the sum of one's beliefs; perceptions create beliefs and beliefs shape identity. Identity represents our current point of consciousness, meaning our sense of "I."

6) Living Symbols - Beliefs made manifest as visible forms that one creates, adopts, or that appear in one's life. These forms include objects, activities, relationships, occurrences, attitudes, conditions, twists of fate, illnesses, ideas, and values. In life, beliefs are the cause and living symbols are the effect.

7) Decisions and Actions - Perceptions create beliefs; beliefs shape identity; identity uses beliefs as a basis for its decisions and actions, which results in one's life; therefore, one's visible life is a literal expression of what one already believes.

THE UNIVERSAL STRUCTURE OF IDENTITY

8) Seen Self - The most influential of the four fundamental elements of identity. It continuously manages identity by perpetuating a self-image that avoids disapproval and rejection by not directly asking for one's emotional longings. The seen self is driven entirely by fear.

9) Hidden Self - One of identity's four fundamental structural elements; its counterpart is the seen self. The hidden self is the unconscious repository for our disowned emotional longings and surrendered personal power. It exists subordinate to the seen self but cannot recognize the seen self's fear-based beliefs, because they do not appear real or true. The hidden self persistently but wordlessly encourages its reintegration with our seen self by embedding our secret emotional longings within every conflict, thus creating choice.

10) Being and Wholeness - Together, the **seen** and **hidden selves** are one's complete identity, meaning who one is. As such, they simultaneously represent both the concept of being (who one is) and potential wholeness (our native condition when divided identity is integrated).

11) Receptive - One of the four fundamental elements of identity. Its function is to open. It initiates belief formation by opening, thus preparing identity to receive perceptions.

12) Active - One of the four fundamental elements of identity. Its function is to think. It initiates the second half of belief formation by thinking about perceptions received so identity can form a belief.

13) Doing and Balance - Together, the inner relationship between one's receptive and active becomes an outer expression of how one performs all of one's actions, which will be either too receptive, too active, or in balance. As such, their relationship represents the principle of balance. Simultaneously, they also represent the concept of doing, meaning how one does what one does, which must be either in or out of balance.

THE UNIVERSAL STRUCTURE OF CONFRONTATION

14) Childhood Beliefs About Disapproval - Beliefs originating in childhood that cause one to hide one's genuine feelings and emotional longings from one's parents (or their proxies) to avoid their disapproval and rejection. The result of repeated, traumatic parent-child collisions while growing up, and the basis for one's fear(s).

15) Masking Behaviors - Any behavior that one uses to hide one's genuine feelings and emotional longings to avoid disapproval; it can appear constructive or destructive. The behavior one uses to avoid disapproval and rejection.

16) Blind Spot - The loss of conscious awareness due to emotional reactivity. This occurs when one is consumed in the present by childhood beliefs about disapproval from the past and then enacts masking behaviors as a coping mechanism.

17) Emotional Longings - Our deepest emotional desires that one surrenders in childhood to avoid parental disapproval and rejection; what one hides in the present to avoid disapproval and rejection.

18) The Path to Consciousness or Unconsciousness - By hiding our emotional longings behind masking behaviors in order to avoid our childhood beliefs about disapproval, we fall into our blind spot—or not. With every decision that we make, we move towards consciousness or unconsciousness.

19) Confrontation - Every confrontation triggers one's fear of disapproval and one's desire for one's emotional longings at the same time. This means that every confrontation presents a critical choice. Do we accept our seen self's fear of disapproval; its hiding of our emotional longings; its acting out of our masking behaviors, or do we embrace our hidden self's belief in the value of owning and expressing our emotional longings and asking directly for what we want? Our choice determines our entire life's direction, which will be toward consciousness or unconsciousness, toward repetitive patterns of pain and dissatisfaction or new patterns of healing and transformation.

A full-page, color version of this chart is available for free download at TheCraftOfLife.com.

Form 1
MASKING BEHAVIORS JOURNAL

Day	Date	Write a Brief Description of Your Confrontation	Name the Emotional Pain You Felt	Write Down Your Reaction ***(your reaction is your masking behavior)***
		Examples		
Thurs	2/25	*My husband told me not to be late again.*	*I felt judged, angry, and insulted.*	*I became enraged and lashed out at him.*
Sat	2/27	*My girlfriend told me my clothes were not good enough for the restaurant we were going to.*	*I felt shamed and embarrassed, as if I'd failed.*	*I became silent and withdrew.*

A full-page, editable version of this form is available for free download at TheCraftOfLife.com.

Form 2 (Father)
IDENTIFYING MY EMOTIONAL LONGINGS

Age	Write a brief description of a childhood memory in which you felt deeply upset and ardently wanted comfort, support, understanding, or help from your **FATHER**, but he could not or would not give these to you.	I Felt	What did you long for from your **FATHER** in this scene? What could he have done to make you feel safe, protected, or loved? These are your **emotional longings**.
3 OR 4	Throwing up on my christmas dress, he almost hit me.	scared	his reassurance. he was always angry when sober.
4 or 5	My cousin accused me of foul assault, he told my mom to keep me away.	confused	His defense. Never defended his daughters.

A full-page, editable version of this form is available for free download at TheCraftOfLife.com.

Form 2 (Mother)
IDENTIFYING MY EMOTIONAL LONGINGS

Age	Write a brief description of a childhood memory in which you felt deeply upset and ardently wanted comfort, support, understanding, or help from your **MOTHER** but she could not or would not give these to you.	I Felt	What did you long for from your **MOTHER** in this scene? What could she have done to make you feel safe, protected, or loved? These are your **emotional longings**.
teen	She was throwing up her meal. Bc she struggled w/ bolimia.	confused	Her honesty, transparency. She lied a lot.
teen	Birth control did a 180 on my mental health and she thought it was a facade.	angry	Reassurance, validation, security.

A full-page, editable version of this form is available for free download at TheCraftOfLife.com.

Form 3
COMPILING MY EMOTIONAL LONGINGS

	Distill these from your Father and Mother columns on the previous pages. Delete duplications, combine ones that are similar. In the end, keep only those for which you feel a strong emotional resonance. ***Minimum of 5, Maximum of 8***
1	
2	
3	
4	
5	
6	
7	
8	

A full-page, editable version of this form is available for free download at TheCraftOfLife.com.

Form 4
IDENTIFYING MY CHILDHOOD BELIEFS ABOUT DISAPPROVAL

	MY EMOTIONAL LONGINGS ARE *From Form 2b, copy your list of emotional longings into the spaces below.*
	Examples *a) To be seen and supported emotionally, especially by my father (or his proxies).* *b) To be met calmly and rationally (instead of with a reactive, irrational response), especially by my mother (or her proxies).*
1	
2	
3	
4	
5	
6	
7	
8	

	MY CHILDHOOD BELIEFS ABOUT DISAPPROVAL ARE *The format is: If I ask to be (**fill in your emotional longing**), I will be disapproved of and rejected.*
	Examples *a) If I ask to be seen or supported, I will be disapproved of and rejected by my father (or his proxies).* *b) If I ask to be met calmly and rationally, I will be disapproved of and rejected, especially by my mother (or her proxies).*
1	
2	
3	
4	
5	
6	
7	
8	

A full-page, editable version of this form is available for free download at TheCraftOfLife.com.

Form 5
MY RESPONSES TO DISAPPROVAL

Name: ______________________________ Date: ______________

When I feel fear or emotional upset in my body, it means I'm having a confrontation in the moment, amplified by parent-child collisions from the past. This tells me that **BOTH** my **childhood beliefs about disapproval AND** my **emotional longings** have become triggered and my **seen** and **hidden selves** are in conflict. My **seen self** pressures me to accept my fear of disapproval, while my **hidden self** simultaneously reminds me to own and act on what I truly want. These represent opposite beliefs, opposite agendas. Now, I must choose to affirm one or the other.

These are my **childhood beliefs about disapproval.** None are true anymore.	
1	
2	
3	
4	
5	
6	
7	
8	

These are the **genuine feelings** I typically hide. My seen self pressures me to conceal these.							
1		3		5		7	
2		4		6		8	

My **masking behaviors** lead me into my blind spot. My seen self pressures me to enact these.			
1		5	
2		6	
3		7	
4		8	

My **emotional longings** are what I want. My seen self pressures me not to ask for or act on these.	
1	
2	
3	
4	
5	
6	
7	
8	

Our **seen self** wants us to remain unconscious by perpetuating our emotional wounds.
When we hide our emotional longings behind our **masking behaviors** because of **childhood fears about disapproval**, then we remain unconscious and our identity cannot change.

Our **hidden self** wants us to become more conscious by healing our emotional wounds.
When we recognize that we are enacting **masking behaviors** because of **childhood beliefs about disapproval** and, instead, act on or ask for what we want, then we are breaking old beliefs and patterns, restoring personal integrity, and building consciousness. And, then, nothing can prevent our identity and our lives from transforming.

A full-page, editable version of this form is available for free download at TheCraftOfLife.com.

Form 6
CONSCIOUS CONFLICT RESOLUTION

Name who the conflict is with (another person, an organization, or yourself?).

Briefly describe the conflict.

Name 3 FEELINGS that this conflict is stirring within you.					
1		2		3	

Briefly explain why you are feeling this way.	
1	
2	
3	

Compare the explanation of your feelings to the parent-child collisions you had growing up.					
1	They are the same	2	They are similar	3	I don't see a connection (If this happens, please look again as there is always a connection between conflict in the moment and our story from the past)

If they appear to be the same or similar, can you recognize your past experience(s) amplifying and affecting your feelings in the present? Can you see how your past experience distorts your present perception?				
1	Yes	2	No	

It is not possible to effectively resolve things in the present when they are comingled with feelings and beliefs from the past. With this understanding, use your will to separate the past from the present. Once you are free of old feelings and old beliefs, describe the present conflict that remains.

Free from past feelings and old beliefs, what do you want from the other in this situation?

Now, ask for or act on what you want, but without concern as to whether you will get it or not. It is the asking, not the getting, that heals our identity; it is the asking that restores our personal integrity. Expect to feel tremendous fear of disapproval inhibiting your asking. Prepare yourself for this emotional challenge.

A full-page, editable version of this form is available for free download at TheCraftOfLife.com.

Form 7
CHALLENGING MY SOURCE BELIEFS IN THE IMPOSSIBILITY OF EMOTIONAL FULFILLMENT

I believed that while growing up my father could not or would not give me:
I believed that while growing up my mother could not or would not give me:

As a result, I still believe that I cannot ask for, have, or am even worthy to receive these things.

DO THIS EXERCISE ONE TIME PER DAY, THEN TWO, THEN THREE

1	A conflict or confrontation occurs. Describe it:
2	Look for your source beliefs. See them. Recognize this proxy for your mother or father. Listen to your seen self's lying words, telling you what you can't have, telling you to be afraid.
3	Now reject your seen self and your source beliefs. They are not true; they are self-defeating lies.
4	Let go of your source belief, even though you are afraid. Stop upholding your belief in the impossibility of emotional fulfillment. Stop turning people into proxies for your wounding mother or father. Stop giving these people the power to hurt, upset, or scare you.
5	Accept the possibility that by asking for what you want you may lose someone or something important or that you might fail. It is far better to accept these potentialities than fearfully resisting their possible outcome. Surrender your fear of what might happen so that you may claim your strength and live conscious and free.
6	Now, ask for or act on what you want. This is what will break your source belief.
7	Affirm that you do not want to live controlled by your source belief any longer. Affirm that you can have what you want instead of believing you cannot.

A full-page, editable version of this form is available for free download at TheCraftOfLife.com.

Acknowledgments

This book would not be possible without the input, effort, and support of many. I thank all of my clients whom I have worked with over the years as I developed this material. I am especially grateful to the men and women who participated in my groups over the past seven years. Interacting with each of you allowed me to explore and refine this model into what it has become. You received me with respect, care, interest, and good humor (along with some brutally honest critiques), which allowed me to polish things to a lovely shine; I am deeply grateful.

Many thanks to Mark Kalina, Bob Angelo, and Joseph Rubano for our long walks and important conversations. Thank you to my dear friend Matt Symczak. We have faced life and death together. You are a true inspiration, buoying my life in hard times, brightening it on regular days. Our Sunday adventures in the ocean keep me happy, healthy, and sane.

There are two people who have so profoundly affected my life that no amount of thanks can ever fully convey my gratitude. Both have changed who I am, what I do, and how I do it. Thank you to my dear friend Michael Rubano for your support, and the countless number of connections you made on my behalf. To have you in my corner has been the greatest of blessings. You are my brother in heart and spirit. Thank you to my dear friend Gary Hooker. I am not sure this book would exist if not for your presence in my life. No one has provided me with the level of support that you have. You gave of yourself freely, lent assistance without condition or judgment, and upheld me through failures and successes. You have taught me more than you know, and I remain grateful beyond words.

When I finally reached the point where I needed someone to read, understand, and edit the manuscript, I turned to another close friend, Glen Slater, Ph.D., who is a professor of Jungian Psychology at Pacifica University. He graciously helped to shape this book into its final form. Thank you, Glen. Your indelible imprint is all over these pages. Your guidance and support came from your heart and was received directly into my own. You have my undying gratitude, dear friend.

Thank you to Ann Webster, Ph.D., for your kind words and gracious foreword.

Thank you to Tawn Babcock for your wonderful book cover design and layout. I appreciate your patience, persistence, and creativity.

Thank you to my brilliant copy editor Paula Fitzgerald. If I could erect a massive billboard that simply says, "Paula is great!" I would do it. Time and again you amazed me with your care, attention to detail, and polished professionalism. I am deeply grateful for your help and your fine work. Your support has been invaluable.

Last but not least, thank you to my wife, Amy, and my daughter, Emily Grace. I hope I have not permanently harmed either of you through exposure, year after year, to the same scene: awakening to find me in my office, typing at my computer in my underwear—a madman relentlessly pursuing his vision. Thank you for your understanding and support. Thank you for your love.

About the Author

Robert Goldstein is an indie publisher, author, and the creator of a practical philosophy called Identity Theory, which he has meticulously developed over the past 35 years. During the day, he is a business executive. At night, he is a successful counselor to individuals, couples, and groups. He writes books and blogs but takes time out weekly to swim with sharks and sea lions in the rejuvenating embrace of the Pacific Ocean. He resides in Encinitas, California, with his wife of 40 years and their lovely daughter. For more information on his methods and future books, visit TheCraftOfLife.com.

Made in the USA
San Bernardino, CA
24 December 2017